748
3380

KU-684-217

FIVE FAMOUS PLAYS

by
ANTON TCHEKOFF

The royalty fees for each and every representation by amateurs of the plays contained in this volume are as follows :—

THE BEAR - - - - - - - -	£1 1s.
THE SEAGULL - - - - - -	£3 3s.
THE THREE SISTERS - - - -	£3 3s.
UNCLE VANYA - - - - - -	£3 3s.
THE CHERRY ORCHARD - - -	£3 3s.

Payable in advance to :—

MESSRS. SAMUEL FRENCH, LTD.
26 Southampton Street,
Strand, London, W.C.2

or their authorized agents who, upon payment of the fee, will issue a licence for the performance to take place. No performance may be given unless this licence has been obtained. The following particulars are needed for the issue of a licence :—

Title of the play or plays.
Name of the town.
Name of the theatre or hall.
Date of the performance or performances.
Name and address of the applicant.
Name of the society.
Amount remitted.

Terms for professional performances quoted on application.

FIVE FAMOUS PLAYS

by

ANTON TCHEKOFF

The Bear, The Three Sisters, The Cherry Orchard
translated from the Russian by Julius West

Uncle Vanya, The Seagull
translated from the Russian by Marian Fell

DUCKWORTH

3 Henrietta Street, London, W.C. 2

RUSSIAN WEIGHTS AND MEASURES AND MONEY EMPLOYED IN THE PLAYS, WITH ENGLISH EQUIVALENTS

$$1 \text{ verst} = 3500 \text{ feet} = \tfrac{2}{3} \text{ mile (almost)}$$
$$1 \text{ arshin} = 28 \text{ inches}$$
$$1 \text{ dessiatin} = 2.7 \text{ acres}$$
$$1 \text{ copeck} = \tfrac{1}{4}d.$$
$$1 \text{ rouble} = 100 \text{ copecks} = 2s. \ 1d.$$

CONTENTS

CHRONOLOGICAL LIST OF THE PRINCIPAL WORKS OF ANTON TCHEKOFF

PLAYS

NOVELS AND SHORT STORIES

MISCELLANEOUS SKETCHES

ANTON TCHEKOFF

By Marian Fell

THE last years of the nineteenth century were for Russia
tinged with doubt and gloom. The high-tide of vitality
that had risen during the Turkish war ebbed in the early
eighties, leaving behind it a dead level of apathy which
lasted until life was again quickened by the high interests
of the Revolution. During these grey years the lonely
country and stagnant provincial towns of Russia buried
a peasantry which was enslaved by want and toil, and an
educated upper class which was enslaved by idleness and
tedium. Most of the " Intellectuals," with no outlet for
their energies, were content to forget their ennui in vodka
and card-playing; only the more idealistic gasped for air
in the stifling atmosphere, crying out in despair against
life as they saw it, and looking forward with a pathetic
hope to happiness for humanity in " two or three hundred
years." It is the inevitable tragedy of their existence,
and the pitiful humour of their surroundings, that are
portrayed with such insight and sympathy by Anton
Tchekoff who is perhaps, of modern writers, the dearest
to the Russian People.

Anton Tchekoff was born in the old Black Sea port of
Taganrog on January 17, 1860. His grandfather had been
a serf; his father married a merchant's daughter and settled
in Taganrog, where, during Anton's boyhood, he carried on
a small and unsuccessful trade in provisions. The young
Tchekoff was soon impressed into the services of the large,
poverty-striken family, and he spoke regretfully in after

7

years of his hard-worked childhood. But he was obedient and good-natured, and worked cheerfully in his father's shop, closely observing the idlers that assembled there, and gathering the drollest stories, which he would afterward whisper in class to his laughing schoolfellows. Many were the punishments which he incurred by this habit, which was incorrigible.

His grandfather had now become manager of an estate near Taganrog, in the wild steppe country of the Don Cossacks, and here the boy spent his summers, fishing in the river, and roving about the countryside as brown as a gipsy, sowing the seeds of that love for nature which he retained all his life. His evenings he liked best to spend in the kitchen of the master's house among the workpeople and peasants who gathered there, taking part in their games, and setting them all laughing by his witty and telling observations.

When Tchekoff was about fourteen, his father moved the family to Moscow, leaving Anton in Taganrog, and now, relieved of work in the shop, his progress at school became remarkable. At seventeen he wrote a long tragedy, which was afterward destroyed, and he already showed flashes of the wit that was soon to blaze into genius.

He graduated from the high school at Taganrog with every honour, entered the University of Moscow as a student of medicine, and threw himself headlong into a double life of student and author, in the attempt to help his struggling family.

His first story appeared in a Moscow paper in 1880, and after some difficulty he secured a position connected with several of the smaller periodicals, for which, during his student years, he poured forth a succession of short stories and sketches of Russian life with incredible rapidity. He wrote, he tells us, during every spare minute, in crowded rooms where there was " no light and less air," and never

spent more than a day on any one story. He also wrote
at this time a very stirring blood-and-thunder play, *The
High Road*, which was suppressed by the censor and only
came to light again in 1915.

His audience demanded laughter above all things, and,
with his deep sense of the ridiculous, Tchekoff asked nothing
better. His stories, though often based on themes profoundly tragic, are penetrated by the light and subtle
satire that has won him his reputation as a great humorist.
But though there was always a smile on his lips, it was a
tender one, and his sympathy with suffering often brought
his laughter near to tears.

This delicate and original genius was at first subjected
to harsh criticism, which Tchekoff felt keenly, and Trigorin's
description in *The Seagull* of the trials of a young author
is a cry from Tchekoff's own soul. A passionate enemy of
all lies and oppression, he already foreshadows in these
early writings the protest against conventions and rules,
which he afterward put into Treplieff's reply to Sorin in
The Seagull : " Let us have new forms, or else nothing at
all."

In 1884 he took his degree as doctor of medicine, and
decided to practise, although his writing had by now taken
on a professional character. He always gave his calling a
high place, and the doctors in his works are drawn with
affection and understanding. If anyone spoke slightingly
of doctors in his presence, he would exclaim : " Stop ! You
don't know what country doctors do for the people ! "

Tchekoff fully realised later the influence which his
profession had exercised on his literary work, and sometimes
regretted the too vivid insight it gave him, but, on the other
hand, he was able to write : " Only a doctor can know
what value my knowledge of science has been to me," and
" It seems to me that as a doctor I have described the
sicknesses of the soul correctly." For instance, Trigorin's

analysis in *The Seagull* of the state of mind of an author
has well been called " artistic diagnosis."

The young doctor-writer is described at this time as
modest and grave, with flashes of brilliant gaiety. A son
of the people, there was in his face an expression that
recalled the simple-hearted village lad ; his eyes were blue,
his glance full of intelligence and kindness, and his manners
unaffected and simple. He was an untiring worker, and
between his patients and his desk he led a life of ceaseless
activity. His restless mind was dominated by a passion
of energy and he thought continually and vividly. Often,
while jesting and talking, he would seem suddenly to plunge
into himself, and his look would grow fixed and deep, as
if he were contemplating something important and strange.
Then he would ask some unexpected question, which
showed how far his mind had roamed.

Success was now rapidly overtaking the young author ;
his first collection of stories appeared in 1887, another
one in the same year had immediate success, and both went
through many editions ; but, at the same time, the shadows
that darkened his later works began to creep over his light-
hearted humour.

His impressionable mind began to take on the grey
tinge of his time, but much of his sadness may also be
attributed to his ever-increasing ill health.

Weary and with an obstinate cough, he went south in
1888, took a little cottage on the banks of a little river
" abounding in fish and crabs," and surrendered himself
to his touching love for nature, happy in his passion for
fishing, in the quiet of the country, and in the music and
gaiety of the peasants. " One would gladly sell one's
soul," he writes, " for the pleasure of seeing the warm
evening sky, and the streams and pools reflecting the darkly
mournful sunset." He described visits to his country
neighbours and long drives in gay company, during which

he says, " we ate every half hour, and laughed to the verge
of colic."

His health, however, did not improve. In 1889 he began
to have attacks of heart trouble, and the sensitive artist's
nature appears in a remark which he made after one of
them. " I walked quickly across the terrace on which the
guests were assembled," he said, " with one idea in my
mind, how awkward it would be to fall down and die in
the presence of strangers."

It was during this transition period of his life, when his
youthful spirits were failing him, that the stage, for which
he had always felt a fascination, tempted him to write
Ivanoff, and also a dramatic sketch in one act entitled
The Swan Song, though he often declared that he had
no ambition to become a dramatist. " The Novel," he
wrote, " is a lawful wife, but the Stage is a noisy, flashy,
and insolent mistress." He has put his opinion of the
stage of his day in the mouth of Treplieff, in *The Seagull*,
and he often refers to it in his letters as " an evil disease of
the towns " and " the gallows on which dramatists are
hanged."

He wrote *Ivanoff* at white-heat in two and a half weeks,
as a protest against a play he had seen at one of the Moscow
theatres. Ivanoff (from Ivan, the commonest of Russian
names) was by no means meant to be a hero, but a most
ordinary, weak man oppressed by the " immortal common-
places of life," with his heart and soul aching in the grip of
circumstances, one of the many " useless people " of Russia
for whose sorrow Tchekoff felt such overwhelming pity.
He saw nothing in their lives that could not be explained
and pardoned, and he returns to his ill-fated, " useless
people " again and again, not to preach any doctrine of
pessimism, but simply because he thought that the world
was the better for a certain fragile beauty of their natures and
their touching faith in the ultimate salvation of humanity.

Both the writing and staging of *Ivanoff* gave Tchekoff
great difficulty. The characters all being of almost equal
importance, he found it hard to get enough good actors to
take the parts, but it finally appeared in Moscow in 1889,
a decided failure! The author had touched sharply several
sensitive spots of Russian life—for instance, in his warning
not to marry a Jewess or a blue-stocking—and the play
was also marred by faults of inexperience, which, however,
he later corrected. The critics were divided in condemning
a certain novelty in it and in praising its freshness and
originality. The character of Ivanoff was not understood,
and the weakness of the man blinded many to the lifelike
portrait. Tchekoff himself was far from pleased with
what he called his " literary abortion," and rewrote it
before it was produced again in St. Petersburg. Here it
was received with the wildest applause, and the morning
after its performance the papers burst into unanimous
praise. The author was enthusiastically fêted, but the
burden of his growing fame was beginning to be very
irksome to him, and he wrote wearily at this time that he
longed to be in the country, fishing in the lake, or lying in
the hay.

His next play to appear was a farce entitled *The Bear*,
which he wrote in a single evening, and which had a great
success. This was followed by *The Demon*, a failure,
rewritten ten years later as *Uncle Vanya*.

All Russia now combined in urging Tchekoff to write
some important work, and this, too, was the writer's
dream ; but his only long story is *The Steppe*, which is,
after all, but a series of sketches, exquisitely drawn, and
strung together on the slenderest connecting thread.
Tchekoff's delicate and elusive descriptive power did not
lend itself to painting on a large canvas, and his strange
little tragi-comedies of Russian life, his *Tedious Tales*,
as he called them, were always to remain his masterpieces.

In 1890 Tchekoff made a journey to the Island of Saghalien, after which his health definitely failed, and the consumption, with which he had long been threatened, finally declared itself. His illness exiled him to the Crimea, and he spent his last ten years there, making frequent trips to Moscow to superintend the production of his four important plays, written during this period of his life.

The Seagull appeared in 1896, and, after a failure in St. Petersburg, won instant success as soon as it was given on the stage of the Artists' Theatre in Moscow. Of all Tchekoff's plays, this one conforms most nearly to our Western conventions, and is therefore most easily appreciated here. In *Trigorin* the author gives us one of the rare glimpses of his own mind, for Tchekoff seldom put his own personality into the pictures of the life in which he took such immense interest.

In *The Seagull* we see clearly the increase of Tchekoff's power of analysis, which is remarkable in his next play, *The Three Sisters*, gloomiest of all his dramas.

The Three Sisters, produced in 1901, depends, even more than most of Tchekoff's plays, on its interpretation, and it is almost essential to its appreciation that it should be seen rather than read. The atmosphere of gloom with which it is pervaded is a thousand times more intense when it comes to us across the foot-lights. In it Tchekoff probes the depths of human life with so sure a touch, and lights them with an insight so piercing, that the play made a deep impression when it appeared. This was also partly owing to the masterly way in which it was acted at the Artists' Theatre in Moscow. The theme is, as usual, the greyness of provincial life, and the night is lit for his little group of characters by a flash of passion so intense that the darkness which succeeds it seems wellnigh intolerable.

Uncle Vanya followed *The Three Sisters*, and the poignant truth of the picture, together with the tender beauty of the last scene, touched his audience profoundly, both on the stage and when the play was afterward published.

The Cherry Orchard appeared in 1904 and was Tchekoff's last play. At its production, just before his death, the author was fêted as one of Russia's greatest dramatists. Here it is not only country life that Tchekoff shows us, but Russian life and character in general, in which the old order is giving place to the new, and we see the practical, modern spirit invading the vague, aimless existence so dear to the owners of the cherry orchard. A new epoch was beginning, and at its dawn the singer of old, dim Russia was silenced.

In the year that saw the production of *The Cherry Orchard*, Tchekoff, the favourite of the Russian people, whom Tolstoi declared to be comparable as a writer of stories only to Maupassant, died suddenly in a little village of the Black Forest, whither he had gone a few weeks before in the hope of recovering his lost health.

Tchekoff, with an art peculiar to himself, in scattered scenes, in haphazard glimpses into the lives of his characters, in seemingly trivial conversations, has succeeded in so concentrating the atmosphere of the Russia of his day that we feel it in every line we read, oppressive as the mists that hang over a lake at dawn, and, like those mists, made visible to us by the light of an approaching day.

THE BEAR

A FARCE IN ONE ACT

CHARACTERS

ELENA IVANOVNA POPOVA, *a landowning little widow,*
with dimples on her cheeks.

GRIGORY STEPANOVITCH SMIRNOV, *a middle-aged*
landowner.

LUKA, *Popova's aged footman.*

THE BEAR

A drawing-room in POPOVA'S *house.*

POPOVA *is in deep mourning and has her eyes fixed on a
photograph.* LUKA *is haranguing her.*

LUKA. It isn't right, madam. . . . You're just destroy-
ing yourself. The maid and the cook have gone off fruit
picking, every living being is rejoicing, even the cat understands how to enjoy herself and walks about in the yard,
catching midges ; only you sit in this room all day, as if
this was a convent, and don't take any pleasure. Yes,
really ! I reckon it's a whole year that you haven't left
the house !

POPOVA. I shall never go out. . . . Why should I ?
My life is already at an end. He is in his grave, and
I have buried myself between four walls. . . . We are
both dead.

LUKA. Well, there you are ! Nicolai Mihailovitch is
dead, well, it's the will of God, and may his soul rest in
peace. . . . You've mourned him—and quite right. But
you can't go on weeping and wearing mourning for ever.
My old woman died too, when her time came. Well ?
I grieved over her, I wept for a month, and that's enough
for her, but if I've got to weep for a whole age, well, the
old woman isn't worth it. [*Sighs*] You've forgotten all
your neighbours. You don't go anywhere, and you see

nobody. We live, so to speak, like spiders, and never see
the light. The mice have eaten my livery. It isn't as
if there were no good people around, for the district's full
of them. There's a regiment quartered at Riblov, and the
officers are such beauties—you can never gaze your fill
at them. And, every Friday, there's a ball at the camp,
and every day the soldier's band plays. . . . Eh, my
lady ! You're young and beautiful, with roses in your
cheek—if you only took a little pleasure. Beauty won't
last long, you know. In ten years' time you'll want to
be a pea-hen yourself among the officers, but they won't
look at you, it will be too late.

POPOVA. [*With determination*] I must ask you never
to talk to me about it ! You know that when Nicolai
Mihailovitch died, life lost all its meaning for me. I vowed
never to the end of my days to cease to wear mourning
or to see the light. . . . You hear ? Let his ghost see
how well I love him. . . . Yes, I know it's no secret to
you that he was often unfair to me, cruel, and . . . . and
even unfaithful, but I shall be true till death, and show
him how I can love. There, beyond the grave, he will see,
me as I was before his death. . . .

LUKA. Instead of talking like that you ought to go and
have a walk in the garden, or else order Toby or Giant
to be harnessed, and then drive out to see some of the
neighbours.

POPOVA. Oh !   [*Weeps.*

LUKA. Madam ! Dear madam ! What is it ?   Bless
you !

POPOVA. He was so fond of Toby ! He always used to
ride on him to the Korchagins and Vlasovs. How well
he could ride ! What grace there was in his figure when
he pulled at the reins with all his strength ! Do you

remember ? Toby, Toby ! Tell them to give him an extra
feed of oats.

LUKA. Yes, madam.   *[A bell rings noisily.*

POPOVA. [*Shaking*] Who's that ? Tell them that I
receive nobody.

LUKA. Yes, madam.   [*Exit.*

POPOVA. [*Looks at the photograph*] You will see, *Nicolas,*
how I can love and forgive. . . . My love will die out with
me, only when this poor heart will cease to beat. [*Laughs
through her tears*] And aren't you ashamed ? I am a good
and virtuous little wife. I've locked myself in, and will
be true to you till the grave, and you . . . aren't you
ashamed, you bad child ? You deceived me, had rows
with me, left me alone for weeks on end . . . .

LUKA *enters in consternation.*

LUKA. Madam, somebody is asking for you. He wants
to see you. . . .

POPOVA. But didn't you tell him that since the death
of my husband I've stopped receiving ?

LUKA. I did, but he wouldn't even listen ; says that
it's a very pressing affair.

POPOVA. I do not re-ceive !

LUKA. I told him so, but the . . . the devil . . . curses
and pushes himself right in. . . . He's in the dining-room
now.

POPOVA. [*Annoyed*] Very well, ask him in. . . . What
manners ! [*Exit* LUKA] How these people annoy me !
What does he want of me ? Why should he disturb my
peace ? [*Sighs*] No, I see that I shall have to go into a
convent after all. [*Thoughtfully*] Yes, into a convent. . . .

[*Enter* LUKA *with* SMIRNOV.

SMIRNOV. [*To* LUKA] You fool, you're too fond of
talking. . . . Ass ! [*Sees* POPOVA *and speaks with respect*]

Madam, I have the honour to present myself, I am Grigory
Stepanovitch Smirnov, landowner and retired lieutenant
of artillery ! I am compelled to disturb you on a very
pressing affair.

POPOVA. [*Not giving him her hand*] What do you want ?

SMIRNOV. Your late husband, with whom I had the
honour of being acquainted, died in my debt for one
thousand two hundred roubles, on two bills of exchange.
As I've got to pay the interest on a mortgage to-morrow,
I've come to ask you, madam, to pay me the money to-day.

POPOVA. One thousand two hundred. . . . And what
was my husband in debt to you for ?

SMIRNOV. He used to buy oats from me.

POPOVA. [*Sighing, to* LUKA] So don't you forget, Luka,
to give Toby an extra feed of oats. [*Exit* LUKA] If Nicolai
Mihailovitch died in debt to you, then I shall certainly pay
you, but you must excuse me to-day, as I haven't any
spare cash. The day after to-morrow my steward will
be back from town, and I'll give him instructions to settle
your account, but at the moment I cannot do as you
wish. . . . Moreover, it's exactly seven months to-day since
the death of my husband, and I'm in a state of mind which
absolutely prevents me from giving money matters my
attention.

SMIRNOV. And I'm in a state of mind which, if I don't pay
the interest due to-morrow, will force me to make a graceful
exit from this life feet first. They'll take my estate !

POPOVA. You'll have your money the day after to-morrow.

SMIRNOV. I don't want the money the day after to-
morrow, I want it to-day.

POPOVA. You must excuse me, I can't pay you.

SMIRNOV. And I can't wait till after to-morrow.

POPOVA. Well, what can I do, if I haven't the money now !

SMIRNOV. You mean to say, you can't pay me ?

POPOVA. I can't.

SMIRNOV. Hm ! Is that the last word you've got to say ?

POPOVA. Yes, the last word.

SMIRNOV. The last word ? Absolutely your last ?

POPOVA. Absolutely.

SMIRNOV. Thank you so much. I'll make a note of it. [*Shrugs his shoulders*] And then people want me to keep calm ! I meet a man on the road, and he asks me : " Why are you always so angry, Grigory Stepanovitch ? " But how on earth am I not to get angry ? I want the money desperately. I rode out yesterday, early in the morning, and called on all my debtors, and not a single one of them paid up ! I was just about dead-beat after it all, slept, goodness knows where, in some inn, kept by a Jew, with a vodka-barrel by my head. At last I get here, seventy versts from home, and hope to get something, and I am received by you with a " state of mind " ! How shouldn't I get angry.

POPOVA. I thought I distinctly said my steward will pay you when he returns from town.

SMIRNOV. I didn't come to your steward, but to you ! What the devil, excuse my saying so, have I to do with your steward !

POPOVA. Excuse me, sir, I am not accustomed to listen to such expressions or to such a tone of voice. I want to hear no more. [*Makes a rapid exit.*

SMIRNOV. Well, there ! " A state of mind." . . . " Husband died seven months ago ! " Must I pay the interest, or mustn't I ? I ask you : Must I pay, or must I not ? Suppose your husband is dead, and you've got a state of mind, and nonsense of that sort. . . . And your steward's gone away somewhere, devil take him, what do you want

me to do ? Do you think I can fly away from my creditors
in a balloon, or what ? Or do you expect me to go and
run my head into a brick wall ? I go to Grusdev and he
isn't at home, Yaroshevitch has hidden himself, I had
a violent row with Kuritsin and nearly threw him out of
the window, Mazugo has something the matter with his
bowels, and this woman has " a state of mind." Not one
of the swine wants to pay me! Just because I'm too
gentle with them, because I'm a rag, just weak wax in
their hands! I'm much too gentle with them! Well,
just you wait! You'll find out what I'm like! I shan't
let you play about with me, confound it! I shall jolly
well stay here until she pays! Brr! . . . How angry
I am to-day, how angry I am! All my inside is quivering
with anger, and I can't even breathe. . . . Foo, my word
I even feel sick! [*Yells*] Waiter!

   Enter LUKA.

LUKA. What is it ?

SMIRNOV. Get me some kvass or water! [*Exit* LUKA],
What a way to reason! A man is in desperate need of
his money, and she won't pay it because, you see, she is
not disposed to attend to money matters! . . . That's
real silly feminine logic. That's why I never did like,
and don't like now, to have to talk to women. I'd rather
sit on a barrel of gunpowder than talk to a woman.
Brr! . . . I feel quite chilly—and it's all on account of
that little bit of fluff! I can't even see one of these
poetic creatures from a distance without breaking out into
a cold sweat out of sheer anger. I can't look at them.

   [*Enter* LUKA *with water.*

LUKA. Madam is ill and will see nobody.

SMIRNOV. Get out! [*Exit* LUKA] Ill and will see nobody! No, it's all right, you don't see me. . . . I'm

going to stay and will sit here till you give me the money.
You can be ill for a week, if you like, and I'll stay here
for a week. . . . If you're ill for a year—I'll stay for a
year. I'm going to get my own, my dear! You don't
get at me with your widow's weeds and your dimpled
cheeks! I know those dimples! [*Shouts through the
window*] Simeon, take them out! We aren't going away
at once! I'm staying here! Tell them in the stable to
give the horses some oats! You fool, you've let the near
horse's leg get tied up in the reins again! [*Teasingly*]
" Never mind. . . ." I'll give it you. " Never mind."
[*Goes away from the window*] Oh, it's bad. . . . The heat's
frightful, nobody pays up. I slept badly, and on top of
everything else here's a bit of fluff in mourning with " a
state of mind." . . . My head's aching. . . . Shall I have
some vodka, what? Yes, I think I will. [*Yells*] Waiter!

    Enter LUKA.

LUKA. What is it?

SMIRNOV. A glass of vodka! [*Exit* LUKA] Ouf! [*Sits
and inspects himself*] I must say I look well! Dust all
over, boots dirty, unwashed, unkempt, straw on my
waistcoat. . . . The dear lady may well have taken me
for a brigand. [*Yawns*] It's rather impolite to come into
a drawing-room in this state, but it can't be helped. . . .
I am not here as a visitor, but as a creditor, and there's
no dress specially prescribed for creditors. . . .

    Enter LUKA *with the vodka.*

LUKA. You allow yourself to go very far, sir. . . .

SMIRNOV. [*Angrily*] What?

LUKA. I . . . er . . . nothing . . . I really . . .

SMIRNOV. Whom are you talking to? Shut up!

LUKA. [*Aside*] The devil's come to stay. . . . Bad luck
that brought him. . . .   [*Exit.*

SMIRNOV. Oh, how angry I am! So angry that I think
I could grind the whole world to dust. . . . I even feel
sick. . . . [*Yells*] Waiter!

Enter POPOVA.

POPOVA. [*Her eyes downcast*] Sir, in my solitude I have
grown unaccustomed to the masculine voice, and I can't
stand shouting. I must ask you not to disturb my peace.

SMIRNOV. Pay me the money, and I'll go.

POPOVA. I told you perfectly plainly; I haven't any
money to spare; wait until the day after to-morrow.

SMIRNOV. And I told you perfectly plainly I don't want
the money the day after to-morrow, but to-day. If you
don't pay me to-day, I'll have to hang myself to-morrow.

POPOVA. But what can I do if I haven't got the money?
You're so strange!

SMIRNOV. Then you won't pay me now? Eh?

POPOVA. I can't. . . .

SMIRNOV. In that case I stay here and shall wait until
I get it. [*Sits down*] You're going to pay me the day after
to-morrow? Very well! I'll stay here until the day
after to-morrow. I'll sit here all the time. . . . [*Jumps
up*] I ask you: Have I got to pay the interest to-morrow,
or haven't I? Or do you think I'm doing this for a joke?

POPOVA. Please don't shout. This isn't a stable!

SMIRNOV. I wasn't asking you about a stable, but
whether I'd got my interest to pay to-morrow or not?

POPOVA. You don't know how to behave before women!

SMIRNOV. No, I do know how to behave before women!

POPOVA. No, you don't! You're a rude, ill-bred man!
Decent people don't talk to a woman like that!

SMIRNOV. What a business! How do you want me to
talk to you? In French, or what? [*Loses his temper and
lisps*] Madame, je vous prie. . . . How happy I am that

you don't pay me. . . . Ah, pardon. I have disturbed
you! Such lovely weather to-day! And how well you
look in mourning!   [*Bows.*

POPOVA. That's silly and rude.

SMIRNOV. [*Teasing her*] Silly and rude! I don't know
how to behave before women! Madam, in my time I've
seen more women than you've seen sparrows! Three
times I've fought duels on account of women. I've refused
twelve women, and nine have refused me! Yes! There
was a time when I played the fool, scented myself, used
honeyed words, wore jewellery, made beautiful bows. . . .
I used to love, to suffer, to sigh at the moon, to get sour,
to thaw, to freeze. . . . I used to love passionately, madly,
every blessed way, devil take me; I used to chatter like
a magpie about emancipation, and wasted half my wealth
on tender feelings, but now—you must excuse me! You
won't get round me like that now! I've had enough!
Black eyes, passionate eyes, ruby lips, dimpled cheeks,
the moon, whispers, timid breathing—I wouldn't give a
brass farthing for the lot, madam! Present company
always excepted, all women, great or little, are insincere,
crooked, backbiters, envious, liars to the marrow of their
bones, vain, trivial, merciless, unreasonable, and, as far
as this is concerned [*taps his forehead*] excuse my out-
spokenness, a sparrow can give ten points to any philosopher in petticoats you like to name! You look at one
of these poetic creatures: all muslin, an ethereal demi-
goddess, you have a million transports of joy, and you
look into her soul—and see a common crocodile! [*He grips
the back of a chair; the chair creaks and breaks*] But the
most disgusting thing of all is that this crocodile for some
reason or other imagines that its *chef d'œuvre*, its privilege
and monopoly, is its tender feelings. Why, confound it,

hang me on that nail feet upwards, if you like, but have
you met a woman who can love anybody except a lapdog ?
When she's in love, can she do anything but snivel and
slobber ? While a man is suffering and making sacrifices
all her love expresses itself in her playing about with her
scarf, and trying to hook him more firmly by the nose.
You have the misfortune to be a woman, you know from
yourself what is the nature of woman. Tell me truth-
fully, have you ever seen a woman who was sincere, faithful, and constant ? You haven't ! Only freaks and old
women are faithful and constant ! You'll meet a cat
with a horn or a white woodcock sooner than a constant
woman !

POPOVA. Then, according to you, who is faithful and
constant in love ? Is it the man ?

SMIRNOV. Yes, the man !

POPOVA. The man ! [*Laughs bitterly*] Men are faithful
and constant in love ! What an idea ! [*With heat*] What
right have you to talk like that ? Men are faithful and
constant. Since we are talking about it, I'll tell you that
of all the men I knew and know, the best was my late
husband. . . . I loved him passionately with all my
being, as only a young and imaginative woman can love.
I gave him my youth, my happiness, my life, my fortune,
I breathed in him, I worshipped him as if I were a heathen,
and . . . and what then ? This best of men shamelessly
deceived me at every step ' After his death I found in
his desk a whole drawerful of love-letters, and when he
was alive—it's an awful thing to remember !—he used to
leave me alone for weeks at a time, and make love to other
women and betray me before my very eyes ; he wasted
my money, and made fun of my feelings. . . . And, in
spite of all that, I loved him and was true to him. . . .

And not only that, but, now that he is dead, I am still
true and constant to his memory. I have shut myself for
ever within these four walls, and will wear these weeds
to the very end. . . .

SMIRNOV. [*Laughs contemptuously*] Weeds ! . . . I don't
understand what you take me for ? As if I don't know
why you wear that black domino and bury yourself between
four walls ! I should say I did ! It's so mysterious, so
poetic ! When some junker* or some tame poet goes past
your windows he'll think : " There lives the mysterious
Tamara who, for the love of her husband, buried herself
between four walls." We know these games !

POPOVA. [*Exploding*] What ? How dare you say all
that to me ?

SMIRNOV. You may have buried yourself alive, but you
haven't forgotten to powder your face !

POPOVA. How dare you speak to me like that ?

SMIRNOV. Please don't shout, I'm not your steward !
You must allow me to call things by their real names. I'm
not a woman, and I'm used to saying what I think straight
out ! Don't you shout, either !

POPOVA. I'm not shouting, it's you ! Please leave me
alone !

SMIRNOV. Pay me my money and I'll go.

POPOVA. I shan't give you any money !

SMIRNOV. Oh, no, you will.

POPOVA. I shan't give you a farthing, just to spite you.
You leave me alone !

SMIRNOV. I have not the pleasure of being either your
husband or your fiancé, so please don't make scenes. [*Sits*]
I don't like it.

POPOVA. [*Choking with rage*] So you sit down ?

* So in the original

SMIRNOV. I do.

POPOVA. I ask you to go away!

SMIRNOV. Give me my money. . . . [*Aside*] Oh, how angry I am! How angry I am!

POPOVA. I don't want to talk to impudent scoundrels! Get out of this! [*Pause*] Aren't you going? No?

SMIRNOV. No.

POPOVA. No.?

SMIRNOV. No!

POPOVA. Very well then! [*Rings, enter* LUKA] Luka, show this gentleman out!

LUKA. [*Approaches* SMIRNOV] Would you mind going out, sir, as you're asked to! You needn't . . .

SMIRNOV. [*Jumps up*] Shut up! Who are you talking to? I'll chop you into pieces!

LUKA. [*Clutches at his heart*] Little fathers! . . . What people! . . . [*Falls into a chair*] Oh, I'm ill, I'm ill! I can't breathe!

POPOVA. Where's Dasha? Dasha! [*Shouts*] Dasha! Pelageya! Dasha!   [*Rings.*

LUKA. Oh! They've all gone out to pick fruit. . . . There's nobody at home! I'm ill! Water!

POPOVA. Get out of this, now.

SMIRNOV. Can't you be more polite?

POPOVA. [*Clenches her fists and stamps her foot*] You're a boor! A coarse bear! A Bourbon! A monster!

SMIRNOV. What? What did you say?

POPOVA. I said you are a bear, a monster!

SMIRNOV. [*Approaching her*] May I ask what right you have to insult me?

POPOVA. And suppose I am insulting you? Do you think I'm afraid of you?

SMIRNOV. And do you think that just because you're a

poetic creature you can insult me with impunity ? Eh ?
We'll fight it out !

LUKA. Little fathers ! . . . What people ! . . . Water !

SMIRNOV. Pistols !

POPOVA. Do you think I'm afraid of you just because
you have large fists and a bull's throat ? Eh ? You
Bourbon !

SMIRNOV. We'll fight it out ! I'm not going to be
insulted by anybody, and I don't care if you are a woman,
one of the " softer sex," indeed !

POPOVA. [*Trying to interrupt him*] Bear ! Bear ! Bear !

SMIRNOV. It's about time we got rid of the prejudice
that only men need pay for their insults. Devil take it,
if you want equality of rights you can have it. We're
going to fight it out !

POPOVA. With pistols ? Very well !

SMIRNOV. This very minute.

POPOVA. This very minute ! My husband had some
pistols. . . . I'll bring them here. [*Is going, but turns
back*] What pleasure it will give me to put a bullet into
your thick head ! Devil take you !   [*Exit.*

SMIRNOV. I'll bring her down like a chicken ! I'm not
a little boy or a sentimental puppy ; I don't care about
this " softer sex."

LUKA. Gracious little fathers ! . . . [*Kneels*] Have pity
on a poor old man, and go away from here ! You've
frightened her to death, and now you want to shoot her !

SMIRNOV. [*Not hearing him*] If she fights, well that's
equality of rights, emancipation, and all that ! Here the
sexes are equal ! I'll shoot her on principle ! But what
a woman ! [*Parodying her*] " Devil take you ! I'll put a
bullet into your thick head." Eh ? How she reddened,
how her cheeks shone ! . . . She accepted my challenge !

My word, it's the first time in my life that I've
seen. . . .

LUKA. Go away, sir, and I'll always pray to God for
you !

SMIRNOV. She is a woman ! That's the sort I can understand ! A real woman ! Not a sour-faced jellybag, but
fire, gunpowder, a rocket ! I'm even sorry to have to kill
her !

LUKA. [*Weeps*] Dear . . . dear sir, do go away !

SMIRNOV. I absolutely like her ! Absolutely ! Even
though her cheeks are dimpled, I like her ! I'm almost
ready to let the debt go . . . and I'm not angry any
longer. . . . Wonderful woman !

    Enter POPOVA *with pistols.*

POPOVA. Here are the pistols. . . . But before we fight
you must show me how to fire. I've never held a pistol
in my hands before.

LUKA. Oh, Lord, have mercy and save her. . . . I'll
go and find the coachman and the gardener. . . . Why
has this infliction come on us. . . .   [*Exit.*

SMIRNOV. [*Examining the pistols*] You see, there are
several sorts of pistols. . . . There are Mortimer pistols
specially made for duels, they fire a percussion-cap. These
are Smith and Wesson revolvers, triple action, with
extractors. . . . These are excellent pistols. They can't
cost less than ninety roubles the pair. . . . You must hold
the revolver like this. . . . [*Aside*] Her eyes, her eyes !
What an inspiring woman !

POPOVA. Like this ?

SMIRNOV. Yes, like this. . . . Then you cock the trigger,
and take aim like this. . . . Put your head back a little !
Hold your arm out properly. . . . Like that. . . . Then
you press this thing with your finger—and that's all.

The great thing is to keep cool and aim steadily. . . . Try not to jerk your arm.

POPOVA. Very well. . . . It's inconvenient to shoot in a room, let's go into the garden.

SMIRNOV. Come along then. But I warn you, I'm going to fire in the air.

POPOVA. That's the last straw! Why?

SMIRNOV. Because . . . because . . . it's my affair.

POPOVA. Are you afraid? Yes? Ah! No, sir, you don't get out of it! You come with me! I shan't have any peace until I've made a hole in your forehead . . . that forehead which I hate so much! Are you afraid?

SMIRNOV. Yes, I am afraid.

POPOVA. You lie! Why won't you fight?

SMIRNOV. Because . . . because you . . . because I like you.

POPOVA. [*Laughs*] He likes me! He dares to say that he likes me! [*Points to the door*] That's the way.

SMIRNOV. [*Loads the revolver in silence, takes his cap and goes to the door. There he stops for half a minute, while they look at each other in silence, then he hesitatingly approaches* POPOVA] Listen. . . . Are you still angry? I'm devilishly annoyed, too . . . but, do you understand . . . how can I express myself? . . . . The fact is, you see, it's like this, so to speak. . . . [*Shouts*] Well, is it my fault that I like you? [*He snatches at the back of a chair; the chair creaks and breaks*] Devil take it, how I'm smashing up your furniture! I like you! Do you understand! I . . . I almost love you!

POPOVA. Get away from me—I hate you!

SMIRNOV. God, what a woman! I've never in my life seen one like her! I'm lost! Done for! Fallen into a mousetrap, like a mouse!

POPOVA. Stand back, or I'll fire !

SMIRNOV. Fire, then ! You can't understand what happiness it would be to die before those beautiful eyes, to be shot by a revolver held in that little, velvet hand. . . . I'm out of my senses ! Think, and make up your mind at once, because if I go out we shall never see each other again ! Decide now. . . . I am a landowner, of respectable character, have an income of ten thousand a year. . . . I can put a bullet through a coin tossed into the air as it comes down. . . . I own some fine horses. . . . Will you be my wife ?

POPOVA. [*Indignantly shakes her revolver*] Let's fight ! Let's go out !

SMIRNOV. I'm mad. . . . I understand nothing. . . . [*Yells*] Waiter, water !

POPOVA. [*Yells*] Let's go out and fight !

SMIRNOV. I'm off my head, I'm in love like a boy, like a fool ! [*Snatches her hand, she screams with pain*] I love you ! [*Kneels*] I love you as I've never loved before ! I've refused twelve women, nine have refused me, but I never loved one of them as I love you. . . . I'm weak, I'm wax, I've melted. . . . I'm on my knees like a fool, offering you my hand. . . . Shame, shame ! I haven't been in love for five years, I'd taken a vow, and now all of a sudden I'm in love, like a fish out of water ! I offer you my hand. Yes or no ? You don't want me ? Very well !

[*Gets up and quickly goes to the door.*

POPOVA. Stop.

SMIRNOV. [*Stops*] Well ?

POPOVA. Nothing, go away . . No, stop. . . . No, go away, go away ! I hate you ! Or no. . . . Don't go away ! Oh, if you knew how angry I am, how angry I am ! [*Throws her revolver on the table*] My fingers have swollen because of all this. . . . [*Tears her handkerchief in temper*] What are you waiting for ? Get out !

SMIRNOV. Good-bye.

POPOVA. Yes, yes, go away ! . . . [*Yells*] Where are you going ? Stop. . . . No, go away. Oh, how angry I am ! Don't come near me, don't come near me !

SMIRNOV. [*Approaching her*] How angry I am with myself ! I'm in love like a student, I've been on my knees. . . . [*Rudely*] I love you ! What do I want to fall in love with you for ? To-morrow I've got to pay the interest, and begin mowing, and here you. . . . [*Puts his arms around her*] I shall never forgive myself for this. . . .

POPOVA. Get away from me ! Take your hands away ! I hate you ! Let's go and fight !

> *A prolonged kiss. Enter* LUKA *with an axe, the* GARDENER *with a rake, the* COACHMAN *with a pitchfork, and* WORKMEN *with poles.*

LUKA. [*Catches sight of the pair kissing*] Little fathers !

> [*Pause.*

POPOVA. [*Lowering her eyes*] Luka, tell them in the stables that Toby isn't to have any oats at all to-day.

Curtain.

THE SEAGULL
A PLAY IN FOUR ACTS

CHARACTERS

IRINA ARKADINA, *an actress.*
CONSTANTINE TREPLIEFF, *her son.*
PETER SORIN, *her brother.*
NINA ZARIETCHNAYA, *a young girl, the daughter of a rich landowner.*
ILIA SHAMRAEFF, *the manager of* SORIN'S *estate.*
PAULINA, *his wife.*
MASHA, *their daughter.*
BORIS TRIGORIN, *an author.*
EUGENE DORN, *a doctor.*
SIMON MEDVIEDENKO, *a schoolmaster.*
JACOB, *a workman.*
A COOK.
A MAIDSERVANT.

The scene is laid on SORIN'S *estate. Two years elapse between the third and fourth acts.*

ACT ONE

The scene is laid in the park on SORIN's *estate. A broad avenue of trees leads away from the audience toward a lake which lies lost in the depths of the park. The avenue is obstructed by a rough stage, temporarily erected for the performance of amateur theatricals, and which screens the lake from view. There is a dense growth of bushes to the left and right of the stage. A few chairs and a little table are placed in front of the stage. The sun has just set.* JACOB *and some other workmen are heard hammering and coughing on the stage behind the lowered curtain.*

MASHA *and* MEDVIEDENKO *come in from the left, returning from a walk.*

MEDVIEDENKO. Why do you always wear mourning ?

MASHA. I dress in black to match my life. I am unhappy.

MEDVIEDENKO. Why should you be unhappy ? [*Thinking it over*] I don't understand it. You are healthy, and though your father is not rich, he has a good competency. My life is far harder than yours. I only have twenty-three roubles a month to live on, but I don't wear mourning.   [*They sit down.*

MASHA. Happiness does not depend on riches ; poor men are often happy.

MEDVIEDENKO. In theory, yes, but not in reality. Take my case, for instance ; my mother, my two sisters, my little brother and I must all live somehow on my

salary of twenty-three roubles a month.   We have to
eat and drink, I take it. You wouldn't have us go without
tea and sugar, would you ? Or tobacco ? Answer me
that, if you can.

MASHA. [*Looking in the direction of the stage*] The play
will soon begin.

MEDVIEDENKO. Yes, Nina Zarietchnaya is going to act
in Treplieff's play. They love one another, and their two
souls will unite to-night in the effort to interpret the same
idea by different means. There is no ground on which
your soul and mine can meet. I love you. Too restless
and sad to stay at home, I tramp here every day, six miles
and back, to be met only by your indifference. I am
poor, my family is large, you can have no inducement to
marry a man who cannot even find sufficient food for his
own mouth.

MASHA. It is not that. [*She takes snuff*] I am touched
by your affection, but I cannot return it, that is all. [*She
offers him the snuff-box*] Will you take some ?

MEDVIEDENKO. No, thank you.   [*A pause.*

MASHA. The air is sultry ; a storm is brewing for
to-night. You do nothing but moralise or else talk about
money. To you, poverty is the greatest misfortune that
can befall a man, but I think it is a thousand times easier
to go begging in rags than to— You wouldn't understand
that, though.

   SORIN *leaning on a cane, and* TREPLIEFF *come in.*

SORIN. For some reason, my boy, country life doesn't
suit me, and I am sure I shall never get used to it. Last
night I went to bed at ten and woke at nine this morning,
feeling as if, from oversleep, my brain had stuck to my
skull. [*Laughing*] And yet I accidentally dropped off to
sleep again after dinner, and feel utterly done up at this
moment. It is like a nightmare.

TREPLIEFF. There is no doubt that you should live in

town. [*He catches sight of* MASHA *and* MEDVIEDENKO] You shall be called when the play begins, my friends, but you must not stay here now. Go away, please.

SORIN. Miss Masha, will you kindly ask your father to leave the dog unchained ? It howled so last night that my sister was unable to sleep.

MASHA. You must speak to my father yourself. Please excuse me ; I can't do so. [*To* MEDVIEDENKO] Come, let us go.

MEDVIEDENKO. You will let us know when the play begins ?

MASHA *and* MEDVIEDENKO *go out.*

SORIN. I foresee that that dog is going to howl all night again. It is always this way in the country ; I have never been able to live as I like here. I come down for a month's holiday, to rest and all, and am plagued so by their nonsense that I long to escape after the first day. [*Laughing*] I have always been glad to get away from this place, but I have been retired now, and this was the only place I had to come to. Willy-nilly, one must live somewhere.

JACOB. [*To* TREPLIEFF] We are going to take a swim, Mr. Constantine.

TREPLIEFF. Very well, but you must be back in ten minutes.

JACOB. We will, sir.

TREPLIEFF. [*Looking at the stage*] Just like a real theatre ! See, there we have the curtain, the foreground, the background, and all. No artificial scenery is needed. The eye travels direct to the lake, and rests on the horizon. The curtain will be raised as the moon rises at half-past eight.

SORIN. Splendid !

TREPLIEFF. Of course the whole effect will be ruined if Nina is late. She should be here by now, but her father and stepmother watch her so closely that it is like stealing her from a prison to get her away from home. [*He straightens* SORIN'S *collar*] Your hair and beard are all on end. Oughtn't you to have them trimmed ?

SORIN. [*Smoothing his beard*] They are the tragedy of my existence. Even when I was young I always looked as if I were drunk, and all. Women have never liked me. [*Sitting down*] Why is my sister out of temper ?

TREPLIEFF. Why ? Because she is jealous and bored. [*Sitting down beside* SORIN] She is not acting this evening, but Nina is, and so she has set herself against me, and against the performance of the play, and against the play itself, which she hates without ever having read it.

SORIN. [*Laughing*] Does she, really ?

TREPLIEFF. Yes, she is furious because Nina is going to have a success on this little stage. [*Looking at his watch*] My mother is a psychological curiosity. Without doubt brilliant and talented, capable of sobbing over a novel, of reciting all Nekrasoff's poetry by heart, and of nursing the sick like an angel of heaven, you should see what happens if anyone begins praising Duse to her ! She alone must be praised and written about, raved over, her marvellous acting in *La Dame aux Camélias* extolled to the skies. As she cannot get all that rubbish in the country, she grows peevish and cross, and thinks we are all against her, and to blame for it all. She is superstitious, too. She dreads burning three candles, and fears the thirteenth day of the month. Then she is stingy. I know for a fact that she has seventy thousand roubles in a bank at Odessa, but she is ready to burst into tears if you ask her to lend you a penny.

SORIN. You have taken it into your head that your mother dislikes your play, and the thought of it has excited you, and all. Keep calm ; your mother adores you.

TREPLIEFF. [*Pulling a flower to pieces*] She loves me, loves me not ; loves—loves me not ; loves—loves me not ! [*Laughing*] You see, she doesn't love me, and why should she ? She likes life and love and gay clothes, and I am already twenty-five years old; a sufficient reminder to her that she is no longer young. When I am away she is only thirty-two, in my presence she is forty-three, and she hates me for it. She knows, too, that I despise the modern stage. She adores it, and imagines that she is working on it for the benefit of humanity and her sacred art, but to me the theatre is merely the vehicle of convention and prejudice. When the curtain rises on that little three-walled room, when those mighty geniuses, those high-priests of art, show us people in the act of eating, drinking, loving, walking, and wearing their coats, and attempt to extract a moral from their insipid talk; when playwrights give us under a thousand different guises the same, same, same old stuff, then I must needs run from it, as Maupassant ran from the Eiffel Tower that was about to crush him by its vulgarity.

SORIN.   But we can't do without a theatre.

TREPLIEFF.   No, but we must have it under a new form. If we can't do that, let us rather not have it at all. [*Looking at his watch*] I love my mother, I love her devotedly, but I think she leads a stupid life. She always has this man of letters of hers on her mind, and the newspapers are always frightening her to death, and I am tired of it. Plain, human egoism sometimes speaks in my heart, and I regret that my mother is a famous actress. If she were an ordinary woman I think I should be a happier man. What could be more intolerable and foolish than my position, Uncle, when I find myself the only nonentity among a crowd of her guests, all celebrated authors and artists ? I feel that they only endure me because I am her son. Personally I am nothing, nobody. I pulled through my third year at college by the skin of my teeth, as they say. I have neither money nor brains, and on my passport you may read that I am simply a citizen of Kiev. So was my father, but he was a well-known actor. When the celebrities that frequent my mother's drawing-room deign to notice me at all, I know they only look at me to measure my insignificance; I read their thoughts, and suffer from humiliation.

SORIN. Tell me, by the way, what is Trigorin like? I can't understand him, he is always so silent.

TREPLIEFF. Trigorin is clever, simple, well-mannered, and a little, I might say, melancholic in disposition. Though still under forty, he is surfeited with praise. As for his stories, they are—how shall I put it?—pleasing, full of talent, but if you have read Tolstoi or Zola you somehow don't enjoy Trigorin.

SORIN. Do you know, my boy, I like literary men. I once passionately desired two things: to marry, and to become an author. I have succeeded in neither. It must be pleasant to be even an insignificant author.

TREPLIEFF. [*Listening*] I hear footsteps! [*He embraces his uncle*] I cannot live without her; even the sound of her footsteps is music to me. I am madly happy. [*He goes quickly to meet* NINA, *who comes in at that moment*] My enchantress! My girl of dreams!

NINA. [*Excitedly*] It can't be that I am late? No, I am not late.

TREPLIEFF. [*Kissing her hands*] No, no, no!

NINA. I have been in a fever all day, I was so afraid my father would prevent my coming, but he and my stepmother have just gone driving. The sky is clear, the moon is rising. How I hurried to get here! How I urged my horse to go faster and faster! [*Laughing*] I am *so* glad to see you!

[*She shakes hands with* SORIN.

SORIN. Oho! Your eyes look as if you had been crying. You mustn't do that.

NINA. It is nothing, nothing. Do let us hurry. I

must go in half an hour. No, no, for heaven's sake do not urge me to stay. My father doesn't know I am here.

TREPLIEFF. As a matter of fact, it is time to begin now. I must call the audience.

SORIN. Let me call them—and all—I am going this minute. [*He goes toward the right, begins to sing " The Two Grenadiers," then stops.*] I was singing that once when a fellow-lawyer said to me : " You have a powerful voice, sir." Then he thought a moment and added, " But it is a disagreeable one ! "

[*He goes out laughing.*

NINA. My father and his wife never will let me come here ; they call this place Bohemia and are afraid I shall become an actress. But this lake attracts me as it does the gulls. My heart is full of you. [*She glances about her.*

TREPLIEFF. We are alone.

NINA. Isn't that someone over there ?

TREPLIEFF. No.   [*They kiss one another.*

NINA. What is that tree ?

TREPLIEFF. An elm.

NINA. Why does it look so dark ?

TREPLIEFF. It is evening ; everything looks dark now. Don't go away early, I implore you.

NINA. I must.

TREPLIEFF. What if I were to follow you, Nina ? I shall stand in your garden all night with my eyes on your window.

NINA. That would be impossible ; the watchman would see you, and Treasure is not used to you yet, and would bark.

TREPLIEFF. I love you.

NINA. Hush !

TREPLIEFF. [*Listening to approaching footsteps*] Who is that ? Is it you, Jacob ?

JACOB. [*On the stage*] Yes, sir.

TREPLIEFF. To your places then. The moon is rising;
the play must commence.

NINA. Yes, sir.

TREPLIEFF. Is the alcohol ready? Is the sulphur
ready? There must be fumes of sulphur in the air when
the red eyes shine out. [*To* NINA] Go, now, everything is
ready. Are you nervous?

NINA. Yes, very. I am not so much afraid of your
mother as I am of Trigorin. I am terrified and ashamed
to act before him; he is so famous. Is he young?

TREPLIEFF. Yes.

NINA. What beautiful stories he writes!

TREPLIEFF. [*Coldly*] I have never read any of them,
so I can't say.

NINA. Your play is very hard to act; there are no
living characters in it.

TREPLIEFF. Living characters! Life must be repre-
sented not as it is, but as it ought to be; as it appears in
dreams.

NINA. There is so little action; it seems more like a
recitation. I think love should always come into every
play.

> NINA *and* TREPLIEFF *go up on to the little stage;*
> PAULINA *and* DORN *come in.*

PAULINA. It is getting damp. Go back and put on
your goloshes.

DORN. I am quite warm.

PAULINA. You never will take care of yourself; you
are quite obstinate about it, and yet you are a doctor, and
know quite well that damp air is bad for you. You like
to see me suffer, that's what it is. You sat out on the
terrace all yesterday evening on purpose.

DORN. [*Sings*]

" Oh, tell me not that youth is wasted."

PAULINA. You were so enchanted by the conversation

of Madame Arkadina that you did not even notice the cold. Confess that you admire her.

DORN. I am fifty-five years old.

PAULINA. A trifle. That is not old for a man. You have kept your looks magnificently, and women still like you.

DORN. What are you trying to tell me ?

PAULINA. You men are all ready to go down on your knees to an actress, all of you.

DORN. [*Sings*]
      " Once more I stand before thee."

It is only right that artists should be made much of by society and treated differently from, let us say, merchants. It is a kind of idealism.

PAULINA. When women have loved you and thrown themselves at your head, has that been idealism ?

DORN. [*Shrugging his shoulders*] I can't say. There has been a great deal that was admirable in my relations with women. In me they liked, above all, the superior doctor. Ten years ago, you remember, I was the only decent doctor they had in this part of the country—and then, I have always acted like a man of honour.

PAULINA. [*Seizes his hand*] Dearest !

DORN. Be quiet ! Here they come.

      ARKADINA *comes in on* SORIN'S *arm ; also* TRIGORIN,
          SHAMRAEFF, MEDVIEDENKO, *and* MASHA.

SHAMRAEFF. She acted most beautifully at the Poltava Fair in 1873 ; she was really magnificent. But tell me, too, where Tchadin the comedian is now ? He was inimitable as Rasplueff, better than Sadofski. Where is he now ?

ARKADINA. Don't ask me where all those antediluvians are ! I know nothing about them.   [*She sits down.*

SHAMRAEFF. [*Sighing*] Pashka Tchadin ! There are none left like him. The stage is not what it was in his time. There were sturdy oaks growing on it then, where now but stumps remain.

DORN. It is true that we have few dazzling geniuses these days, but, on the other hand, the average of acting is much higher.

SHAMRAEFF. I cannot agree with you; however, that is a matter of taste, *de gustibus*.

Enter TREPLIEFF *from behind the stage.*

ARKADINA. When will the play begin, my dear boy?

TREPLIEFF. In a moment. I must ask you to have patience.

ARKADINA. [*Quoting from Hamlet*] My son,
"Thou turn'st mine eyes into my very soul;
And there I see such black grained spots
As will not leave their tinct."

[*A horn is blown behind the stage.*

TREPLIEFF. Attention, ladies and gentlemen! The play is about to begin. [*A pause*] I shall commence. [*He taps the door with a stick, and speaks in a loud voice*] O, ye time-honoured, ancient mists that drive at night across the surface of this lake, blind you our eyes with sleep, and show us in our dreams that which will be in twice ten thousand years!

SORIN. There won't be anything in twice ten thousand years.

TREPLIEFF. Then let them now show us that nothingness.

ARKADINA. Yes, let them—we are asleep.

The curtain rises. A vista opens across the lake. The moon hangs low above the horizon and is reflected in the water. NINA, *dressed in white, is seen seated on a great rock.*

NINA. All men and beasts, lions, eagles, and quails, horned stags, geese, spiders, silent fish that inhabit the waves, star-fish from the sea, and creatures invisible to the eye—in one word, life—all, all life, completing the dreary round imposed upon it, has died out at last. A thousand years have passed since the earth last bore a living creature on her breast, and the unhappy moon now lights her lamp in vain. No longer are the cries of storks heard in the meadows, or the drone of beetles in the groves of limes, All is cold, cold. All is void, void, void. All is terrible, terrible—[*A pause*] The bodies of all living creatures have dropped to dust, and eternal matter has transformed them into stones and water and clouds; but their spirits have flowed together into one, and that great world-soul am I! In me is the spirit of the great Alexander, the spirit of Napoleon, of Caesar, of Shakespeare, and of the tiniest leech that swims. In me the consciousness of man has joined hands with the instinct of the animal; I understand all, all, all, and each life lives again in me.

[*The will-o'-the-wisps flicker out along the lake shore.*]

ARKADINA. [*Whispers*] What decadent rubbish is this?

TREPLIEFF. [*Imploringly*] Mother!

NINA. I am alone. Once in a hundred years my lips are opened, my voice echoes mournfully across the desert earth, and no one hears. And you, poor lights of the marsh, you do not hear me. You are engendered at sunset in the putrid mud, and flit wavering about the lake till dawn, unconscious, unreasoning, unwarmed by the breath of life. Satan, father of eternal matter, trembling lest the spark of life should glow in you, has ordered an unceasing movement of the atoms that compose you, and so you shift and change for ever. I, the spirit of the universe, I alone am immutable and eternal. [*A pause*] Like a captive in a dungeon deep and void, I know not where I am, nor what awaits me. One thing only is not hidden from me: in my fierce and obstinate battle with Satan, the sources of the forces of matter, I am destined to be victorious in the end. Matter and spirit will then be one at last in glorious harmony, and the reign of freedom will begin on earth. But this can only come to pass by slow degrees, when after countless æons the moon and earth and shining Sirius himself shall fall to dust. Until that hour, oh, horror! horror! horror! [*A pause. Two glowing red points are seen shining across the lake*] Satan, my mighty foe, advances; I see his dread and lurid eyes.

ARKADINA. I smell sulphur. Is that done on purpose?

TREPLIEFF. Yes.

ARKADINA. Oh, I see; that is part of the effect.

TREPLIEFF. Mother!

NINA. He longs for man——

PAULINA. [*To* DORN] You have taken off your hat again! Put it on, you will catch cold.

ARKADINA. The doctor has taken off his hat to Satan, father of eternal matter——

TREPLIEFF. [*Loudly and angrily*] Enough of this! There's an end to the performance. Down with the curtain!

ARKADINA. Why, what are you so angry about?

TREPLIEFF. [*Stamping his foot*] The curtain; down with it! [*The curtain falls*] Excuse me, I forgot that only a chosen few might write plays or act them. I have infringed the monopoly. I—I——

He would like to say more, but waves his hand instead. and goes out to the left.

ARKADINA. What is the matter with him?

SORIN. You should not handle youthful egoism so roughly, sister.

ARKADINA. What did I say to him?

SORIN. You hurt his feelings.

ARKADINA. But he told me himself that this was all in fun, so I treated his play as if it were a comedy.

SORIN. Nevertheless——

ARKADINA. Now it appears that he has produced a masterpiece, if you please! I suppose it was not meant to

amuse us at all, but that he arranged the performance and
fumigated us with sulphur to demonstrate to us how plays
should be written, and what is worth acting. I am tired
of him. No one could stand his constant thrusts and
sallies. He is a wilful, egotistic boy.

SORIN. He had hoped to give you pleasure.

ARKADINA. Is that so ? I notice, though, that he
did not choose an ordinary play, but forced his decadent
trash on us. I am willing to listen to any raving, so long
as it is not meant seriously, but in showing us this, he
pretended to be introducing us to a new form of art, and
inaugurating a new era. In my opinion, there was nothing
new about it, it was simply an exhibition of bad temper.

TRIGORIN. Everybody must write as he feels, and as
best he may.

ARKADINA. Let him write as he feels and can, but let
him spare me his nonsense.

DORN. Thou art angry, O Jove !

ARKADINA. I am a woman, not Jove. [*She lights a
cigarette*] And I am not angry, I am only sorry to see a
young man foolishly wasting his time. I did not mean to
hurt him.

MEDVIEDENKO. No one has any ground for separating
life from matter, as the spirit may well consist of the union
of material atoms. [*Excitedly, to* TRIGORIN] Some day you
should write a play, and put on the stage the life of a
schoolmaster. It is a hard, hard life.

ARKADINA. I agree with you, but do not let us talk
about plays or atoms now. This is such a lovely evening.
Listen to the singing, friends, how sweet it sounds.

PAULINA. Yes, they are singing across the water.
                                              [*A pause.*

ARKADINA. [*To* TRIGORIN] Sit down beside me here. Ten
or fifteen years ago we had music and singing on this
lake almost all night. There are six houses on its shores.

                                                       D

All was noise and laughter and romance then, such romance !
The young star and idol of them all in those days was this
man here, [*Nods towards* DORN] Doctor Eugene Dorn.
He is fascinating now, but he was irresistible then. But
my conscience is beginning to prick me. Why did I
hurt my poor boy ? I am uneasy about him. [*Loudly*]
Constantine ! Constantine !

MASHA. Shall I go and find him ?

ARKADINA. If you please, my dear.

MASHA. [*Goes off to the left, calling*] Mr. Constantine !
Oh, Mr. Constantine !

NINA. [*Comes in from behind the stage*] I see that the
play will never be finished, so now I can go home. Good
evening.   [*She kisses* ARKADINA *and* PAULINA.

SORIN. Bravo ! Bravo !

ARKADINA. Bravo ! Bravo ! We were quite charmed
by your acting. With your looks and such a lovely voice
it is a crime for you to hide yourself in the country. You
must be very talented. It is your duty to go on the stage,
do you hear me ?

NINA. It is the dream of my life, which will never come
true.

ARKADINA. Who knows ? Perhaps it will. But let me
present Monsieur Boris Trigorin.

NINA. I am delighted to meet you. [*Embarrassed*]
I have read all your books.

ARKADINA. [*Drawing* NINA *down beside her*] Don't be
afraid of him, dear. He is a simple, good-natured soul,
even if he is a celebrity. See, he is embarrassed himself.

DORN. Couldn't the curtain be raised now ? It is
depressing to have it down.

SHAMRAEFF. [*Loudly*] Jacob, my man ! Raise the
curtain !

NINA. [*To* TRIGORIN] It was a curious play, wasn't it ?

TRIGORIN. Very. I couldn't understand it at all, but

I watched it with the greatest pleasure because you acted with such sincerity, and the setting was beautiful. [*A pause*] There must be a lot of fish in this lake.

NINA. Yes, there are.

TRIGORIN. I love fishing. I know of nothing pleasanter than to sit on a lake shore in the evening with one's eyes on a floating cork.

NINA. Why, I should think that for one who has tasted the joys of creation, no other pleasure could exist.

ARKADINA. Don't talk like that. He always begins to flounder when people say nice things to him.

SHAMRAEFF. I remember when the famous Silva was singing once in the Opera House at Moscow, how delighted we all were when he took the low C. Well, you can imagine our astonishment when one of the church cantors, who happened to be sitting in the gallery, suddenly boomed out " Bravo Silva ! " a whole octave lower. Like this : [*In a deep bass voice*] " Bravo, Silva ! " The audience was left breathless. [*A pause.*

DORN. An angel of silence is flying over our heads.

NINA. I must go. Good-bye.

ARKADINA. Where to ? Where must you go so early ? We shan't allow it.

NINA. My father is waiting for me.

ARKADINA. How cruel he is, really. [*They kiss each other*] Then I suppose we can't keep you, but it is very hard indeed to let you go.

NINA. If you only knew how hard it is for me to leave you all.

ARKADINA. Somebody must see you home, my pet.

NINA. [*Startled*] No, no !

SORIN. [*Imploringly*] Don't go !

NINA. I must.

SORIN. Stay just one hour more, and all. Come now, really, you know.

NINA. [*Struggling against her desire to stay; through her tears*] No, no, I can't.

[*She shakes hands with him and quickly goes out.*

ARKADINA. An unlucky girl! They say that her mother left the whole of an immense fortune to her husband, and now the child is penniless because the father has already willed everything away to his second wife. It is pitiful.

DORN. Yes, her papa is a perfect beast, and I don't mind saying so—it is what he deserves.

SORIN. [*Rubbing his chilled hands*] Come, let us go in; the night is damp, and my legs are aching.

ARKADINA. Yes, you act as if they were turned to stone; you can hardly move them. Come, you unfortunate old man.

[*She takes his arm.*

SHAMRAEFF. [*Offering his arm to his wife*] Permit me, madam.

SORIN. I hear that dog howling again. Won't you please have it unchained, Shamraeff?

SHAMRAEFF. No, I really can't, sir. The granary is full of millet, and I am afraid thieves might break in if the dog were not there. [*Walking beside* MEDVIEDENKO] Yes, a whole octave lower: " Bravo, Silva ! " and he wasn't a singer either, just a simple church cantor.

MEDVIEDENKO. What salary does the church pay its singers ?   [*All go out except* DORN.

DORN. I may have lost my judgment and my wits, but I must confess I liked that play. There was something in it. When the girl spoke of her solitude and the Devil's eyes gleamed across the lake, I felt my hands shaking with excitement. It was so fresh and naïve. But here he comes; let me say something pleasant to him.

TREPLIEFF *comes in.*

TREPLIEFF. All gone already ?

DORN. I am here.

TREPLIEFF. Masha has been yelling for me all over the park. An insufferable creature.

DORN. Constantine, your play delighted me. It was strange, of course, and I did not hear the end, but it made a deep impression on me. You have a great deal of talent, and must persevere in your work.

TREPLIEFF *seizes his hand and squeezes it hard, then kisses him impetuously.*

DORN. Tut, tut! how excited you are. Your eyes are full of tears. Listen to me. You chose your subject in the realm of abstract thought, and you did quite right. A work of art should invariably embody some lofty idea. Only that which is seriously meant can ever be beautiful. How pale you are!

TREPLIEFF. So you advise me to persevere?

DORN. Yes, but use your talent to express only deep and eternal truths. I have led a quiet life, as you know, and am a contented man, but if I should ever experience the exaltation that an artist feels during his moments of creation, I think I should spurn this material envelope of my soul and everything connected with it, and should soar away into heights above this earth.

TREPLIEFF. I beg your pardon, but where is Nina?

DORN. And yet another thing: every work of art should have a definite object in view. You should know why you are writing, for if you follow the road of art without a goal before your eyes, you will lose yourself, and your genius will be your ruin.

TREPLIEFF. [*Impetuously*] Where is Nina?

DORN. She has gone home.

TREPLIEFF. [*In despair*] Gone home? What *shall* I do? I want to see her; I must see her! I shall follow her.

DORN. My dear boy, keep quiet.

TREPLIEFF. I am going. I must go.

MASHA *comes in.*

MASHA. Your mother wants you to come in, Mr. Constantine. She is waiting for you, and is very uneasy.

TREPLIEFF. Tell her I have gone away. And for heaven's sake, all of you, leave me alone! Go away! Don't follow me about!

DORN. Come, come, old chap, don't act like this; it isn't kind at all.

TREPLIEFF. [*Through his tears*] Good-bye, doctor, and thank you.

TREPLIEFF *goes out*.

DORN. [*Sighing*] Ah, youth, youth!

MASHA. It is always " Youth, youth," when there is nothing else to be said.

She takes snuff. DORN *takes the snuff-box out of her hands and flings it into the bushes.*

DORN. Don't do that, it is horrid. [*A pause*] I hear music in the house. I must go in.

MASHA. Wait a moment.

DORN. What do you want?

MASHA. Let me tell you again. I feel like talking. [*She grows more and more excited*] I do not love my father, but my heart turns to you. For some reason, I feel with all my soul that you are near to me. Help me! Help me, or I shall do something foolish and mock at my life, and ruin it. I am at the end of my strength.

DORN. What is the matter? How can I help you?

MASHA. I am in agony. No one, no one can imagine how I suffer. [*She lays her head on his shoulder and speaks softly*] I love Constantine.

DORN. Oh, how excitable you all are! And how much love there is about this lake of spells! [*Tenderly*] But what can I do for you, my child? What? What?

The curtain falls.

ACT TWO

The lawn in front of SORIN'S *house. The house stands in the background, on a broad terrace. The lake, brightly reflecting the rays of the sun, lies to the left. There are flowerbeds here and there. It is noon ; the day is hot.* ARKADINA, DORN, *and* MASHA *are sitting on a bench on the lawn, in the shade of an old linden. An open book is lying on* DORN'S *knees.*

ARKADINA. [*To* MASHA] Come, get up. [*They both get up*] Stand beside me. You are twenty-two and I am almost twice your age. Tell me, Doctor, which of us is the younger looking ?

DORN. You are, of course.

ARKADINA. You see ! Now why is it ? Because I work ; my heart and mind are always busy, whereas you never move off the same spot. You don't live. It is a maxim of mine never to look into the future. I never admit the thought of old age or death, and just accept what comes to me.

MASHA. I feel as if I had been in the world a thousand years, and I trail my life behind me like an endless scarf. Often I have no desire to live at all. Of course that is foolish. One ought to pull oneself together and shake off such nonsense.

DORN. [*Sings softly*]
　　　"Tell her, oh flowers—"

ARKADINA. And then I keep myself as correct-looking as an Englishman. I am always well-groomed, as the saying is, and carefully dressed, with my hair neatly arranged. Do you think I should ever permit myself to leave the house half-dressed, with untidy hair ? Certainly not ! I have kept my looks by never letting myself slump as some women do. [*She puts her arms akimbo, and walks up and down on the lawn*] See me, tripping on tiptoe like a fifteen-year-old girl.

DORN. I see. Nevertheless, I shall continue my reading. [*He takes up his book*] Let me see, we had come to the grain-dealer and the rats.

ARKADINA. And the rats. Go on. [*She sits down*] No, give me the book, it is my turn to read. [*She takes the book and looks for the place*] And the rats. Ah, here it is. [*She reads*] " It is as dangerous for society to attract and indulge authors as it is for grain-dealers to raise rats in their granaries. Yet society loves authors. And so, when a woman has found one whom she wishes to make her own, she lays siege to him by indulging and flattering him." That may be so in France, but it certainly is not so in Russia. We do not carry out a programme like that. With us, a woman is usually head over ears in love with an author before she attempts to lay siege to him. You have an example before your eyes, in me and Trigorin.

> SORIN *comes in leaning on a cane, with* NINA *beside him.* MEDVIEDENKO *follows, pushing an arm-chair.*

SORIN. [*In a caressing voice, as if speaking to a child*] So we are happy now, eh ? We are enjoying ourselves to-day, are we ? Father and stepmother have gone away to Tver, and we are free for three whole days !

NINA. [*Sits down beside* ARKADINA, *and embraces her*] I am so happy. I belong to you now.

SORIN. [*Sits down in his arm-chair*] She looks lovely to-day.

ARKADINA. Yes, she has put on her prettiest dress, and

looks sweet. That was nice of you. [*She kisses* NINA] But
we mustn't praise her too much ; we shall spoil her. Where
is Trigorin ?

NINA. He is fishing off the wharf.

ARKADINA. I wonder he isn't bored.

[*She begins to read again.*

NINA. What are you reading ?

ARKADINA. " On the Water," by Maupassant. [*She
reads a few lines to herself*] But the rest is neither true nor
interesting. [*She lays down the book*] I am uneasy about
my son. Tell me, what is the matter with him ? Why is
he so dull and depressed lately ? He spends all his days on
the lake, and I scarcely ever see him any more.

MASHA. His heart is heavy. [*Timidly, to* NINA] Please
recite something from his play.

NINA. [*Shrugging her shoulders*] Shall I ? Is it so
interesting ?

MASHA. [*With suppressed rapture*] When he recites, his
eyes shine and his face grows pale. His voice is beautiful
and sad, and he has the ways of a poet.

SORIN *begins to snore.*

DORN. Pleasant dreams !

ARKADINA. Peter !

SORIN. Eh ?

ARKADINA. Are you asleep ?

SORIN. Not a bit of it.   [*A pause.*

ARKADINA. You don't do a thing for your health, brother,
but you really ought to.

DORN. The idea of doing anything for one's health at
sixty-five.

SORIN. One still wants to live at sixty-five.

DORN. [*Crossly*] Ho ! Take some camomile tea.

ARKADINA. I think a journey to some watering-place
would be good for him.

DORN. Why, yes ; he might go as well as not.

ARKADINA. You don't understand.

DORN. There is nothing to understand in this case; it is quite clear.   [*A pause.*

MEDVIEDENKO. He ought to give up smoking.

SORIN. What nonsense!

DORN. No, that is not nonsense. Wine and tobacco destroy the individuality. After a cigar or a glass of vodka you are no longer Peter Sorin, but Peter Sorin plus somebody else. Your ego breaks in two: you begin to think of yourself in the third person.

SORIN. It is easy for you to condemn smoking and drinking; you have known what life is, but what about me? I have served in the Department of Justice for twenty-eight years, but I have never lived, I have never had any experiences. You are satiated with life, and that is why you have an inclination for philosophy, but I want to live, and that is why I drink my wine for dinner and smoke cigars, and all.

DORN. One must take life seriously, and to take a cure at sixty-five and regret that one did not have more pleasure in youth is, forgive my saying so, trifling.

MASHA. It must be lunch-time. [*She walks away languidly, with a dragging step*] My foot has gone to sleep.

DORN. She is going to have a couple of drinks before lunch.

SORIN. The poor soul is unhappy.

DORN. That is a trifle, your honour.

SORIN. You judge her like a man who has obtained all he wants in life.

ARKADINA. Oh, what could be duller than this dear tedium of the country? The air is hot and still, nobody does anything but sit and philosophise about life. It is pleasant, my friends, to sit and listen to you here, but I had rather a thousand times sit alone in the room of a hotel learning a rôle by heart.

NINA. [*With enthusiasm*] You are quite right. I understand how you feel.

SORIN. Of course it is pleasanter to live in town. One can sit in one's library with a telephone at one's elbow, no one comes in without being first announced by the footman, the streets are full of cabs, and all——

DORN. [*Sings*]

" Tell her, oh flowers—"

SHAMRAEFF *comes in, followed by* PAULINA.

SHAMRAEFF. Here they are. How do you do ? [*He kisses* ARKADINA'S *hand and then* NINA'S] I am delighted to see you looking so well. [*To* ARKADINA] My wife tells me that you mean to go to town with her to-day. Is that so ?

ARKADINA. Yes, that is what I had planned to do.

SHAMRAEFF. H'm—that is splendid, but how do you intend to get there, madam ? We are hauling rye to-day, and all the men are busy. What horses would you take ?

ARKADINA. What horses ? How do I know what horses we shall have ?

SORIN. Why, we have the carriage horses.

SHAMRAEFF. The carriage horses ! And where am I to find the harness for them ? This is astonishing ! My dear madam, I have the greatest respect for your talents, and would gladly sacrifice ten years of my life for you, but I cannot let you have any horses to-day.

ARKADINA. But if I must go to town ? What an extraordinary state of affairs !

SHAMRAEFF. You do not know, madam, what it is to run a farm.

ARKADINA. [*In a burst of anger*] That is an old story ! Under these circumstances I shall go back to Moscow this very day. Order a carriage for me from the village, or I shall go to the station on foot.

SHAMRAEFF. [*Losing his temper*] Under these circumstances I resign my position. You must find yourself another manager. [*He goes out.*

ARKADINA. It is like this every summer : every summer I am insulted here. I shall never set foot here again.

> *She goes out to the left, in the direction of the wharf. In a few minutes she is seen entering the house, followed by* TRIGORIN, *who carries a bucket and fishing-rod.*

SORIN. [*Losing his temper*] What the deuce did he mean by his impudence ? I want all the horses brought here at once !

NINA. [*To* PAULINA] How could he refuse anything to Madame Arkadina, the famous actress ? Is not every wish, every caprice even, of hers, more important than any farm work ? This is incredible.

PAULINA. [*In despair*] What can I do about it ? Put yourself in my place and tell me what I can do.

SORIN. [*To* NINA] Let us go and find my sister, and all beg her not to go. [*He looks in the direction in which* SHAMRAEFF *went out*] That man is insufferable ; a regular tyrant.

NINA. [*Preventing him from getting up*] Sit still, sit still, and let us wheel you. [*She and* MEDVIEDENKO *push the chair before them*] This is terrible !

SORIN. Yes, yes, it is terrible ; but he won't leave. I shall have a talk with him in a moment.

> [*They go out. Only* DORN *and* PAULINA *are left.*

DORN. How tiresome people are ! Your husband deserves to be thrown out of here neck and crop, but it will all end by this old granny Sorin and his sister asking the man's pardon. See if it doesn't.

PAULINA. He has sent the carriage horses into the fields too. These misunderstandings occur every day. If you only knew how they excite me ! I am ill ; see ! I am trembling all over ! I cannot endure his rough ways.

[*Imploringly*] Eugene, my darling, my beloved, take me to you. Our time is short; we are no longer young; let us end deception and concealment, even though it is only at the end of our lives.

[*A pause.*

DORN. I am fifty-five years old. It is too late now for me to change my ways of living.

PAULINA. I know that you refuse me because there are other women who are near to you, and you cannot take everybody. I understand. Excuse me—I see I am only bothering you.

NINA *is seen near the house picking a bunch of flowers.*

DORN. No, it is all right.

PAULINA. I am tortured by jealousy. Of course you are a doctor and cannot escape from women. I understand.

DORN. [*To* NINA, *who comes toward him*] How are things in there?

NINA. Madame Arkadina is crying, and Sorin is having an attack of asthma.

DORN. Let us go and give them both some camomile tea.

NINA. [*Hands him the bunch of flowers*] Here are some flowers for you.

DORN. Thank you.   [*He goes into the house.*

PAULINA. [*Following him*] What pretty flowers! [*As they reach the house she says in a low voice*] Give me those flowers! Give them to me!

DORN *hands her the flowers; she tears them to pieces and flings them away. They both go into the house.*

NINA. [*Alone*] How strange to see a famous actress weeping, and for such a trifle! Is it not strange, too, that a famous author should sit fishing all day? He is the idol of the public, the papers are full of him, his photograph is for sale everywhere, his works have been translated into many foreign languages, and yet he is overjoyed if he

catches a couple of minnows. I always thought famous
people were distant and proud; I thought they despised
the common crowd which exalts riches and birth, and
avenged themselves on it by dazzling it with the inextin-
guishable honour and glory of their fame. But here I
see them weeping and playing cards and flying into passions
like everybody else.

> TREPLIEFF *comes in without a hat on, carrying a gun
> and a dead seagull.*

TREPLIEFF. Are you alone here?

NINA. Yes.

> TREPLIEFF *lays the seagull at her feet.*

NINA. What do you mean by this?

TREPLIEFF. I was base enough to-day to kill this gull.
I lay it at your feet.

NINA. What is happening to you?

> [*She picks up the gull and stands looking at it.*

TREPLIEFF. [*After a pause*] So shall I soon end my own
life.

NINA. You have changed so that I fail to recognise you.

TREPLIEFF. Yes, I have changed since the time when
I ceased to recognise you. You have failed me; your
look is cold; you do not like to have me near you.

NINA. You have grown so irritable lately, and you talk
so darkly and symbolically that you must forgive me if I
fail to follow you. I am too simple to understand you.

TREPLIEFF. All this began when my play failed so
dismally. A woman never can forgive failure. I have
burnt the manuscript to the last page. Oh, if you could
only fathom my unhappiness! Your estrangement is to
me terrible, incredible; it is as if I had suddenly waked to
find this lake dried up and sunk into the earth. You say
you are too simple to understand me; but oh, what is there
to understand? You disliked my play, you have no faith
in my powers, you already think of me as commonplace

and worthless, as many are. [*Stamping his foot*] How well
I can understand your feelings ! And that understanding
is to me like a dagger in the brain. May it be accursed,
together with my stupidity, which sucks my life-blood
like a snake ! [*He sees* TRIGORIN, *who approaches reading a
book*] There comes real genius, striding along like another
Hamlet, and with a book, too. [*Mockingly*] " Words,
words, words." You feel the warmth of that sun already,
you smile, your eyes melt and glow liquid in its rays. I
shall not disturb you.   [*He goes out.*

TRIGORIN. [*Making notes in his book*] Takes snuff and
drinks vodka ; always wears black dresses ; is loved by a
school teacher——

NINA. How do you do ?

TRIGORIN. How are you, Miss Nina ? Owing to an
unforeseen development of circumstances, it seems that
we are leaving here to-day. You and I shall probably
never see each other again, and I am sorry for it. I seldom
meet a young and pretty girl now ; I can hardly remember
how it feels to be nineteen, and the young girls in my books
are seldom living characters. I should like to change places
with you, if but for an hour, to look out at the world
through your eyes, and so find out what sort of a little
person you are.

NINA. And I should like to change places with you.

TRIGORIN. Why ?

NINA. To find out how a famous genius feels. What is it
like to be famous ? What sensations does it give you ?

TRIGORIN. What sensations ? I don't believe it gives
any. [*Thoughtfully*] Either you exaggerate my fame, or
else, if it exists, all I can say is that one simply doesn't
feel fame in any way.

NINA. But when you read about yourself in the papers ?

TRIGORIN. If the critics praise me, I am happy ; if
they condemn me, I am out of sorts for the next two days.

NINA. This is a wonderful world. If you only knew how I envy you! Men are born to different destinies. Some dully drag a weary, useless life behind them, lost in the crowd, unhappy, while to one out of a million, as to you, for instance, comes a bright destiny full of interest and meaning. You are lucky.

TRIGORIN. 1, lucky ? [*He shrugs his shoulders*] H'm—I hear you talking about fame, and happiness, and bright destinies, and those fine words of yours mean as much to me —forgive my saying so—as sweetmeats do, which I never eat. You are very young, and very kind.

NINA. Your life is beautiful.

TRIGORIN. I see nothing especially lovely about it. [*He looks at his watch*] Excuse me, I must go at once, and begin writing again. I am in a hurry. [*He laughs*] You have stepped on my pet corn, as they say, and I am getting excited, and a little cross. Let us discuss this bright and beautiful life of mine, though. [*After a few moments' thought*] Violent obsessions sometimes lay hold of a man : he may, for instance, think day and night of nothing but the moon. I have such a moon. Day and night I am held in the grip of one besetting thought, to write, write, write ! Hardly have I finished one book than something urges me to write another, and then a third, and then a fourth—I write ceaselessly. I am, as it were, on a treadmill. I hurry for ever from one story to another, and can't help myself. Do you see anything bright and beautiful in that ? Oh, it is a wild life ! Even now, thrilled as I am by talking to you, I do not forget for an instant that an unfinished story is awaiting me. My eye falls on that cloud there, which has the shape of a grand piano ; I instantly make a mental note that I must remember to mention in my story a cloud floating by that looked like a grand piano. I smell heliotrope ; I mutter to myself : a sickly smell, the colour worn by widows ; I must remember that in

writing my next description of a summer evening. I
catch an idea in every sentence of yours or of my own, and
hasten to lock all these treasures in my literary store-room,
thinking that some day they may be useful to me. As
soon as I stop working I rush off to the threatre or go
fishing, in the hope that I may find oblivion there, but no!
Some new subject for a story is sure to come rolling through
my brain like an iron cannon-ball. I hear my desk calling,
and have to go back to it and begin to write, write, write,
once more. And so it goes on for ever. I cannot escape
myself, though I feel that I am consuming my life. To
prepare the honey I feed to unknown crowds, I am doomed
to brush the bloom from my dearest flowers, to tear them
from their stems, and trample the roots that bore them
underfoot. Am I not a madman? Should I not be
treated by those who know me as one mentally diseased?
Yet it is always the same, same old story, till I begin to
think that all this praise and admiration must be a
deception, that I am being hoodwinked because they know
I am crazy, and I sometimes tremble lest I should be grabbed
from behind and whisked off to a lunatic asylum. The best
years of my youth were made one continual agony for me
by my writing. A young author, especially if at first he
does not make a success, feels clumsy, ill-at-ease, and
superfluous in the world. His nerves are all on edge and
stretched to the point of breaking; he is irresistibly
attracted to literary and artistic people, and hovers about
them unknown and unnoticed, fearing to look them bravely
in the eye, like a man with a passion for gambling, whose
money is all gone. I did not know my readers, but for
some reason I imagined they were distrustful and unfriendly;
I was mortally afraid of the public, and when my first play
appeared, it seemed to me as if all the dark eyes in the
audience were looking at it with enmity, and all the blue

E

ones with cold indifference. Oh, how terrible it was!
What agony!

NINA. But don't your inspiration and the act of creation
give you moments of lofty happiness?

TRIGORIN. Yes. Writing is a pleasure to me, and so is
reading the proofs, but no sooner does a book leave the
press than it becomes odious to me; it is not what I meant
it to be; I made a mistake to write it at all; I am provoked
and discouraged. Then the public reads it and says:
"Yes, it is clever and pretty, but not nearly as good as
Tolstoi," or "It is a lovely thing, but not as good as
Turgenieff's *Fathers and Sons*," and so it will always be.
To my dying day I shall hear people say: "Clever and
pretty; clever and pretty," and nothing more; and when
I am gone, those that knew me will say as they pass my
grave: "Here lies Trigorin, a clever writer, but not as
good as Turgenieff."

NINA. You must excuse me, but I decline to understand
what you are talking about. The fact is, you have been
spoilt by your success.

TRIGORIN. What success have I had? I have never
pleased myself; as a writer, I do not like myself at all.
The trouble is that I am made giddy, as it were, by the
fumes of my brain, and often hardly know what I
am writing. I love this lake, these trees, the blue heaven;
nature's voice speaks to me and wakes a feeling of passion
in my heart, and I am overcome by an uncontrollable
desire to write. But I am not only a painter of landscapes,
I am a man of the city besides. I love my country,
too, and her people; I feel that, as a writer, it is my duty
to speak of their sorrows, of their future, also of science,
of the rights of man, and so forth. So I write on every
subject, and the public hounds me on all sides, sometimes
in anger, and I race and dodge like a fox with a pack of
hounds on his trail. I see life and knowledge flitting away

before me. I am left behind them like a peasant who has missed his train at a station, and finally I come back to the conclusion that all I am fit for is to describe landscapes, and that whatever else I attempt rings abominably false.

NINA. You work too hard to realise the importance of your writings. What if you are discontented with yourself ? To others you appear a great and splendid man. If I were a writer like you I should devote my whole life to the service of the Russian people, knowing at the same time that their welfare depended on their power to rise to the heights I had attained, and the people should send me before them in a chariot of triumph.

TRIGORIN. In a chariot ? Do you think I am Agamemnon ?   [*They both smile.*

NINA. For the bliss of being a writer or an actress I could endure want, and disillusionment, and the hatred of my friends, and the pangs of my own dissatisfaction with myself ; but I should demand in return fame, real, resounding fame ! [*She covers her face with her hands*] Whew ! My head reels !

THE VOICE OF ARKADINA. [*From inside the house*] Boris ! Boris !

TRIGORIN. She is calling me, probably to come and pack, but I don't want to leave this place. [*His eyes rest on the lake*] What a blessing such beauty is !

NINA. Do you see that house there, on the far shore ?

TRIGORIN. Yes.

NINA. That was my dead mother's home. I was born there, and have lived all my life beside this lake. I know every little island in it.

TRIGORIN. This is a beautiful place to live. [*He catches sight of the dead seagull*] What is that ?

NINA. A gull. Constantine shot it.

TRIGORIN. What a lovely bird ! Really, I can't bear to go away. Can't you persuade Irina to stay ?

[He writes something in his note-book.

NINA. What are you writing ?

TRIGORIN. Nothing much, only an idea that occurred to me. *[He puts the book back in his pocket]* An idea for a short story. A young girl grows up on the shores of a lake, as you have. She loves the lake as the gulls do, and is as happy and free as they. But a man sees her who chances to come that way, and he destroys her out of idleness, as this gull here has been destroyed.

[A pause. ARKADINA appears at one of the windows.

ARKADINA. Boris ! Where are you ?

TRIGORIN. I am coming this minute.

He goes toward the house, looking back at NINA. ARKADINA remains at the window.

TRIGORIN. What do you want ?

ARKADINA. We are not going away, after all.

TRIGORIN goes into the house. NINA comes forward and stands lost in thought.

NINA. It is a dream !

The curtain falls.

ACT THREE

The dining-room of SORIN'S *house. Doors open out of it to the right and left. A table stands in the centre of the room. Trunks and boxes encumber the floor, and preparations for departure are evident.* TRIGORIN *is sitting at a table eating his breakfast, and* MASHA *is standing beside him.*

MASHA. I am telling you all these things because you write books and they may be useful to you. I tell you honestly, I should not have lived another day if he had wounded himself fatally. Yet I am courageous; I have decided to tear this love of mine out of my heart by the roots.

TRIGORIN. How will you do it?

MASHA. By marrying Medviedenko.

TRIGORIN. The school teacher?

MASHA. Yes.

TRIGORIN. I don't see the necessity for that.

MASHA. Oh, if you knew what it is to love without hope for years and years, to wait for ever for something that will never come! I shall not marry for love, but marriage will at least be a change, and will bring new cares to deaden the memories of the past. Shall we have another drink?

TRIGORIN. Haven't you had enough?

MASHA. Fiddlesticks! [*She fills a glass*] Don't look at me with that expression on your face. Women drink oftener than you imagine, but most of them do it in secret, and not openly, as I do. They do indeed, and it is always

either vodka or brandy. [*They touch glasses*] To your good
health! You are so easy to get on with that I am sorry
to see you go. [*They drink.*

Trigorin. And I am sorry to leave.

Masha. You should ask her to stay.

Trigorin. She would not do that now. Her son has
been behaving outrageously. First he attempted suicide,
and now I hear he is going to challenge me to a duel,
though what his provocation may be I can't imagine.
He is always sulking and sneering and preaching about a
new form of art, as if the field of art were not large enough
to accommodate both old and new without the necessity
of jostling.

Masha. It is jealousy. However, that is none of my
business. [*A pause. JACOB walks through the room carrying
a trunk; NINA comes in and stands by the window*] That
school teacher of mine is none too clever, but he is very
good, poor man, and he loves me dearly, and I am sorry for
him. However, let me say good-bye and wish you a
pleasant journey. Remember me kindly in your thoughts.
[*She shakes hands with him*] Thanks for your goodwill.
Send me your books, and be sure to write something in
them; nothing formal, but simply this: "To Masha,
who, forgetful of her origin, for some unknown reason is
living in this world." Good-bye. [*She goes out.*

Nina. [*Holding out her closed hand to* Trigorin] Is it odd
or even?

Trigorin. Even.

Nina. [*With a sigh*] No, it is odd. I had only one pea
in my hand. I wanted to see whether I was to become
an actress or not. If only someone would advise me what
to do!

Trigorin. One cannot give advice in a case like this.

[*A pause.*

Nina. We shall soon part, perhaps never to meet again.

I should like you to accept this little medallion as a remembrance of me. I have had your initials engraved on it, and on this side is the name of one of your books : *Days and Nights*.

TRIGORIN. How sweet of you ! [*He kisses the medallion*] Iti s a lovely present.

NINA. Think of me sometimes.

TRIGORIN. I shall never forget you. I shall always remember you as I saw you that bright day—do you recall it ?—a week ago, when you wore your light dress, and we talked together, and the white seagull lay on the bench beside us.

NINA. [*Lost in thought*] Yes, the seagull. [*A pause*] I beg you to let me see you alone for two minutes before you go.

> *She goes out to the left. At the same moment* ARKADINA *comes in from the right, followed by* SORIN *in a long coat, with his orders on his breast, and by* JACOB, *who is busy packing.*

ARKADINA. Stay here at home, you poor old man. How could you pay visits with that rheumatism of yours ? [*To* TRIGORIN] Who left the room just now, was it Nina ?

TRIGORIN. Yes.

ARKADINA. I beg your pardon ; I am afraid we interrupted you. [*She sits down*] I think everything is packed. I am absolutely exhausted.

TRIGORIN. [*Reading the inscription on the medallion*] "*Days and Nights,* page 121, lines 11 and 12."

JACOB. [*Clearing the table*] Shall I pack your fishing-rods, too, sir ?

TRIGORIN. Yes, I shall need them, but you can give my books away.

JACOB. Very well, sir.

TRIGORIN. [*To himself*] Page 121, lines 11 and 12. [*To* ARKADINA] Have we my books here in the house ?

ARKADINA. Yes, they are in my brother's library, in the corner cupboard.

TRIGORIN. Page 121——   [*He goes out.*

SORIN. You are going away, and I shall be lonely without you.

ARKADINA. What would you do in town ?

SORIN. Oh, nothing in particular, but somehow—[*He laughs*] They are soon to lay the corner-stone of the new court-house here. How I should like to leap out of this minnow-pond, if but for an hour or two ! I am tired of lying here like an old cigarette stump. I have ordered the carriage for one o'clock. We can go away together.

ARKADINA. [*After a pause*] No, you must stay here. Don't be lonely, and don't catch cold. Keep an eye on my boy. Take good care of him ; guide him along the proper paths. [*A pause*] I am going away, and so shall never find out why Constantine shot himself, but I think the chief reason was jealousy, and the sooner I take Trigorin away, the better.

SORIN. There were—how shall I explain it to you ?— other reasons besides jealousy for his act. Here is a clever young chap living in the depths of the country, without money or position, with no future ahead of him, and with nothing to do. He is ashamed and afraid of being so idle. I am devoted to him and he is fond of me, but nevertheless he feels that he is useless here, that he is little more than a dependant in this house. It is the pride in him.

ARKADINA. He is a misery to me ! [*Thoughtfully*] He might possibly enter the army.

SORIN. [*Gives a whistle, and then speaks with hesitation*] It seems to me that the best thing for him would be if you were to let him have a little money. For one thing, he ought to be allowed to dress like a human being. See how he looks ! Wearing the same little old coat that he has had for three years, and he doesn't even possess an overcoat! [*Laughing*] And it wouldn't hurt the youngster to sow a few wild oats ; let him go abroad, say, for a time. It wouldn't cost much.

ARKADINA. Yes, but— However, I think I might manage about his clothes, but I couldn't let him go abroad. And no, I don't think I can let him have his clothes even, now. [*Decidedly*] I have no money at present.

SORIN *laughs.*

ARKADINA. I haven't indeed.

SORIN. [*Whistles*] Very well. Forgive me, darling ; don't be angry. You are a noble, generous woman !

ARKADINA. [*Weeping*] I really haven't the money.

SORIN. If I had any money of course I should let him have some myself, but I haven't even a penny. The farm manager takes my pension from me and puts it all into the farm or into cattle or bees, and in that way it is always lost for ever. The bees die, the cows die, they never let me have a horse.

ARKADINA. Of course I have some money, but I am an actress and my expenses for dress alone are enough to bankrupt me.

SORIN. You are a dear, and I am very fond of you, indeed I am. But something is the matter with me again. [*He staggers*] I feel giddy. [*He leans against the table*] I feel faint, and all.

ARKADINA. [*Frightened*] Peter ! [*She tries to support him*] Peter ! dearest ! [*She calls*] Help ! Help !

TREPLIEFF *and* MEDVIEDENKO *come in ;* TREPLIEFF
has a bandage around his head.

ARKADINA. He is fainting !

SORIN. I am all right. [*He smiles and drinks some water*] It is all over now.

TREPLIEFF. [*To his mother*] Don't be frightened, mother, these attacks are not dangerous ; my uncle often has them now. [*To his uncle*] You must go and lie down, uncle.

SORIN. Yes, I think I shall, for a few minutes. I am going to Moscow all the same, but I shall lie down a bit before I start.   [*He goes out leaning on his cane.*

MEDVIEDENKO. [*Giving him his arm*] Do you know this riddle ? On four legs in the morning ; on two legs at noon ; and on three legs in the evening ?

SORIN. [*Laughing*] Yes, exactly, and on one's back at night. Thank you, I can walk alone.

MEDVIEDENKO. Dear me, what formality !

[*He and* SORIN *go out.*

ARKADINA. He gave me a dreadful fright.

TREPLIEFF. It is not good for him to live in the country. Mother, if you would only untie your purse-strings for once, and lend him a thousand roubles ! He could then spend a whole year in town.

ARKADINA. I have no money. I am an actress and not a banker.   [*A pause.*

TREPLIEFF. Please change my bandage for me, mother, you do it so gently.

ARKADINA *goes to the cupboard and takes out a box of bandages and a bottle of iodoform.*

ARKADINA. The doctor is late.

TREPLIEFF. Yes, he promised to be here at nine, and now it is noon already.

ARKADINA. Sit down. [*She takes the bandage off his head*] You look as if you had a turban on. A stranger that was in the kitchen yesterday asked to what nationality you belonged. Your wound is almost healed. [*She kisses his head*] You won't be up to any more of these silly tricks again, will you, when I am gone ?

TREPLIEFF. No, mother, I did that in a moment of insane despair, when I had lost all control over myself. It will never happen again. [*He kisses her hand*] Your touch is golden. I remember when you were still acting at the State Theatre, long ago, when I was still a little chap, there was a fight one day in our court, and a poor washerwoman was almost beaten to death. She was picked up unconscious, and you nursed her till she was well, and bathed her children in the washtubs. Have you forgotten it ?

ARKADINA. Yes, entirely. [*She puts on a new bandage.*

TREPLIEFF. Two ballet dancers lived in the same house, and they used to come and drink coffee with you.

ARKADINA. I remember that.

TREPLIEFF. They were very pious. [*A pause*] I love you again, these last few days, as tenderly and trustingly as I did as a child. I have no one left me now but you. Why, why do you let yourself be controlled by that man ?

ARKADINA. You don't understand him, Constantine. He has a wonderfully noble personality.

TREPLIEFF. Nevertheless, when he has been told that I wish to challenge him to a duel his nobility does not prevent him from playing the coward. He is about to beat an ignominious retreat.

ARKADINA. What nonsense ! I have asked him myself to go.

TREPLIEFF. A noble personality indeed ! Here we are almost quarrelling over him, and he is probably in the garden laughing at us at this very moment, or else enlightening Nina's mind and trying to persuade her into thinking him a man of genius.

ARKADINA. You enjoy saying unpleasant things to me. I have the greatest respect for that man, and I must ask you not to speak ill of him in my presence.

TREPLIEFF. I have no respect for him at all. You want me to think him a genius, as you do, but I refuse to lie : his books make me sick.

ARKADINA. You envy him. There is nothing left for people with no talent and mighty pretensions to do but to criticise those who are really gifted. I hope you enjoy the consolation it brings.

TREPLIEFF. [*With irony*] Those who are really gifted, indeed! [*Angrily*] I am cleverer than any of you, if it comes to that! [*He tears the bandage off his head*] You are the slaves of convention, you have seized the upper hand and now lay down as law everything that you do; all else you strangle and trample on. I refuse to accept your point of view, yours and his, I refuse!

ARKADINA. That is the talk of a decadent.

TREPLIEFF. Go back to your beloved stage and act the miserable ditch-water plays you so much admire!

ARKADINA. I never acted in a play like that in my life. You couldn't write even the trashiest music-hall farce, you idle good-for-nothing!

TREPLIEFF. Miser!

ARKADINA. Rag-bag!

TREPLIEFF *sits down and begins to cry softly.*

ARKADINA. [*Walking up and down in great excitement*] Don't cry! You mustn't cry! [*She bursts into tears*] You really mustn't. [*She kisses his forehead, his cheeks, his head*] My darling child, forgive me. Forgive your wicked mother.

TREPLIEFF. [*Embracing her*] Oh, if you could only know what it is to have lost everything under heaven! She does not love me. I see I shall never be able to write. Every hope has deserted me.

ARKADINA. Don't despair. This will all pass. He is going away to-day, and she will love you once more. [*She wipes away his tears*] Stop crying. We have made peace again.

TREPLIEFF. [*Kissing her hand*] Yes, mother.

ARKADINA. [*Tenderly*] Make your peace with him, too. Don't fight with him. You surely won't fight?

TREPLIEFF. I won't, but you must not insist on my seeing him again, mother, I couldn't stand it. [TRIGORIN *comes in*] There he is; I am going. [*He quickly puts the medicines away in the cupboard*] The doctor will attend to my head.

TRIGORIN. [*Looking through the pages of a book*] Page 121, lines 11 and 12; here it is. [*He reads*] " If at any time you should have need of my life, come and take it."

TREPLIEFF *picks up the bandage off the floor and goes out.*

ARKADINA. [*Looking at her watch*] The carriage will soon be here.

TRIGORIN. [*To himself*] If at any time you should have need of my life, come and take it.

ARKADINA. I hope your things are all packed.

TRIGORIN. [*Impatiently*] Yes, yes. [*In deep thought*] Why do I hear a note of sadness that wrings my heart in this cry of a pure soul ? If at any time you should have need of my life, come and take it. [*To* ARKADINA] Let us stay here one more day !

ARKADINA *shakes her head.*

TRIGORIN. Do let us stay !

ARKADINA. I know, dearest, what keeps you here, but you must control yourself. Be sober ; your emotions have intoxicated you a little.

TRIGORIN. You must be sober, too. Be sensible ; look upon what has happened as a true friend would. [*Taking her hand*] You are capable of self-sacrifice. Be a friend to me and release me !

ARKADINA. [*In deep excitement*] Are you so much in love ?

TRIGORIN. I am irresistibly impelled toward her. It may be that this is just what I need.

ARKADINA What, the love of a country girl ? Oh, how little you know yourself !

TRIGORIN. People sometimes walk in their sleep, and so I feel as if I were asleep, and dreaming of her as I stand here talking to you. My imagination is shaken by the sweetest and most glorious visions. Release me!

ARKADINA. [*Shuddering*] No, no! I am only an ordinary woman; you must not say such things to me. Do not torment me, Boris; you frighten me.

TRIGORIN. You could be an extraordinary woman if you only would. Love alone can bring happiness on earth, love the enchanting, the poetical love of youth, that sweeps away the sorrows of the world. I had no time for it when I was young and struggling with want and laying siege to the literary fortress, but now at last this love has come to me. I see it beckoning; why should I fly?

ARKADINA. [*With anger*] You are mad!

TRIGORIN. Release me.

ARKADINA. You have all conspired together to torture me to-day.   [*She weeps.*

TRIGORIN. [*Clutching his head desperately*] She doesn't understand me! She won't understand me!

ARKADINA. Am I then so old and ugly already that you can talk to me like this without any shame about another woman? [*She embraces and kisses him*] Oh, you have lost your senses! My splendid, my glorious friend, my love for you is the last chapter of my life. [*She falls on her knees*] You are my pride, my joy, my light. [*She embraces his knees*] I could never endure it should you desert me, if only for an hour; I should go mad. Oh, my wonder, my marvel, my king!

TRIGORIN. Someone might come in. [*He helps her to rise.*

ARKADINA. Let them come! I am not ashamed of my love. [*She kisses his hands*] My jewel! My despair! You want to do a foolish thing, but I don't want you to do it. I shan't let you do it! [*She laughs*] You are mine, you are mine! This forehead is mine, these eyes are mine, this silky hair is mine. All your being is mine. You are so clever, so wise, the first of all living writers ; you are the only hope of your country. You are so fresh, so simple, so deeply humorous. You can bring out every feature of a man or of a landscape in a single line, and your characters live and breathe. Do you think that these words are but the incense of flattery ? Do you think I am not speaking the truth ? Come, look into my eyes ; look deep ; do you find lies there ? No, you see that I alone know how to treasure you. I alone tell you the truth. Oh, my very dear, you will go with me ? You will ? You will not forsake me ?

TRIGORIN. I have no will of my own ; I never had. I am too indolent, too submissive, too phlegmatic, to have any. Is it possible that women like that ? Take me. Take me away with you, but do not let me stir a step from your side.

ARKADINA. [*To herself*] Now he is mine ! [*Carelessly, as if nothing unusual had hapened*] Of course you must stay here if you really want to. I shall go, and you can follow in a week's time. Yes, really, why should you hurry away ?

TRIGORIN. Let us go together.

ARKADINA. As you like. Let us go together then. [*A pause.* TRIGORIN *writes something in his note-book*] What are you writing ?

TRIGORIN. A happy expression I heard this morning : "A grove of maiden pines." It may be useful. [*He yawns*] So we are really off again, condemned once more to railway carriages, to stations and restaurants, to Hamburger steaks and endless arguments !

SHAMRAEFF *comes in.*

SHAMRAEFF. I am sorry to have to inform you that your carriage is at the door. It is time to start, honoured madam, the train leaves at two-five. Would you be kind enough, madam, to remember to inquire for me where Suzdaltzeff the actor is now ? Is he still alive, I wonder ? Is he well ? He and I have had many a jolly time together. He was inimitable in *The Stolen Mail*. A tragedian called Izmailoff was in the same company, I remember, who was also quite remarkable. Don't hurry, madam, you still have five minutes. They were both of them conspirators once, in the same melodrama, and one night when in the course of the play they were suddenly discovered, instead of saying " We have been trapped ! " Izmailoff cried out : " We have been rapped ! " [*He laughs*] Rapped !

> *While he has been talking,* JACOB *has been busy with the trunks, and the maid has brought* ARKADINA *her hat, coat, parasol, and gloves. The cook looks hesitatingly through the door on the right, and finally comes into the room.* PAULINA *comes in.* MEDVIEDENKO *comes in.*

PAULINA. [*Presenting* ARKADINA *with a little basket*] Here are some plums for the journey. They are very sweet ones. You may want to nibble something good on the way.

ARKADINA. You are very kind, Paulina.

PAULINA. Good-bye, my dearie. If things have not been quite as you could have wished, please forgive us.

> [*She weeps.*

ARKADINA. It has been delightful, delightful. You mustn't cry.

> SORIN *comes in through the door on the left, dressed in a long coat with a cape, and carrying his hat and cane. He crosses the room.*

SORIN. Come, sister, it is time to start, unless you want to miss the train. I am going to get into the carriage.

> [*He goes out.*

MEDVIEDENKO. I shall walk quickly to the station and see you off there.   [*He goes out.*

ARKADINA. Good-bye, all! We shall meet again next summer if we live. [*The maidservant,* JACOB, *and the cook kiss her hand*] Don't forget me. [*She gives the cook a rouble*] There is a rouble for all three of you.

THE COOK. Thank you, mistress; a pleasant journey to you.

JACOB. God bless you, mistress.

SHAMRAEFF. Send us a line to cheer us up. [*To* TRIGORIN] Good-bye, sir.

ARKADINA. Where is Constantine? Tell him I am starting. I must say good-bye to him. [*To* JACOB] I gave the cook a rouble for all three of you.

> *All go out through the door on the right. The stage remains empty. Soun ds of farewell are heard. The maid comes running b ck to fetch the basket of plums which has been forgotten.* TRIGORIN *comes back.*

TRIGORIN. I had forgotten my cane. I think I left it on the terrace. [*He goes toward the door on the right and meets* NINA, *who comes in at that moment*] Is that you? We are off.

NINA. I knew we should meet again. [*With emotion*] I have come to an irrevocable decision, the die is cast: I am going on the stage. I am deserting my father and abandoning everything. I am beginning life anew. I am going, as you are, to Moscow. We shall meet there.

TRIGORIN. [*Glancing about him*] Go to the Hotel Slavianski Bazar. Let me know as soon as you get there. I shall be at the Grosholski House in Moltchanofka Street. I must go now.   [*A pause.*

NINA. Just one more minute!

TRIGORIN. [*In a low voice*] You are so beautiful! What

F

bliss to think that I shall see you again so soon ! [*She sinks on his breast*] I shall see those glorious eyes again, that wonderful, ineffably tender smile, those gentle features with their expression of angelic purity ! My darling !
[*A prolonged kiss.*

The curtain falls.

Two years elapse between the third and fourth acts.

ACT FOUR

A sitting-room in SORIN'S *house, which has been converted into
a writing-room for* TREPLIEFF. *To the right and left are
doors leading into inner rooms, and in the centre is a glass
door opening on to a terrace. Besides the usual furniture
of a sitting-room there is a writing-desk in the right-hand
corner of the room. There is a Turkish divan near the
door on the left, and shelves full of books stand against
the walls. Books are lying scattered about on the window-
sills and chairs. It is evening. The room is dimly
lighted by a shaded lamp on a table. The wind moans
in the tree tops and whistles down the chimney. The*
WATCHMAN *in the garden is heard sounding his rattle.*
MEDVIEDENKO *and* MASHA *come in.*

MASHA. [*Calling* TREPLIEFF] Mr. Constantine, where
are you ? [*Looking about her*] There is no one here. His
old uncle is for ever asking for Constantine, and can't live
without him for an instant.

MEDVIEDENKO. He dreads being left alone. [*Listening
to the wind*] This is a wild night. We have had this storm
for two days.

MASHA. [*Turning up the lamp*] The waves on the lake
are enormous.

MEDVIEDENKO. It is very dark in the garden. Do you
know, I think that old theatre ought to be knocked down.
It is still standing there, naked and hideous as a skeleton,
with the curtain flapping in the wind. I thought I heard a
voice weeping in it as I passed there last night.

MASHA. What an idea ! [*A pause.*

MEDVIEDENKO.   Come home with me, Masha.

MASHA.   [*Shaking her head*] I shall spend the night here.

MEDVIEDENKO.   [*Imploringly*] Do come, Masha.   The baby must be hungry.

MASHA.   Nonsense, Matriona will feed it.   [*A pause.*

MEDVIEDENKO.   It is a pity to leave him three nights without his mother.

MASHA.   You are getting too tiresome.   You used sometimes to talk of other things besides home and the baby, home and the baby.   That is all I ever hear from you now.

MEDVIEDENKO.   Come home, Masha.

MASHA.   You can go home if you want to.

MEDVIEDENKO.   Your father won't give me a horse.

MASHA.   Yes, he will; ask him.

MEDVIEDENKO.   I think I shall.   Are you coming home to-morrow ?

MASHA.   Yes, yes, to-morrow.

> *She takes snuff.* TREPLIEFF *and* PAULINA *come in.* TREPLIEFF *is carrying some pillows and a blanket, and* PAULINA *is carrying sheets and pillow cases. They lay them on the divan, and* TREPLIEFF *goes and sits down at his desk.*

MASHA.   Who is that for, mother ?

PAULINA.   Mr. Sorin asked to sleep in Constantine's room to-night.

MASHA.   Let me make the bed.

> *She makes the bed.* PAULINA *goes up to the desk and looks at the manuscripts lying on it.*   [*A pause.*

MEDVIEDENKO.   Well, I am going.   Good-bye, Masha. [*He kisses his wife's hand*] Good-bye, mother.

> [*He tries to kiss his mother-in-law's hand.*

PAULINA.   [*Crossly*] Be off, in God's name !

TREPLIEFF *shakes hands with him in silence, and*
MEDVIEDENKO *goes out.*

PAULINA. [*Looking at the manuscripts*] No one ever
dreamed, Constantine, that you would one day turn into a
real author.   The magazines pay you well for your stories.
[*She strokes his hair.*]   You have grown handsome, too.
Dear, kind Constantine, be a little nicer to my Masha.

MASHA. [*Still making the bed*] Leave him alone, mother.

PAULINA.   She is a sweet child.   [*A pause*] A woman,
Constantine, asks only for kind looks.   I know that from
experience.

> TREPLIEFF *gets up from his desk and goes out without
> a word.*

MASHA.   There now !   You have vexed him.   I told
you not to bother him.

PAULINA.   I am sorry for you, Masha.

MASHA.   Much I need your pity !

PAULINA.   My heart aches for you.   I see how things
are, and understand.

MASHA.   You see what doesn't exist.   Hopeless love
is only found in novels.   It is a trifle ; all one has to do is
to keep a tight rein on oneself, and keep one's head clear.
Love must be plucked out the moment it springs up in
the heart.   My husband has been promised a school in
another district, and when we have once left this place I
shall forget it all.   I shall tear my passion out by the roots.

> [*The notes of a melancholy waltz are heard in the
> distance.*

PAULINA.   Constantine is playing.   That means he is sad.

> MASHA *silently waltzes a few turns to the music.*

MASHA.   The great thing, mother, is not to have him
continually in sight.   If my Simon could only get his
remove I should forget it all in a month or two.   It is a
trifle.

DORN *and* MEDVIEDENKO *come in through the door on the left, wheeling* SORIN *in an arm-chair.*

MEDVIEDENKO. I have six mouths to feed now, and flour is at seventy kopecks.

DORN. A hard riddle to solve !

MEDVIEDENKO. It is easy for you to make light of it. You are rich enough to scatter money to your chickens, if you wanted to.

DORN. You think I am rich ? My friend, after practising for thirty years, during which I could not call my soul my own for one minute of the night or day, I succeeded at last in scraping together one thousand roubles, all of which went, not long ago, in a trip which I took abroad. I haven't a penny.

MASHA. [*To her husband*] So you didn't go home after all ?

MEDVIEDENKO. [*Apologetically*] How can I go home when they won't give me a horse ?

MASHA. [*Under her breath, with bitter anger*] Would I might never see your face again !

SORIN *in his chair is wheeled to the left-hand side of the room.* PAULINA, MASHA, *and* DORN *sit down beside him.* MEDVIEDENKO *stands sadly aside.*

DORN. What a lot of changes you have made here ! You have turned this sitting-room into a library.

MASHA. Constantine likes to work in this room, because from it he can step out into the garden to meditate whenever he feels like it.   [*The* WATCHMAN'S *rattle is heard.*

SORIN. Where is my sister ?

DORN. She has gone to the station to meet Trigorin. She will soon be back.

SORIN. I must be dangerously ill if you had to send for my sister. [*He falls silent for a moment*] A nice business this is ! Here I am dangerously ill, and you won't even give me any medicine.

DORN. What shall I prescribe for you ? Camomile tea ? Soda ? Quinine ?

SORIN. Don't inflict any of your discussions on me again. [*He nods toward the sofa*] Is that bed for me ?

PAULINA. Yes, for you, sir.

SORIN. Thank you.

DORN. [*Sings*] " The moon swims in the sky to-night."

SORIN. I am going to give Constantine an idea for a story. It shall be called " The Man Who Wished— *L'Homme qui a voulu.*" When I was young, I wished to become an author ; I failed. I wished to be an orator ; I speak abominably [*Exciting himself*] with my eternal " and all, and all," dragging each sentence on and on until I sometimes break out into a sweat all over. I wished to marry, and I didn't ; I wished to live in the city, and here I am ending my days in the country, and all.

DORN. You wished to become State Councillor, and— you are one !

SORIN. [*Laughing*] I didn't try for that, it came of its own accord.

DORN. Come, you must admit that it is petty to cavil at life at sixty-two years of age.

SORIN. You are pig-headed ! Can't you see I want to live ?

DORN. That is futile. Nature has commanded that every life shall come to an end.

SORIN. You speak like a man who is satiated with life. Your thirst for it is quenched, and so you are calm and indifferent, but even you dread death.

DORN. The fear of death is an animal passion which must be overcome. Only those who believe in a future life and tremble for sins committed, can logically fear death ; but you, for one thing, don't believe in a future life, and for another, you haven't committed any sins. You have served as a Councillor for twenty-five years, that is all.

SORIN. [*Laughing*] Twenty-eight years!

    TREPLIEFF *comes in and sits down on a stool at*
        SORIN'S *feet.* MASHA *fixes her eyes on his face and*
        never once tears them away.

DORN. We are keeping Constantine from his work.

TREPLIEFF. No matter.   [*A pause.*

MEDVIEDENKO. Of all the cities you visited when you
were abroad, Doctor, which one did you like the best?

DORN. Genoa.

TREPLIEFF. Why Genoa?

DORN. Because there is such a splendid crowd in its
streets. When you leave the hotel in the evening, and
throw yourself into the heart of that throng, and move with
it without aim or object, swept along, hither and thither,
their life seems to be yours, their soul flows into you, and
you begin to believe at last in a great world spirit, like the
one in your play that Nina Zarietchnaya acted. By the
way, where is Nina now? Is she well?

TREPLIEFF. I believe so.

DORN. I hear she has led rather a strange life; what
happened?

TREPLIEFF. It is a long story, Doctor.

DORN. Tell it shortly.   [*A pause.*

TREPLIEFF. She ran away from home and joined
Trigorin; you know that?

DORN. Yes.

TREPLIEFF. She had a child that died. Trigorin
soon tired of her and returned to his former ties, as might
have been expected. He had never broken them, indeed,
but out of weakness of character had always vacillated
between the two. As far as I can make out from what
I have heard, Nina's domestic life has not been altogether a
success.

DORN. What about her acting?

TREPLIEFF. I believe she made an even worse failure of

that. She made her début on the stage of the Summer Theatre in Moscow, and afterward made a tour of the country towns. At that time I never let her out of my sight, and wherever she went I followed. She always attempted great and difficult parts, but her delivery was harsh and monotonous, and her gestures heavy and crude. She shrieked and died well at times, but those were but moments.

DORN. Then she really has a talent for acting ?

TREPLIEFF. I never could make out. I believe she has. I saw her, but she refused to see me, and her servant would never admit me to her rooms. I appreciated her feelings, and did not insist upon a meeting. [*A pause*] What more can I tell you ? She sometimes writes to me now that I have come home, such clever, sympathetic letters, full of warm feeling. She never complains, but I can tell that she is profoundly unhappy ; not a line but speaks to me of an aching, breaking nerve. She has one strange fancy ; she always signs herself " The Seagull." The miller in *Rusalka* called himself " The Crow," and so she repeats in all her letters that she is a seagull. She is here now.

DORN. What do you mean by " here ? "

TREPLIEFF. In the village, at the inn. She has been there for five days. I should have gone to see her, but Masha here went, and she refuses to see anyone. Someone told me she had been seen wandering in the fields a mile from here yesterday evening.

MEDVIEDENKO. Yes, I saw her. She was walking away from here in the direction of the village. I asked her why she had not been to see us. She said she would come.

TREPLIEFF. But she won't. [*A pause*] Her father and stepmother have disowned her. They have even put watchmen all around their estate to keep her away. [*He goes with the doctor toward the desk*] How easy it is, Doctor, to be a philosopher on paper, and how difficult in real life !

SORIN. She was a beautiful girl. Even the State Councillor himself was in love with her for a time.

DORN. You old Lovelace, you!

SHAMRAEFF'S *laugh is heard.*

PAULINA. They are coming back from the station.

TREPLIEFF. Yes, I hear my mother's voice.

ARKADINA *and* TRIGORIN *come in, followed by* SHAMRAEFF.

SHAMRAEFF. We all grow old and wither, my lady, while you alone, with your light dress, your gay spirits, and your grace, keep the secret of eternal youth.

ARKADINA. You are still trying to turn my head, you tiresome old man.

TRIGORIN. [*To* SORIN] How do you do, Peter? What, still ill? How silly of you! [*With evident pleasure, as he catches sight of* MASHA] How are you, Miss Masha?

MASHA. So you recognised me? [*She shakes hands with him.*]

TRIGORIN. Did you marry him?

MASHA. Long ago.

TRIGORIN. You are happy now? [*He bows to* DORN *and* MEDVIEDENKO, *and then goes hesitatingly toward* TREPLIEFF] Your mother says you have forgotten the past and are no longer angry with me.

TREPLIEFF *gives him his hand.*

ARKADINA. [*To her son*] Here is a magazine that Boris has brought you with your latest story in it.

TREPLIEFF. [*To* TRIGORIN, *as he takes the magazine*] Many thanks; you are very kind.

TRIGORIN. Your admirers all send you their regards. Everyone in Moscow and St. Petersburg is interested in you, and all ply me with questions about you. They ask me what you look like, how old you are, whether you are fair or dark. For some reason they all think that you are no longer young, and no one knows who you are, as you

always write under an assumed name. You are as great
a mystery as the Man in the Iron Mask.

TREPLIEFF. Do you expect to be here long ?

TRIGORIN. No, I must go back to Moscow to-morrow. I
am finishing another novel, and have promised something
to a magazine besides. In fact, it is the same old business.

> *During their conversation* ARKADINA *and* PAULINA
> *have put up a card-table in the centre of the room ;*
> SHAMRAEFF *lights the candles and arranges the
> chairs, then fetches a box of lotto from the cupboard.*

TRIGORIN. The weather has given me a rough welcome.
The wind is frightful. If it goes down by morning I shall
go fishing in the lake, and shall have a look at the garden
and the spot—do you remember ?—where your play was
given. I remember the piece very well, but should like
to see again where the scene was laid.

MASHA. [*To her father*] Father, do please let my husband
have a horse. He ought to go home.

SHAMRAEFF. [*Angrily*] A horse to go home with !
[*Sternly*] You know the horses have just been to the station.
I can't send them out again.

MASHA. But there are other horses. [*Seeing that her
father remains silent*] You are impossible !

MEDVIEDENKO. I shall go on foot, Masha.

PAULINA. [*With a sigh*] On foot in this weather ? [*She
takes a seat at the card-table*] Shall we begin ?

MEDVIEDENKO. It is only six miles. Good-bye. [*He
kisses his wife's hand*] Good-bye, mother. [*His mother-in-
law gives him her hand unwillingly*] I should not have
troubled you all, but the baby— [*He bows to everyone*]
Good-bye.

> [*He goes out with an apologetic air.*

SHAMRAEFF. He will get there all right, he is not a
major-general.

PAULINA. Come, let us begin. Don't let us waste time, we shall soon be called to supper.

SHAMRAEFF, MASHA, *and* DORN *sit down at the card-table.*

ARKADINA. [*To* TRIGORIN] When the long autumn evenings descend on us we while away the time here by playing lotto. Look at this old set ; we used it when our mother played with us as children. Don't you want to take a hand in the game with us until supper time ? [*She and* TRIGORIN *sit down at the table*] It is a monotonous game, but it is all right when one gets used to it.

[*She deals three cards to each of the players.*

TREPLIEFF. [*Looking through the pages of the magazine*] He has read his own story, and hasn't even cut the pages of mine.

> *He lays the magazine on his desk and goes toward the door on the right, stopping as he passes his mother to give her a kiss.*

ARKADINA. Won't you play, Constantine ?

TREPLIEFF. No, excuse me please, I don't feel like it. I am going to take a turn through the rooms. [*He goes out.*

MASHA. Are you all ready ? I shall begin : twenty-two.

ARKADINA. Here it is.

MASHA. Three.

DORN. Right.

MASHA. Have you put down three ? Eight. Eighty-one. Ten.

SHAMRAEFF. Don't go so fast.

ARKADINA. Could you believe it ? I am still dazed by the reception they gave me in Kharkoff.

MASHA. Thirty-four.

[*The notes of a melancholy waltz are heard.*

ARKADINA. The students gave me an ovation ; they sent me three baskets of flowers, a wreath, and this thing here.

She unclasps a brooch from her breast and lays it on the table.

SHAMRAEFF. There is something worth while!

MASHA. Fifty.

DORN. Fifty, did you say?

ARKADINA. I wore a perfectly magnificent dress; I am no fool when it comes to clothes.

PAULINA. Constantine is playing again; the poor boy is sad.

SHAMRAEFF. He has been severely criticised in the papers.

MASHA. Seventy-seven.

ARKADINA. They want to attract attention to him.

TRIGORIN. He doesn't seem able to make a success, he can't somehow strike the right note. There is an odd vagueness about his writings that sometimes verges on delirium. He has never created a single living character.

MASHA. Eleven.

ARKADINA. Are you bored, Peter? [*A pause*] He is asleep.

DORN. The Councillor is taking a nap.

MASHA. Seven. Ninety.

TRIGORIN. Do you think I should write if I lived in such a place as this, on the shore of this lake? Never! I should overcome my passion, and give my life up to the catching of fish.

MASHA. Twenty-eight.

TRIGORIN. And if I caught a perch or a bass, what bliss it would be!

DORN. I have great faith in Constantine. I know there is something in him. He thinks in images; his stories are vivid and full of colour, and always affect me deeply. It is only a pity that he has no definite object in view. He creates impressions, and nothing more, and one cannot go

far on impressions alone. Are you glad, madam, that you
have an author for a son ?

ARKADINA.   Just think, I have never read anything of
his ; I never have time.

MASHA.   Twenty-six.

> TREPLIEFF *comes in quietly and sits down at his table.*

SHAMRAEFF. [*To* TRIGORIN] We have something here
that belongs to you, sir.

TRIGORIN.   What is it ?

SHAMRAEFF.   You told me to have the seagull stuffed
that Mr. Constantine killed some time ago.

TRIGORIN.   Did I ? [*Thoughtfully*] I don't remember.

MASHA.   Sixty-one.   One.

> TREPLIEFF *throws open the window and stands
> listening.*

TREPLIEFF.   How dark the night is ! I wonder what
makes me so restless.

ARKADINA.   Shut the window, Constantine, there is a
draught here.

> TREPLIEFF *shuts the window.*

MASHA.   Ninety-eight.

TRIGORIN.   See, my card is full.

ARKADINA.   [*Gaily*] Bravo ! Bravo !

SHAMRAEFF.   Bravo !

ARKADINA.   Wherever he goes and whatever he does,
that man always has good luck. [*She gets up*] And now,
come to supper. Our renowned guest did not have any
dinner to-day. We can continue our game later. [*To
her son*] Come, Constantine, leave your writing and come
to supper.

TREPLIEFF.   I don't want anything to eat, mother ;
I am not hungry.

ARKADINA.   As you please. [*She wakes* SORIN] Come
to supper, Peter. [*She takes* SHAMRAEFF'S *arm*] Let me
tell you about my reception in Kharkoff.

PAULINA *blows out the candles on the table, then she and* DORN *roll* SORIN'S *chair out of the room, and all go out through the door on the left, except* TREPLIEFF, *who is left alone.* TREPLIEFF *prepares to write. He runs his eye over what he has already written.*

TREPLIEFF. I have talked a great deal about new forms of art, but I feel myself gradually slipping into the beaten track. [*He reads*] " The placard cried it from the wall—a pale face in a frame of dusky hair "—cried—frame —that is stupid. [*He scratches out what he has written*] I shall begin again from the place where my hero is wakened by the noise of the rain, but what follows must go. This description of a moonlight night is long and stilted. Trigorin has worked out a process of his own, and descriptions are easy for him. He writes that the neck of a broken bottle lying on the bank glittered in the moonlight, and that the shadows lay black under the mill-wheel. There you have a moonlight night before your eyes, but I speak of the shimmering light, the twinkling stars, the distant sounds of a piano melting into the still and scented air, and the result is abominable. [*A pause*] The conviction is gradually forcing itself upon me that good literature is not a question of forms new or old, but of ideas that must pour freely from the author's heart, without his bothering his head about any forms whatsoever. [*A knock is heard at the window nearest the table*] What was that ? [*He looks out of the window*] I can't see anything. [*He opens the glass door and looks out into the garden*] I heard someone run down the steps. [*He calls*] Who is there ? [*He goes out, and is heard walking quickly along the terrace. In a few minutes he comes back with* NINA ZARIETCHNAYA] Oh, Nina, Nina !

NINA *lays her head on* TREPLIEFF'S *breast and stifles her sobs.*

TREPLIEFF. [*Deeply moved*] Nina, Nina ! It is you—you!

I felt you would come ; all day my heart has been aching for you. [*He takes off her hat and cloak*] My darling, my beloved has come back to me ! We mustn't cry, we mustn't cry.

NINA. There is someone here.

TREPLIEFF. No one is here.

NINA. Lock the door, someone might come.

TREPLIEFF. No one will come in.

NINA. I know your mother is here. Lock the door.

TREPLIEFF *locks the door on the right and comes back to* NINA.

TREPLIEFF. There is no lock on that one. I shall put a chair against it. [*He puts an arm-chair against the door*] Don't be frightened, no one shall come in.

NINA. [*Gazing intently into his face*] Let me look at you. [*She looks about her*] It is warm and comfortable in here. This used to be a sitting-room. Have I changed much ?

TREPLIEFF. Yes, you have grown thinner, and your eyes are larger than they were. Nina, it seems so strange to see you ! Why didn't you let me go to you ? Why didn't you come sooner to me ? You have been here nearly a week, I know. I have been several times each day to where you live, and have stood like a beggar beneath your window.

NINA. I was afraid you might hate me. I dream every night that you look at me without recognising me. I have been wandering about on the shores of the lake ever since I came back. I have often been near your house, but I have never had the courage to come in. Let us sit down. [*They sit down*] Let us sit down and talk our hearts out. It is so quiet and warm in here. Do you hear the wind whistling outside ? As Turgenieff says, " Happy is he who can sit at night under the roof of his home, who has a warm corner in which to take refuge." I am a seagull—and yet —no. [*She passes her hand across her forehead*] What was

I saying ? Oh, yes, Turgenieff. He says, " and God help all houseless wanderers."   [*She sobs.*

TREPLIEFF. Nina ! You are crying again, Nina !

NINA. It is all right. I shall feel better after this. I have not cried for two years. I went into the garden last night to see if our old theatre were still standing. I see it is. I wept there for the first time in two years, and my heart grew lighter, and my soul saw more clearly again. See, I am not crying now. [*She takes his hand in hers*] So you are an author now, and I am an actress. We have both been sucked into the whirlpool. My life used to be as happy as a child's ; I used to wake singing in the morning; I loved you and dreamt of fame, and what is the reality ? To-morrow morning early I must start for Eltz by train in a third-class carriage, with a lot of peasants, and at Eltz the educated trades-people will pursue me with compliments. It is a rough life.

TREPLIEFF. Why are you going to Eltz ?

NINA. I have accepted an engagement there for the winter. It is time for me to go.

TREPLIEFF. Nina, I have cursed you, and hated you, and torn up your photograph, and yet I have known every minute of my life that my heart and soul were yours for ever. To cease from loving you is beyond my power. I have suffered continually from the time I lost you and began to write, and my life has been almost unendurable. My youth was suddenly plucked from me then, and I seem now to have lived in this world for ninety years. I have called out to you, I have kissed the ground you walked on, wherever I looked I have seen your face before my eyes, and the smile that had illumined for me the best years of my life.

NINA. [*Despairingly*] Why, why does he talk to me like this ?

TREPLIEFF. I am quite alone, unwarmed by any

G

attachment. I am as cold as if I were living in a cave. Whatever I write is dry and gloomy and harsh. Stay here, Nina, I beseech you, or else let me go away with you.

NINA *quickly puts on her coat and hat.*

TREPLIEFF. Nina, why do you do that ? For God's sake, Nina ! [*He watches her as she dresses. A pause.*

NINA. My carriage is at the gate. Do not come out to see me off. I shall find the way alone. [*Weeping*] Let me have some water.

TREPLIEFF *hands her a glass of water.*

TREPLIEFF. Where are you going ?

NINA. Back to the village. Is your mother here ?

TREPLIEFF. Yes, my uncle fell ill on Thursday, and we telegraphed for her to come.

NINA. Why do you say that you have kissed the ground I walked on ? You should kill me rather. [*She bends over the table*] I am so tired. If I could only rest—rest. [*She raises her head*] I am a seagull—no—no, I am an actress. [*She hears* ARKADINA *and* TRIGORIN *laughing in the distance, runs to the door on the left and looks through the keyhole*] He is there too. [*She goes back to* TREPLIEFF] Ah, well—no matter. He does not believe in the theatre ; he used to laugh at my dreams, so that little by little I became down-hearted and ceased to believe in it too. Then came all the cares of love, the continual anxiety about my little one, so that I soon grew trivial and spiritless, and played my parts without meaning. I never knew what to do with my hands, and I could not walk properly or control my voice. You cannot imagine the state of mind of one who knows as he goes through a play how terribly badly he is acting. I am a seagull—no—no, that is not what I meant to say. Do you remember how you shot a seagull once ? A man chanced to pass that way and destroyed it out of idleness. That is an idea for a short story, but it is not what I meant to say. [*She passes her hand across her*

forehead] What was I saying ? Oh, yes, the stage. I have
changed now. Now I am a real actress. I act with joy,
with exaltation, I am intoxicated by it, and feel that I am
superb. I have been walking and walking, and thinking
and thinking, ever since I have been here, and I feel the
strength of my spirit growing in me every day. I know
now, I understand at last, Constantine, that for us, whether
we write or act, it is not the honour and glory of which I
have dreamt that is important, it is the strength to endure.
One must know how to bear one's cross, and one must have
faith. I believe, and so do not suffer so much, and when
I think of my calling I do not fear life.

TREPLIEFF. [*Sadly*] You have found your way, you
know where you are going, but I am still groping in a chaos
of phantoms and dreams, not knowing whom and what end
I am serving by it all. I do not believe in anything, and
I do not know what my calling is.

NINA. [*Listening*] Hush ! I must go. Good-bye. When
I have become a famous actress you must come and see
me. Will you promise to come ? But now—[*She takes
his hand*] it is late. I can hardly stand. I am fainting.
I am hungry.

TREPLIEFF. Stay, and let me bring you some supper.

NINA. No, no—and don't come out, I can find the way
alone. My carriage is not far away. So she brought him
back with her ? However, what difference can that make
to me ? Don't tell Trigorin anything when you see him.
I love him—I love him even more than I used to. It is an
idea for a short story. I love him—I love him passionately
—I love him to despair. Have you forgotten, Constantine,
how pleasant the old times were ? What a gay, bright
gentle, pure life we led ? How a feeling as sweet and tender
as a flower blossomed in our hearts ? Do you remember
[*She recites*] " All men and beasts, lions, eagles, and quails,
horned stags, geese, spiders, silent fish that inhabit the

waves, starfish from the sea, and creatures invisible to the eye—in one word, life—all, all life, completing the dreary round set before it, has died out at last. A thousand years have passed since the earth last bore a living creature on its breast, and the unhappy moon now lights her lamp in vain. No longer are the cries of storks heard in the meadows, or the drone of beetles in the groves of limes——"

> *She embraces* TREPLIEFF *impetuously and runs out on to the terrace.*

TREPLIEFF. [*After a pause*] It would be a pity if she were seen in the garden. My mother would be distressed.

> *He stands for several minutes tearing up his manuscripts and throwing them under the table, then unlocks the door on the right and goes out.*

DORN. [*Trying to force open the door on the left*] Odd ! This door seems to be locked. [*He comes in and puts the chair back in its former place*] This is like a hurdle race.

> ARKADINA *and* PAULINA *come in, followed by* JACOB *carrying some bottles; then come* MASHA, SHAMRAEFF, *and* TRIGORIN.

ARKADINA. Put the claret and the beer here, on the table, so that we can drink while we are playing. Sit down, friends.

PAULINA. And bring the tea at once.

> *She lights the candles and takes her seat at the card-table.* SHAMRAEFF *leads* TRIGORIN *to the cupboard.*

SHAMRAEFF. Here is the stuffed seagull I was telling you about. [*He takes the seagull out of the cupboard*] You told me to have it done.

TRIGORIN. [*Looking at the bird*] I don't remember a thing about it, not a thing.

> [*A shot is heard. Everyone jumps.*

ARKADINA. [*Frightened*] What was that ?

DORN. Nothing at all ; probably one of my medicine bottles has blown up. Don't worry. [*He goes out through*

the door on the right, and comes back in a few moments] It is
as I thought, a flask of ether has exploded. [*He sings.*]
   " Spellbound once more I stand before thee."

ARKADINA. [*Sitting down at the table*] Heavens! I
was really frightened. That noise reminded me of—
[*She covers her face with her hands*] Everything is black
before my eyes.

DORN. [*Looking through the pages of a magazine, to*
TRIGORIN] There was an article from America in this
magazine about two months ago that I wanted to ask you
about, among other things. [*He leads* TRIGORIN *to the front
of the stage*] I am very much interested in this question.
[*He lowers his voice and whispers*] You must take Madame
Arkadina away from here ; what I wanted to say was,
that Constantine has shot himself.

The curtain falls.

THE THREE SISTERS

A DRAMA IN FOUR ACTS

CHARACTERS

ANDREY SERGEYEVITCH PROSOROV

NATALIA IVANOVNA (NATASHA), *his fianceé, later his wife* (28)

OLGA ⎫
MASHA ⎬ *his sisters*
IRINA ⎭

FEODOR ILITCH KULIGIN, *high school teacher, married to MASHA* (20)

ALEXANDER IGNATEYEVITCH VERSHININ, *lieutenant-colonel in charge of a battery* (42)

NICOLAI LVOVITCH TUZENBACH, *baron, lieutenant, in the army* (30)

VASSILI VASSILEVITCH SOLENI, *captain*

IVAN ROMANOVITCH CHEBUTIKIN, *army doctor* (60)

ALEXEY PETROVITCH FEDOTIK, *sub-lieutenant*

VLADIMIR CARLOVITCH RODE, *sub-lieutenant*

FERAPONT, *door-keeper at local council offices, an old man*

ANFISA, *nurse* (80)

The action takes place in a provincial town.

[Ages are stated in brackets.]

THE THREE SISTERS

A DRAMA IN FOUR ACTS

ACT ONE

In PROSOROV'S *house. A sitting-room with pillars ; behind is seen a large dining-room. It is midday, the sun is shining brightly outside. In the dining-room the table is being laid for lunch.*

OLGA, *in the regulation blue dress of a teacher at a girl's high school, is walking about correcting exercise books ;* MASHA, *in a black dress, with a hat on her knees, sits and reads a book ;* IRINA, *in white, stands about, with a thoughtful expression.*

OLGA. It's just a year since father died last May the fifth, on your name-day, Irina. It was very cold then, and snowing. I thought I would never survive it, and you were in a dead faint. And now a year has gone by and we are already thinking about it without pain, and you are wearing a white dress and your face is happy. [*Clock strikes twelve.* And the clock struck just the same way then. [*Pause*] I remember that there was music at the funeral, and they fired a volley in the cemetery. He was a general in command of a brigade but there were few people present. Of course, it was raining then, raining hard, and snowing.

IRINA. Why think about it !

BARON TUZENBACH, CHEBUTIKIN *and* SOLENI *appear by the table in the dining-room, behind the pillars.*

OLGA. It's so warm to-day that we can keep the windows open, though the birches are not yet in flower. Father was put in command of a brigade, and he rode out of Moscow with us eleven years ago. I remember perfectly that it was early in May and that everything in Moscow was flowering then. It was warm too, everything was bathed in sunshine. Eleven years have gone, and I remember everything as if we rode out only yesterday. Oh, God! When I awoke this morning and saw all the light and the spring, joy entered my heart, and I longed passionately to go home.

CHEBUTIKIN. Will you take a bet on it?

TUZENBACH. Oh, nonsense.

MASHA, *lost in a reverie over her book, whistles softly*.

OLGA. Don't whistle, Masha. How can you! [*Pause*] I'm always having headaches from having to go to the High School every day and then teach till evening. Strange thoughts come to me, as if I were already an old woman. And really, during these four years that I have been working here, I have been feeling as if every day my strength and youth have been squeezed out of me, drop by drop. And only one desire grows and gains in strength . . .

IRINA. To go away to Moscow. To sell the house, drop everything here, and go to Moscow. . . .

OLGA. Yes! To Moscow, and as soon as possible.

CHEBUTIKIN *and* TUZENBACH *laugh*.

IRINA. I expect Andrey will become a professor, but still, he won't want to live here. Only poor Masha must go on living here.

OLGA. Masha can come to Moscow every year, for the whole summer.

MASHA *is whistling gently*.

IRINA. Everything will be arranged, please God. [*Looks out of the window*] It's nice out to-day. I don't know why I'm so happy : I remembered this morning that it was my name-day, and I suddenly felt glad and remembered my childhood, when mother was still with us. What beautiful thoughts I had, what thoughts !

OLGA. You're all radiance to-day, I've never seen you look so lovely. And Masha is pretty, too. Andrey wouldn't be bad-looking, if he wasn't so stout ; it does spoil his appearance. But I've grown old and very thin, I suppose it's because I get angry with the girls at school. To-day I'm free. I'm at home. I haven't got a headache, and I feel younger than I was yesterday. I'm only twenty-eight. . . . All's well, God is everywhere, but it seems to me that if only I were married and could stay at home all day, it would be even better. [*Pause*] I should love my husband.

TUZENBACH. [*To* SOLENI] I'm tired of listening to the rot you talk. [*Entering the sitting-room*] I forgot to say that Vershinin, our new lieutenant-colonel of artillery, is coming to see us to-day.   [*Sits down to the piano.*

OLGA. That's good. I'm glad.

IRINA. Is he old ?

TUZENBACH. Oh, no. Forty or forty-five, at the very outside. [*Plays softly*] He seems rather a good sort. He's certainly no fool, only he likes to hear himself speak.

IRINA. Is he interesting ?

TUZENBACH. Oh, he's all right, but there's his wife, his mother-in-law, and two daughters. This is his second wife. He pays calls and tells everybody that he's got a wife and two daughters. He'll tell you so here. The wife isn't all there, she does her hair like a flapper and gushes extremely. She talks philosophy and tries to commit suicide every now and again, apparently in order to annoy

her husband. I should have left her long ago, but he bears
up patiently, and just grumbles.

SOLENI. [*Enters with* CHEBUTIKIN *from the dining-room*]
With one hand I can only lift fifty-four pounds, but with
both hands I can lift 180, or even 200 pounds. From this I
conclude that two men are not twice as strong as one, but
three times, perhaps even more. . . .

CHEBUTIKIN. [*Reads a newspaper as he walks*] If your
hair is coming out . . . take an ounce of naphthaline and
half a bottle of spirit . . . dissolve and use daily. . . .
[*Makes a note in his pocket diary*] When found make a note
of! Not that I want it though. . . . [*Crosses it out*] It
doesn't matter.

IRINA. Ivan Romanovitch, dear Ivan Romanovitch!

CHEBUTIKIN. What does my own little girl want?

IRINA. Ivan Romanovitch, dear Ivan Romanovitch! I
feel as if I were sailing under the broad blue sky with great
white birds around me. Why is that? Why?

CHEBUTIKIN. [*Kisses her hands, tenderly*] My white
bird. . . .

IRINA. When I woke up to-day and got up and dressed
myself, I suddenly began to feel as if everything in this life
was open to me, and that I knew how I must live. Dear
Ivan Romanovitch, I know everything. A man must work,
toil in the sweat of his brow, whoever he may be, for that
is the meaning and object of his life, his happiness, his
enthusiasm. How fine it is to be a workman who gets up
at daybreak and breaks stones in the street, or a shepherd,
or a schoolmaster, who teaches children, or an engine-driver
on the railway. . . . My God, let alone a man, it's better to
be an ox, or just a horse, so long as it can work, than a
young woman who wakes up at twelve o'clock, has her
coffee in bed, and then spends two hours dressing. . . .

Oh it's awful! Sometimes when it's hot, your thirst can be just as tiresome as my need for work. And if I don't get up early in future and work, Ivan Romanovitch, then you may refuse me your friendship.

CHEBUTIKIN. [*Tenderly*] I'll refuse, I'll refuse. . . .

OLGA. Father used to make us get up at seven. Now Irina wakes at seven and lies and meditates about something till nine at least. And she looks so serious ! [*Laughs.*

IRINA. You're so used to seeing me as a little girl that it seems queer to you when my face is serious. I'm twenty !

TUZENBACH. How well I can understand that craving for work, oh God ! I've never worked once in my life. I was born in Petersburg, a chilly, lazy place, in a family which never knew what work or worry meant. I remember that when I used to come home from my regiment, a footman used to have to pull off my boots while I fidgeted and my mother looked on in adoration and wondered why other people didn't see me in the same light. They shielded me from work ; but only just in time ! A new age is dawning, the people are marching on us all, a powerful, health-giving storm is gathering, it is drawing near, soon it will be upon us and it will drive away laziness, indifference, the prejudice against labour, and rotten dullness from our society. I shall work, and in twenty-five or thirty years, every man will have to work. Every one !

CHEBUTIKIN. I shan't work.

TUZENBACH. You don't matter.

SOLENI. In twenty-five years' time, we shall all be dead, thank the Lord. In two or three years' time apoplexy will carry you off, or else I'll blow your brains out, my pet.

> *Takes a scent-bottle out of his pocket and sprinkles his chest and hands.*

CHEBUTIKIN. [*Laughs*] It's quite true, I never have

worked. After I came down from the university I never
stirred a finger or opened a book, I just read the papers. . . .
[*Takes another newspaper out of his pocket*] Here we are. . . .
I've learnt from the papers that there used to be one,
Dobrolubov,* for instance, but what he wrote—I don't
know . . . God only knows. . . . [*Somebody is heard
tapping on the floor from below*] There. . . . They're calling
me downstairs, somebody's come to see me. I'll be back in a
minute . . . won't be long. . . .

[*Exit hurriedly, scratching his beard.*

IRINA. He's up to something.

TUZENBACH. Yes, he looked so pleased as he went out
that I'm pretty certain he'll bring you a present in a
moment.

IRINA. How unpleasant !

OLGA. Yes, it's awful. He's always doing silly things.

MASHA. "There stands a green oak by the sea.

And a chain of bright gold is around it . . .

And a chain of bright gold is around it. . . ."

[*Gets up and sings softly.*

OLGA. You're not very bright to-day, Masha. [MASHA
sings, putting on her hat] Where are you off to ?

MASHA. Home.

IRINA. That's odd. . . .

TUZENBACH. On a name-day, too !

MASHA. It doesn't matter. I'll come in the evening.
Good-bye, dear. [*Kisses* IRINA] Many happy returns,
though I've said it before. In the old days when father was
alive, every time we had a name-day, thirty or forty officers
used to come, and there was lots of noise and fun, and
to-day there's only a man and a half, and it's as quiet as a

* Dobrolubov (1836–61), in spite of the shortness of his career,
established himself as one of the classic literary critics of Russia.

desert . . . I'm off . . . I've got the hump to-day, and am not at all cheerful, so don't you mind me. [*Laughs through her tears*] We'll have a talk later on, but good-bye for the present, my dear ; I'll go somewhere.

IRINA. [*Displeased*] You are queer. . . .

OLGA. [*Crying*] I understand you, Masha.

SOLENI. When a man talks philosophy, well, it is philosophy or at any rate sophistry ; but when a woman, or two women, talk philosophy—it's all my eye.

MASHA. What do you mean by that, you very awful man ?

SOLENI. Oh, nothing. You came down on me before I could say . . . help ! [*Pause.*

MASHA. [*Angrily, to* OLGA] Don't cry !

    Enter ANFISA *and* FERAPONT *with a cake.*

ANFISA. This way, my dear. Come in, your feet are clean. [*To* IRINA] From the District Council, from Mihail Ivanitch Protopopov . . . a cake.

IRINA. Thank you. Please thank him. [*Takes the cake.*

FERAPONT. What ?

IRINA. [*Louder*] Please thank him.

OLGA. Give him a pie, nurse. Ferapont, go, she'll give you a pie.

FERAPONT. What ?

ANFISA. Come on, gran'fer, Ferapont Spiridonitch. Come on. [*Exeunt.*

MASHA. I don't like this Mihail Potapitch or Ivanitch, Protopopov. We ought'nt to invite him here.

IRINA. I never asked him.

MASHA. That's all right.

    Enter CHEBUTIKIN *followed by a soldier with a silver samovar ; there is a rumble of dissatisfied surprise.*

OLGA. [*Covers her face with her hands*] A samovar !

That's awful !   [*Exit into the dining-room, to the table.*

IRINA. My dear Ivan Romanovitch, what are you doing !

TUZENBACH. [*Laughs*] I told you so !

MASHA. Ivan Romanovitch, you are simply shameless !

CHEBUTIKIN. My dear good girl, you are the only thing, and the dearest thing I have in the world. I'll soon be sixty.   I'm an old man, a lonely worthless old man.   The only good thing in me is my love for you, and if it hadn't been for that, I would have been dead long ago. . . . [*To* IRINA] My dear little girl, I've known you since the day of your birth, I've carried you in my arms . . . I loved your dead mother. . . .

MASHA. But your presents are so expensive !

CHEBUTIKIN. [*Angrily, through his tears*] Expensive presents. . . . You really are ! . . . [*To the orderly*] Take the samovar in there. . . . [*Teasing*] Expensive presents !

> *The orderly goes into the dining-room with the samovar.*

ANFISA. [*Enters and crosses stage*] My dear, there's a strange Colonel come ! He's taken off his coat already. Children, he's coming here.   Irina darling, you'll be a nice and polite little girl, won't you. . . . Should have lunched a long time ago. . . . Oh, Lord. . . .   [*Exit.*

TUZENBACH. It must be Vershinin. [*Enter* VERSHININ] Lieutenant-Colonel Vershinin !

VERSHININ. [*To* MASHA *and* IRINA] I have the honour to introduce myself, my name is Vershinin.   I am very glad indeed to be able to come at last.   How you've grown ! Oh ! oh !

IRINA. Please sit down.   We're very glad you've come.

VERSHININ. [*Gaily*] I am glad, very glad !   But there are three sisters, surely.   I remember—three little girls. I forget your faces, but your father, Colonel Prosorov, used to have three little girls, I remember that perfectly, I saw

them with my own eyes. How time does fly! Oh, dear,
how it flies!

TUZENBACH. Alexander Ignateyevitch comes from Moscow.

IRINA. From Moscow? Are you from Moscow?

VERSHININ. Yes, that's so. Your father used to be in
charge of a battery there, and I was an officer in the same
brigade. [*To* MASHA] I seem to remember your face a little.

MASHA. I don't remember you.

IRINA. Olga! Olga! [*Shouts into the dining-room*] Olga!
Come along! [OLGA *enters from the dining-room*] Lieutenant-
Colonel Vershinin comes from Moscow, as it happens.

VERSHININ. I take it that you are Olga Sergeyevna, the
eldest, and that you are Maria . . . and you are Irina, the
youngest. . . .

OLGA. So you come from Moscow?

VERSHININ. Yes. I went to school in Moscow and began
my service there; I was there for a long time until at last
I got my battery and moved over here, as you see. I don't
really remember you, I only remember that there used to
be three sisters. I remember your father well; I have
only to shut my eyes to see him as he was. I used to come
to your house in Moscow. . . .

OLGA. I used to think I remembered everybody, but . .

VERSHININ. My name is Alexander Ignateyevitch.

IRINA. Alexander Ignateyevitch, you've come from
Moscow. That is really quite a surprise!

OLGA. We are going to live there, you see.

IRINA. We think we may be there this autumn. It's
our native town, we were born there. In Old Basmanni
Road. . . .   [*They both laugh for joy.*

MASHA. We've unexpectedly met a fellow countryman.
[*Briskly*] I remember: Do you remember, Olga, they

H

used to speak at home of a " lovelorn Major." You were
only a Lieutenant then, and in love with somebody, but for
some reason they always called you a Major for fun.

VERSHININ. [*Laughs*] That's it . . . the lovelorn Major,
that's got it !

MASHA. You only wore moustaches then. You have
grown older ! [*Through her tears*] You have grown older !

VERSHININ. Yes, when they used to call me the lovelorn
Major, I was young and in love. I've grown out of both
now.

OLGA. But you haven't a single white hair yet. You're
older, but you're not yet old.

VERSHININ. I'm forty-two, anyway. Have you been
away from Moscow long ?

IRINA. Eleven years. What are you crying for, Masha,
you little fool. . . . [*Crying*] And I'm crying too.

MASHA. It's all right. And where did you live ?

VERSHININ. Old Basmanni Road.

OLGA. Same as we.

VERSHININ. Once I used to live in German Street. That
was when the Red Barracks were my headquarters. There's
an ugly bridge in between, where the water rushes under-
neath. One gets melancholy when one is alone there.
[*Pause*] Here the river is so wide and fine ! It's a splendid
river !

OLGA. Yes, but it's so cold. It's very cold here, and the
midges. . . .

VERSHININ. What are you saying ! Here you've got
such a fine healthy Russian climate. You've a forest, a
river . . . and birches. Dear, modest birches, I like them
more than any other tree. It's good to live here. Only it's
odd that the railway station should be thirteen miles away.
. . . Nobody knows why.

SOLENI. I know why. [*All look at him*] Because if it was near it wouldn't be far off, and if it's far off, it can't be near.
[*An awkward pause.*

TUZENBACH. Funny man.

OLGA. Now I know who you are. I remember.

VERSHININ. I used to know your mother.

CHEBUTIKIN. She was a good woman, rest her soul.

IRINA. Mother is buried in Moscow.

OLGA. At the Novo-Devichi Cemetery.

MASHA. Do you know, I'm beginning to forget her face. We'll be forgotten in just the same way.

VERSHININ. Yes, they'll forget us. It's our fate, it can't be helped. A time will come when everything that seems serious, significant, or very important to us will be forgotten, or considered trivial. [*Pause*] And the curious thing is that we can't possibly find out what will come to be regarded as great and important, and what will be feeble, or silly. Didn't the discoveries of Copernicus, or Columbus, say, seem unnecessary and ludicrous at first, while wasn't it thought that some rubbish written by a fool, held all the truth ? And it may so happen that our present existence, with which we are so satisfied, will in time appear strange, inconvenient, stupid, unclean, perhaps even sinful. . . .

TUZENBACH. Who knows ? But on the other hand, they may call our life noble and honour its memory. We've abolished torture and capital punishment, we live in security, but how much suffering there is still !

SOLENI. [*In a feeble voice*] There, there. . . . The Baron will go without his dinner if you only let him talk philosophy.

TUZENBACH. Vassili Vassilevitch, kindly leave me alone. [*Changes his chair*] You're very dull, you know.

SOLENI. [*Feebly*] There, there, there.

TUZENBACH. [*To* VERSHININ] The sufferings we see

to-day—there are so many of them !—still indicate a certain moral improvement in society.

VERSHININ. Yes, yes, of course.

CHEBUTIKIN. You said just now, Baron, that they may call our life noble ; but we are very petty. . . . [*Stands up*] See how little I am.   [*Violin played behind.*

MASHA. That's Andrey playing—our brother.

IRINA. He's the learned member of the family. I expect he will be a professor some day. Father was a soldier, but his son chose an academic career for himself.

MASHA. That was father's wish.

OLGA. We ragged him to-day. We think he's a little in love.

IRINA. To a local lady. She will probably come here to-day.

MASHA. You should see the way she dresses ! Quite prettily, quite fashionably too, but so badly ! Some queer bright yellow skirt with a wretched little fringe and a red bodice. And such a complexion ! Andrey isn't in love. After all he has taste, he's simply making fun of us. I heard yesterday that she was going to marry Protopopov, the chairman of the Local Council. That would do her nicely. . . . [*At the side door*] Andrey, come here ! Just for a minute, dear !   [*Enter* ANDREY.

OLGA. My brother, Andrey Sergeyevitch.

VERSHININ. My name is Vershinin.

ANDREY. Mine is Prosorov. [*Wipes his perspiring hands*] You've come to take charge of the battery ?

OLGA. Just think, Alexander Ignateyevitch comes from Moscow.

ANDREY. That's all right. Now my little sisters won't give you any rest.

VERSHININ. I've already managed to bore your sisters.

IRINA. Just look what a nice little photograph frame Andrey gave me to-day. [*Shows it*] He made it himself.

VERSHININ. [*Looks at the frame and does not know what to say*] Yes. . . . It's a thing that . . .

IRINA. And he made that frame there, on the piano as well   [*Andrey waves his hand and walks away.*

OLGA. He's got a degree, and plays the violin, and cuts all sorts of things out of wood, and is really a domestic Admirable Crichton. Don't go away, Andrey! He's got into the habit of always going away. Come here!

> MASHA *and* IRINA *take his arms and laughingly lead him back.*

MASHA. Come on, come on!

ANDREY. Please leave me alone.

MASHA. You are funny. Alexander Ignateyevitch used to be called the lovelorn Major, but he never minded.

VERSHININ. Not the least.

MASHA. I'd like to call you the lovelorn fiddler!

IRINA. Or the lovelorn professor!

OLGA. He's in love! little Andrey is in love!

IRINA. [*Applauds*] Bravo, bravo! Encore! Little Andrey is in love.

CHEBUTIKIN. [*Goes up behind* ANDREY *and takes him round the waist with both arms*] Nature only brought us into the world that we should love!

> *Roars with laughter, then sits down and reads a news-paper which he takes out of his pocket.*

ANDREY. That's enough, quite enough. . . . [*Wipes his face*] I couldn't sleep all night and now I can't quite find my feet, so to speak. I read until four o'clock, then tried to sleep, but nothing happened. I thought about one thing and another, and then it dawned and the sun crawled into my bedroom. This summer, while I'm here, I want to translate a book from the English. . . .

VERSHININ. Do you read English ?

ANDREY. Yes ; father, rest his soul, educated us almost violently. It may seem funny and silly, but it's neverthe-less true, that after his death I began to fill out and get rounder, as if my body had had some great pressure taken off it. Thanks to father, my sisters and I know French, German, and English, and Irina knows Italian as well. But we paid dearly for it all !

MASHA. A knowledge of three languages is an unnecessary luxury in this town. It isn't even a luxury but a sort of useless extra, like a sixth finger. We know a lot too much.

VERSHININ. Well, I say ! [Laughs] You know a lot too much ! I don't think there can really be a town so dull and stupid as to have no place for a clever, cultured person. Let us suppose even that among the hundred thousand inhabitants of this backward and uneducated town, there are only three persons like yourself. It stands to reason that you won't be able to conquer that dark mob around you ; little by little as you grow older you will be bound to give way and lose yourselves in this crowd of a hundred thousand human beings ; their life will suck you up in itself, but still, you won't disappear having influenced nobody ; later on, others like you will come, perhaps six of them, then twelve, and so on, until at last your sort will be in the majority. In two or three hundred years' time life on this earth will be unimaginably beautiful and wonderful. Man-kind needs such a life, and if it is not ours to-day then we must look ahead for it, wait, think, prepare for it. We must see and know more than our fathers and grandfathers saw and knew. [Laughs] And you complain that you know too much.

MASHA. [*Takes off her hat*] I'll stay to lunch.

IRINA. [*Sighs*] Yes, all that ought to be written down.

ANDREY *has gone out quietly.*

TUZENBACH. You say that many years later on, life on this earth will be beautiful and wonderful. That's true. But to share in it now, even though at a distance, we must prepare by work. . . .

VERSHININ. [*Gets up*] Yes. What a lot of flowers you have. [*Looks round*] It's a beautiful flat. I envy you! I've spent my whole life in rooms with two chairs, one sofa, and fires which always smoke. I've never had flowers like these in my life. . . . [*Rubs his hands*] Well, well!

TUZENBACH. Yes, we must work. You are probably thinking to yourself : the German lets himself go. But I assure you I'm a Russian, I can't even speak German. My father belonged to the Orthodox Church. . . .   [*Pause.*

VERSHININ. [*Walks about the stage*] I often wonder : suppose we could begin life over again, knowing what we were doing ? Suppose we could use one life, already ended, as a sort of rough draft for another ? I think that every one of us would try, more than anything else, not to repeat himself, at the very least he would rearrange his manner of life, he would make sure of rooms like these, with flowers and light. . . . I have a wife and two daughters, my wife's health is delicate and so on and so on, and if I had to begin life all over again I would not marry. . . . No, no !

Enter KULIGIN *in a regulation jacket.*

KULIGIN. [*Going up to* IRINA] Dear sister, allow me to congratulate you on the day sacred to your good angel and to wish you, sincerely and from the bottom of my heart, good health and all that one can wish for a girl of your years. And then let me offer you this book as a present.

[*Gives it to her*] It is the history of our High School during the last fifty years, written by myself. The book is worthless, and written because I had nothing to do, but read it all the same. Good day, gentlemen! [*To* VERSHININ] My name is Kuligin, I am a master of the local High School.* [*To* IRINA] In this book you will find a list of all those who have taken the full course at our High School during these fifty years. *Feci quod potui, faciant meliora potentes.*

[*Kisses* MASHA.

IRINA. But you gave me one of these at Easter.

KULIGIN. [*Laughs*] I couldn't have, surely! You'd better give it back to me in that case, or else give it to the Colonel. Take it, Colonel. You'll read it some day when you're bored.

VERSHININ. Thank you. [*Prepares to go*] I am extremely happy to have made the acquaintance of . . .

OLGA. Must you go? No, not yet?

IRINA. You'll stop and have lunch with us. Please do.

OLGA. Yes, please!

VERSHININ. [*Bows*] I seem to have dropped in on your name-day. Forgive me, I didn't know, and I didn't offer you my congratulations. . . .

[*Goes with* OLGA *into the dining-room.*

KULIGIN. To-day is Sunday, the day of rest, so let us rest and rejoice, each in a manner compatible with his age and disposition. The carpets will have to be taken up for the summer and put away till the winter . . . Persian powder or naphthaline. . . . The Romans were healthy because they knew both how to work and how to rest, they had *mens sana in corpore sano.* Their life ran along certain

---

* He adds that he is a *Nadvorny Sovetnik* (almost the same as a German *Hofrat*), an undistinguished civilian title with no English equivalent.

recognized patterns. Our director says : " The chief thing about each life is its pattern. Whoever loses his pattern is lost himself "—and it's just the same in our daily life· [*Takes* MASHA *by the waist, laughing*] Masha loves me. My wife loves me. And you ought to put the window curtains away with the carpets. . . . I'm feeling awfully pleased with life to-day. Masha, we've got to be at the director's at four. They're getting up a walk for the pedagogues and their families.

MASHA. I shan't go.

KULIGIN. [*Hurt*] My dear Masha, why not ?

MASHA. I'll tell you later. . . . [*Angrily*] All right, I'll go, only please stand back. . . .   [*Steps away.*

KULIGIN. And then we're to spend the evening at the director's. In spite of his ill-health that man tries, above everything else, to be sociable. A splendid, illuminating personality. A wonderful man. After yesterday's com- mittee he said to me : " I'm tired, Feodor Ilitch, I'm tired ! " [*Looks at the clock, then at his watch*] Your clock is seven minutes fast. " Yes," he said, " I'm tired."

[*Violin played off.*

OLGA. Let's go and have lunch ! There's to be a master- piece of baking !

KULIGIN. Oh my dear Olga, my dear. Yesterday I was working till eleven o'clock at night, and got awfully tired. To-day I'm quite happy. [*Goes into dining-room*] My dear . . .

CHEBUTIKIN. [*Puts his paper into his pocket, and combs his beard*] A pie ? Splendid !

MASHA. [*Severely to* CHEBUTIKIN] Only mind ; you're not to drink anything to-day. Do you hear ? It's bad for you.

CHEBUTIKIN. Oh, that's all right. I haven't been

drunk for two years. And it's all the same, anyway!

MASHA. You're not to dare to drink, all the same. [*Angrily, but so that her husband should not hear*] Another dull evening at the director's, confound it!

TUZENBACH. I shouldn't go if I were you. . . . It's quite simple.

CHEBUTIKIN. Don't go.

MASHA. Yes, " don't go. . . ." It's a cursed, unbearable life. . . .   [*Goes into dining-room.*

CHEBUTIKIN. [*Follows her*] It's not so bad.

SOLENI. [*Going into the dining-room*] There, there, there. . . .

TUZENBACH. Vassili Vassilevitch, that's enough. Be quiet!

SOLENI. There, there, there. . . .

KULIGIN. [*Gaily*] Your health, Colonel! I'm a pedagogue and not quite at home here. I'm Masha's husband. . . . She's a good sort, a very good sort. . . .

VERSHININ. I'll have some of this black vodka. . . . [*Drinks*] Your health! [*To* OLGA] I'm very comfortable here!

    Only IRINA *and* TUZENBACH *are now left in the sitting-room.*

IRINA. Masha's out of sorts to-day. She married when she was eighteen, when he seemed to her the wisest of men. And now it's different. He's the kindest man, but not the wisest.

OLGA. [*Impatiently*] Andrey, when are you coming?

ANDREY. [*Off*] One minute. [*Enters and goes to the table.*

TUZENBACH. What are you thinking about?

IRINA. I don't like this Soleni of yours and I'm afraid of him. He only says silly things.

TUZENBACH. He's a queer man. I'm sorry for him,
though he vexes me. I think he's shy. When there
are just the two of us he's quite all right and very good
company; when other people are about he's rough and
hectoring. Don't let's go in, let them have their meal without us. Let me stay with you. What are you thinking
of ? [*Pause*] You're twenty. I'm not yet thirty. How
many years are there left to us, with their long, long lines of
days, filled with my love for you. . . .

IRINA. Nicolai Lvovitch, don't speak to me of love.

TUZENBACH. [*Does not hear*] I've a great thirst for life,
struggle, and work, and this thirst has united with my love
for you, Irina, and you're so beautiful, and life seems so
beautiful to me ! What are you thinking about ?

IRINA. You say that life is beautiful. Yes, if only it
seems so ! The life of us three hasn't been beautiful yet ;
it has been stifling us as if it was weeds . . . I'm crying. I
oughtn't. . . . [*Dries her tears, smiles*] We must work,
work. That is why we are unhappy and look at the world
so sadly ; we don't know what work is. Our parents
despised work. . . .

> *Enter* NATALIA IVANOVNA ; *she wears a pink dress
> and a green sash.*

NATASHA. They're already at lunch . . . I'm late . . .
[*Carefully examines herself in a mirror, and puts herself
straight*] I think my hair's done all right. . . . [*Sees* IRINA]
Dear Irina Sergeyevna, I congratulate you ! [*Kisses
her firmly and at length*] You've so many visitors, I'm really
ashamed. . . . How do you do, Baron !

OLGA. [*Enters from dining-room*] Here's Natalia Ivanovna. How are you, dear !   [*They kiss.*

NATASHA. Happy returns. I'm awfully shy, you've
so many people here.

OLGA. All our friends. [*Frightened, in an undertone*] You're wearing a green sash ! My dear, you shouldn't !

NATASHA. Is it a sign of anything ?

OLGA. No, it simply doesn't go well . . . and it looks so queer.

NATASHA. [*In a tearful voice*] Yes ? But it isn't really green, it's too dull for that.

[*Goes into dining-room with* OLGA.
They have all sat down to lunch in the dining-room, the sitting-room is empty.

KULIGIN. I wish you a nice *fiancé*, Irina. It's quite time you married.

CHEBUTIKIN. Natalia Ivanovna, I wish you the same.

KULIGIN. Natalia Ivanovna has a *fiancé* already.

MASHA. [*Raps with her fork on a plate*] Let's all get drunk and make life purple for once !

KULIGIN. You've lost three good conduct marks.

VERSHININ. This is a nice drink. What's it made of ?

SOLENI. Blackbeetles.

IRINA. [*Tearfully*] Phoo ! How disgusting !

OLGA. There is to be a roast turkey and a sweet apple pie for dinner. Thank goodness I can spend all day and the evening at home. You'll come in the evening, ladies and gentlemen. . . .

VERSHININ. And please may I come in the evening !

IRINA. Please do.

NATASHA. They don't stand on ceremony here.

CHEBUTIKIN. Nature only brought us into the world that we should love !   [*Laughs.*

ANDREY. [*Angrily*] Please don't ! Aren't you tired of it ?

Enter FEDOTIK *and* RODE *with a large basket of flowers.*

FEDOTIK. They're lunching already.

RODE. [*Loudly and thickly*] Lunching ? Yes, so they are. . . .

FEDOTIK. Wait a minute ! [*Takes a photograph*] That's one. No, just a moment. . . . [*Takes another*] That's two. Now we're ready !

> *They take the basket and go into the dining-room, where they have a noisy reception.*

RODE. [*Loudly*] Congratulations and best wishes ! Lovely weather to-day, simply perfect. Was out walking with the High School students all the morning. I take their drills.

FEDOTIK. You may move, Irina Sergeyevna ! [*Takes a photograph*] You look well to-day. [*Takes a humming-top out of his pocket*] Here's a humming-top, by the way. It's got a lovely note !

IRINA. How awfully nice !

MASHA. " There stands a green oak by the sea,

> And a chain of bright gold is around it . . .
> And a chain of bright gold is around it . . ."

[*Tearfully*] What am I saying that for ? I've had those words running in my head all day. . . .

KULIGIN. There are thirteen at table !

RODE. [*Aloud*] Surely you don't believe in that superstition ? [*Laughter.*

KULIGIN. If there are thirteen at table then it means there are lovers present. It isn't you, Ivan Romanovitch, hang it all. . . . [*Laughter.*

CHEBUTIKIN. I'm a hardened sinner, but I really don't see why Natalia Ivanovna should blush. . . .

> *Loud laughter ;* NATASHA *runs out into the sitting-room, followed by* ANDREY.

ANDREY. Don't pay any attention to them ! Wait . . . do stop, please. . . .

NATASHA. I'm shy . . . I don't know what's the matter with me and they're all laughing at me. It wasn't nice of me to leave the table like that, but I can't . . . I can't.

[Covers her face with her hands.

ANDREY. My dear, I beg you. I implore you not to excite yourself. I assure you they're only joking, they're kind people. My dear, good girl, they're all kind and sincere people, and they like both you and me. Come here to the window, they can't see us here. . . . *[Looks round.*

NATASHA. I'm so unaccustomed to meeting people!

ANDREY. Oh your youth, your splendid, beautiful youth! My darling, don't be so excited! Believe me, believe me . . . I'm so happy, my soul is full of love, of ecstasy. . . . They don't see us! They can't! Why, why or when did I fall in love with you—Oh, I can't understand anything. My dear, my pure darling, be my wife! I love you, love you . . . as never before. . . . *[They kiss.*

Two officers come in and, seeing the lovers kiss, stop in astonishment.

Curtain.

ACT TWO

Scene as before. It is 3 p.m. Somebody is heard playing a concertina outside in the street. There is no fire. NATALYA IVANOVNA *enters in indoor dress carrying a candle ; she stops by the door which leads into* ANDREY'S *room.*

NATASHA. What are you doing, Andrey ? Are you reading ? It's nothing, only I. . . . [*She opens another door, and looks in, then closes it*] Isn't there any fire. . . .

ANDREY. [*Enters with book in hand*] What are you doing, Natasha ?

NATASHA. I was looking to see if there wasn't a fire. It's Shrovetide, and the servant is simply beside herself ; I must look out that something doesn't happen. When I came through the dining-room yesterday midnight, there was a candle burning. I couldn't get her to tell me who had lighted it. [*Puts down her candle*] What's the time ?

ANDREY. [*Looks at his watch*] A quarter past eight.

NATASHA. And Olga and Irina aren't in yet. The poor things are still at work. Olga at the teachers' council, Irina at the telegraph office. . . . [*Sighs*] I said to your sister this morning, " Irina, darling, you must take care of yourself." But she pays no attention. Did you say it was a quarter past eight ? I am afraid little Bobby is quite ill. Why is he so cold ? He was feverish yesterday, but to-day he is quite cold . . . I am so frightened !

ANDREY. It's all right, Natasha. The boy is well.

127

NATASHA. Still, I think we ought to put him on a diet·
I am so afraid. And the entertainers were to be here after
nine ; they had better not come, Andrey.

ANDREY. I don't know. After all, they were asked.

NATASHA. This morning, when the little boy woke up and
saw me he suddenly smiled ; that means he knew me.
" Good morning, Bobby ! " I said, " good morning, darling."
And he laughed. Children understand, they understand
very well. So I'll tell them, Andrey dear, not to receive
the entertainers.

ANDREY. [*Hesitatingly*] But what about my sisters.
This is their flat.

NATASHA. They'll do as I want them. They are so kind.
. . . [*Going*] I ordered sour milk for supper. The doctor
says you must eat sour milk and nothing else, or you won't
get thin. [*Stops*] Bobby is so cold. I'm afraid his room is
too cold for him. It would be nice to put him into another
room till the warm weather comes. Irina's room, for
instance, is just right for a child : it's dry and has the sun
all day. I must tell her, she can share Olga's room. . . .
It isn't as if she was at home in the daytime, she only sleeps
here. . . . [*A pause*] Andrey, darling, why are you so
silent ?

ANDREY. I was just thinking. . . . There is really nothing to say. . . .

NATASHA. Yes . . . there was something I wanted to
tell you. . . . Oh, yes. Ferapont has come from the
Council offices, he wants to see you.

ANDREY. [*Yawns*] Call him here.

> NATASHA *goes out ;* ANDREY *reads his book, stooping
> over the candle she has left behind.* FERAPONT
> *enters ; he wears a tattered old coat with the collar
> up. His ears are muffled.*

ANDREY. Good morning, grandfather. What have you to say ?

FERAPONT. The Chairman sends a book and some documents or other. Here. . . .

[*Hands him a book and a packet.*

ANDREY. Thank you. It's all right. Why couldn't you come earlier ? It's past eight now.

FERAPONT. What ?

ANDREY. [*Louder*] I say you've come late, it's past eight.

FERAPONT. Yes, yes. I came when it was still light, but they wouldn't let me in. They said you were busy. Well, what was I to do. If you're busy, you're busy, and I'm in no hurry. [*He thinks that* ANDREY *is asking him something*] What ?

ANDREY. Nothing. [*Looks through the book*] To-morrow's Friday. I'm not supposed to go to work, but I'll come— all the same . . . and do some work. It's dull at home. . . . [*Pause*] Oh, my dear old man, how strangely life changes, and how it deceives ! To-day, out of sheer boredom, I took up this book—old university lectures, and I couldn't help laughing. My God, I'm secretary of the local district council, the council which has Protopopov for its chairman, yes, I'm the secretary, and the summit of my ambitions is—to become a member of the council ! I to be a member of the local district council, I, who dream every night that I'm a professor of Moscow University, a famous scholar of whom all Russia is proud !

FERAPONT. I can't tell . . . I'm hard of hearing. . . .

ANDREY. If you weren't, I don't suppose I should talk to you. I've got to talk to somebody, and my wife doesn't understand me, and I'm a bit afraid of my sisters—I don't know why unless it is that they may make fun of me and make me feel ashamed . . . I don't drink, I don't like

I

public-houses, but how I should like to be sitting just now in Tyestov's place in Moscow, or at the Great Moscow, old fellow !

FERAPONT. Moscow ? That's where a contractor was once telling that some merchants or other were eating pancakes ; one ate forty pancakes and he went and died, he was saying. Either forty or fifty, I forget which.

ANDREY. In Moscow you can sit in an enormous restaurant where you don't know anybody and where nobody knows you, and you don't feel all the same that you're a stranger. And here you know everybody and everybody knows you, and you're a stranger . . . and a lonely stranger.

FERAPONT. What ? And the same contractor was telling —perhaps he was lying—that there was a cable stretching right across Moscow.

ANDREY. What for ?

FERAPONT. I can't tell. The contractor said so.

ANDREY. Rubbish. [*He reads*] Were you ever in Moscow ?

FERAPONT. [*After a pause*] No. God did not lead me there. [*Pause*] Shall I go ?

ANDREY. You may go. Good-bye. [FERAPONT *goes*] Good-bye. [*Reads*] You can come to-morrow and fetch these documents. . . . Go along. . . . [*Pause*] He's gone. [*A ring*] Yes, yes. . . .

> [*Stretches himself and slowly goes into his own room. Behind the scene the nurse is singing a lullaby to the child.* MASHA *and* VERSHININ *come in. While they talk, a maidservant lights candles and a lamp.*

MASHA. I don't know. [*Pause*] I don't know. Of course, habit counts for a great deal. After father's death, for instance, it took us a long time to get used to the absence of orderlies. But, apart from habit, it seems to me in all fairness that, however it may be in other towns, the best and most-educated people are army men.

VERSHININ. I'm thirsty. I should like some tea.

MASHA. [*Glancing at her watch*] They'll bring some soon. I was given in marriage when I was eighteen, and I was afraid of my husband because he was a teacher and I'd only just left school. He then seemed to me frightfully wise and learned and important. And now, unfortunately, that has changed.

VERSHININ. Yes . . . yes.

MASHA. I don't speak of my husband, I've grown used to him, but civilians in general are so often coarse, impolite, uneducated. Their rudeness offends me, it angers me. I suffer when I see that a man isn't quite sufficiently refined, or delicate, or polite. I simply suffer agonies when I happen to be among schoolmasters, my husband's colleagues.

VERSHININ. Yes. . . . It seems to me that civilians and army men are equally interesting, in this town, at any rate. It's all the same ! If you listen to a member of the local intelligentsia, whether to civilian or military, he will tell you that he's sick of his wife, sick of his house, sick of his estate, sick of his horses. . . . We Russians are extremely gifted in the direction of thinking on an exalted plane, but, tell me, why do we aim so low in real life ? Why ?

MASHA. Why ?

VERSHININ. Why is a Russian sick of his children, sick of his wife ? And why are his wife and children sick of him ?

MASHA. You're a little downhearted to-day.

VERSHININ. Perhaps I am. I haven't had any dinner, I've had nothing since the morning. My daughter is a little unwell, and when my girls are ill, I get very anxious and my conscience tortures me because they have such a mother.   Oh, if you had seen her to-day !   What a trivial personality !   We began quarrelling at seven in the morning and at nine I slammed the door and went out. [*Pause*] I never speak of her, it's strange that I bear my complaints to you alone. [*Kisses her hand*] Don't be angry with me. I haven't anybody but you, nobody at all. . . .   [*Pause.*

MASHA.   What a noise in the oven.   Just before father's death there was a noise in the pipe, just like that.

VERSHININ.   Are you superstitious ?

MASHA.   Yes.

VERSHININ.   That's strange. [*Kisses her hand*] You are a splendid, wonderful woman.   Splendid, wonderful !   It is dark here, but I see your sparkling eyes.

MASHA. [*Sits on another chair*] There is more light here.

VERSHININ.   I love you, love you, love you . . . I love your eyes, your movements, I dream of them. . . . Splendid, wonderful woman !

MASHA. [*Laughing*] When you talk to me like that, I laugh ; I don't know why, for I'm afraid.   Don't repeat it, please. . . . [*In an undertone*] No, go on, it's all the same to me. . . . [*Covers her face with her hands*] Somebody's coming, let's talk about something else. . . .

> IRINA *and* TUZENBACH *come in through the dining-room.*

TUZENBACH.   My surname is really triple.   I am called Baron Tuzenbach-Krone-Altschauer, but I am Russian and Orthodox, the same as you.   There is very little German left in me, unless perhaps it is the patience and the obstinacy with which I bore you.   I see you home every night.

IRINA.   How tired I am !

TUZENBACH.   And I'll come to the telegraph office to see you home every day for ten or twenty years, until you drive me away. [*He sees* MASHA *and* VERSHININ ; *joyfully*] Is that you ? How do you do.

IRINA. Well, I am home at last. [*To* MASHA] A lady came to-day to telegraph to her brother in Saratov that her son died to-day, and she couldn't remember the address anyhow. So she sent the telegram without an address, just to Saratov. She was crying. And for some reason or other I was rude to her. " I've no time," I said. It was so stupid. Are the entertainers coming to-night ?

MASHA. Yes.

IRINA. [*Sitting down in an armchair*] I want a rest. I am tired.

TUZENBACH. [*Smiling*] When you come home from your work you seem so young, and so unfortunate. . . .

[*Pause.*

IRINA. I am tired. No, I don't like the telegraph office, I don't like it.

MASHA. You've grown thinner. . . . [*Whistles a little*] And you look younger, and your face has become like a boy's.

TUZENBACH. That's the way she does her hair.

IRINA. I must find another job, this one won't do for me. What I wanted, what I hoped to get, just that is lacking here. Labour without poetry, without ideas. . . . [*A knock on the floor*] The doctor is knocking. [*To* TUZEN- BACH] Will you knock, dear. I can't . . . I'm tired. . . . [TUZENBACH *knocks*] He'll come in a minute. Something ought to be done. Yesterday the doctor and Andrey played cards at the club and lost money. Andrey seems to have lost 200 roubles.

MASHA. [*with indifference*] What can we do now ?

IRINA. He lost money a fortnight ago, he lost money in December. Perhaps if he lost everything we should go away from this town Oh, my God, I dream of Moscow every night. I'm just like a lunatic. [*Laughs*] We go there in June, and before June there's still . . . February, March, April, May . . . nearly half a year !

MASHA. Only Natasha mustn't get to know of these losses.

IRINA. I expect it will be all the same to her.

CHEBUTIKIN, *who has only just got out of bed—he was resting after dinner—comes into the dining-room and combs his beard. He then sits by the table and takes a newspaper from his pocket.*

MASHA. Here he is. . . . Has he paid his rent ?

IRINA. [*Laughs*] No. He's been here eight months and hasn't paid a copeck. Seems to have forgotten.

MASHA. [*Laughs*] What dignity in his pose !

[*They all laugh. A pause.*

IRINA. Why are you so silent, Alexander Ignateyevitch ?

VERSHININ. I don't know. I want some tea. Half my life for a tumbler of tea : I haven't had anything since morning.

CHEBUTIKIN. Irina Sergeyevna !

IRINA. What is it ?

CHEBUTIKIN. Please come here, *Venez ici.* [IRINA *goes and sits by the table*] I can't do without you.

[IRINA *begins to play patience.*

VERSHININ. Well, if we can't have any tea, let's philosophize, at any rate.

TUZENBACH. Yes, let's. About what ?

VERSHININ. About what ? Let us meditate . . . about life as it will be after our time ; for example, in two or three hundred years.

TUZENBACH. Well ? After our time people will fly about in balloons, the cut of one's coat will change, perhaps they'll discover a sixth sense and develop it, but life will remain the same, laborious, mysterious, and happy. And in a thousand years' time, people will still be sighing : " Life is hard ! "—and at the same time they'll be just as afraid of death, and unwilling to meet it, as we are.

VERSHININ. [*Thoughtfully*] How can I put it ? It seems to me that everything on earth must change, little by little, and is already changing under our very eyes. After two or three hundred years, after a thousand—the actual time doesn't matter—a new and happy age will begin. We, of course, shall not take part in it, but we live and work and even suffer to-day that it should come. We create it—and in that one object is our destiny and, if you. like, our happiness.

MASHA *laughs softly.*

TUZENBACH. What is it ?

MASHA. I don't know. I've been laughing all day, ever since morning.

VERSHININ. I finished my education at the same point as you, I have not studied at universities ; I read a lot, but I cannot choose my books and perhaps what I read is not at all what I should, but the longer I live, the more I want to know. My hair is turning white, I am nearly an old man now, but I know so little, oh, so little ! But I think I know the things that matter most, and that are most real. I know them well. And I wish I could make you understand that there is no happiness for us, that there should not and cannot be. . . . We must only work and work, and happiness is only for our distant posterity. [*Pause*] If not for me, then for the descendants of my descendants.

FEDOTIK *and* RODE *come into the dining-room ; they sit and sing softly, strumming on a guitar.*

TUZENBACH. According to you, one should not even think about happiness ! But suppose I am happy !

VERSHININ. No.

TUZENBACH. [*Moves his hands and laughs*] We do not seem to understand each other. How can I convince you ? [MASHA *laughs quietly*, TUZENBACH *continues, pointing at her*] Yes, laugh ! [*To* VERSHININ] Not only after two or three centuries, but in a million years, life will still be as it was ; life does not change, it remains for ever, following its own laws which do not concern us, or which, at any rate, you will never find out. Migrant birds, cranes for example, fly and fly, and whatever thoughts, high or low, enter their heads, they will still fly and not know why or where. They fly and will continue to fly, whatever philosophers come to life among them ; they may philosophize as much as they like, only they will fly. . . .

MASHA. Still, is there a meaning ?

TUZENBACH. A meaning. . . . Now the snow is falling. What meaning ?   [*Pause.*

MASHA. It seems to me that a man must have faith, or must search for a faith, or his life will be empty, empty. . . . To live and not to know why the cranes fly, why babies are born, why there are stars in the sky. . . . Either you must know why you live, or everything is trivial, not worth a straw.   [*A pause.*

VERSHININ. Still, I am sorry that my youth has gone.

MASHA. Gogol says : life in this world is a dull matter, my masters !

TUZENBACH. And I say it's difficult to argue with you, my masters ! Hang it all.

CHEBUTIKIN. [*Reading*] Balzac was married at Berdichev. [IRINA *is singing softly*] That's worth making a note of. [*He makes a note*] Balzac was married at Berdichev.

                                          [*Goes on reading.*

IRINA. [*Laying out cards, thoughtfully*] Balzac was married at Berdichev.

TUZENBACH. The die is cast. I've handed in my resignation, Maria Sergeyevna.

MASHA. So I heard. I don't see what good it is ; I don't like civilians.

TUZENBACH. Never mind. . . . [*Gets up*] I'm not handsome ; what use am I as a soldier ? Well, it makes no difference . . . I shall work. If only just once in my life I could work so that I could come home in the evening, fall exhausted on my bed, and go to sleep at once. [*Going into the dining-room*] Workmen, I suppose, do sleep soundly !

FEDOTIK. [*To* IRINA] I bought some coloured pencils for you at Pizhikov's in the Moscow Road, just now. And here is a little knife.

IRINA. You have got into the habit of behaving to me as if I am a little girl, but I am grown up. [*Takes the pencils and the knife, then, with joy*] How lovely !

FEDOTIK. And I bought myself a knife . . . look at it . . . one blade, another, a third, an ear-scoop, scissors, nail-cleaners. . . .

RODE. [*Loudly*] Doctor, how old are you ?

CHEBUTIKIN. I ? Thirty-two.   [*Laughter.*

FEDOTIK. I'll show you another kind of patience. . . .
                                           [*Lays out cards.*

    A samovar is brought in ; ANFISA *attends to it ; a little later* NATASHA *enters and helps by the table ;* SOLENI *arrives and, after greetings, sits by the table.*

VERSHININ. What a wind !

MASHA. Yes. I'm tired of winter. I've already forgotten what summer's like.

IRINA. It's coming out, I see. We're going to Moscow.

FEDOTIK. No, it won't come out. Look, the eight was on the two of spades. [*Laughs*] That means you won't go to Moscow.

CHEBUTIKIN. [*Reading paper*] Tsitsigar. Smallpox is raging here.

ANFISA. [*Coming up to* MASHA] Masha, have some tea, little mother. [*To* VERSHININ] Please have some, sir . . . excuse me, but I've forgotten your name. . . .

MASHA. Bring some here, nurse. I shan't go over there.

IRINA. Nurse !

ANFISA. Coming, coming !

NATASHA. [*To* SOLENI] Children at the breast understand perfectly. I said " Good morning, Bobby ; good morning, dear ! " And he looked at me in quite an unusual way. You think it's only the mother in me that is speaking : I assure you that isn't so ! He's a wonderful child.

SOLENI. If he was my child I'd roast him on a frying-pan and eat him.

> *Takes his tumbler into the drawing-room and sits in a corner.*

NATASHA. [*Covers her face in her hands*] Vulgar, ill-bred man !

MASHA. He's lucky who doesn't notice whether it's winter now, or summer. I think that if I were in Moscow, I shouldn't mind about the weather.

VERSHININ. A few days ago I was reading the prison diary of a French minister. He had been sentenced on account of the Panama scandal. With what joy, what delight, he speaks of the birds he saw through the prison windows, which he had never noticed while he was a minister. Now, of course, that he is at liberty, he notices birds no more than he did before. When you go to live in Moscow you'll not notice it, in just the same way

There can be no happiness for us, it only exists in our wishes.

TUZENBACH. [*Takes cardboard box from the table*] Where are the pastries ?

IRINA. Soleni has eaten them.

TUZENBACH. All of them ?

ANFISA. [*Serving tea*] There's a letter for you.

VERSHININ. For me ? [*Takes the letter*] From my daughter. [*Reads*] Yes, of course . . . I will go quietly. Excuse me, Maria Sergeyevna. I shan't have any tea. [*Stands up, excited*] That eternal story. . . .

MASHA. What is it ? Is it a secret ?

VERSHININ. [*Quietly*] My wife has poisoned herself again. I must go. I'll go out quietly. It's all awfully unpleasant. [*Kisses* MASHA's *hand*] My dear, my splendid, good woman . . . I'll go this way, quietly.   [*Exit.*

ANFISA. Where has he gone ? And I'd served tea. . . . What a man.

MASHA. [*Angrily*] Be quiet ! You bother so one can't have a moment's peace. . . . [*Goes to the table with her cup*] I'm tired of you, old woman !

ANFISA. My dear ! Why are you offended !

ANDREY'S VOICE. Anfisa !

ANFISA. [*Mocking*] Anfisa ! He sits there and . . . [*Exit.*

MASHA. [*In the dining-room, by the table angrily*] Let me sit down ! [*Disturbs the cards on the table*] Here you are, spreading your cards out. Have some tea !

IRINA. You are cross, Masha.

MASHA. If I am cross, then don't talk to me. Don't touch me !

CHEBUTIKIN. Don't touch her, don't touch her. . . .

MASHA. You're sixty, but you're like a boy, always up to some beastly nonsense.

NATASHA. [*Sighs*] Dear Masha, why use such expressions? With your beautiful exterior you would be simply fascinating in good society, I tell you so directly, if it wasn't for your words. *Je vous prie, pardonnez moi, Marie, mais vous avez des manières un peu grossières.*

TUZENBACH. [*Restraining his laughter*] Give me . . . give me . . . there's some cognac, I think.

NATASHA. *Il parait, que mon Bobick déja ne dort pas*, he has awakened. He isn't well to-day. I'll go to him, excuse me. . . . [*Exit.*

IRINA. Where has Alexander Ignateyevitch gone ?

MASHA. Home. Something extraordinary has happened to his wife again.

TUZENBACH. [*Goes to* SOLENI *with a cognac-flask in his hands*] You go on sitting by yourself, thinking of something —goodness knows what. Come and let's make peace Let's have some cognac. [*They drink*] I expect I'll have to play the piano all night, some rubbish most likely . . . well, so be it !

SOLENI. Why make peace ? I haven't quarrelled with you.

TUZENBACH. You always make me feel as if something has taken place between us. You've a strange character, you must admit.

SOLENI. [*Declaims*] " I am strange, but who is not ? Don't be angry, Aleko ! "

TUZENBACH. And what has Aleko to do with it ?

[*Pause.*

SOLENI. When I'm with one other man I behave just like everybody else, but in company I'm dull and shy and . . . talk all manner of rubbish. But I'm more honest and more honourable than very, very many people. And I can prove it.

TUZENBACH. I often get angry with you, you always fasten on to me in company, but I like you all the same. I'm going to drink my fill to-night, whatever happens. Drink, now!

SOLENI. Let's drink. [*They drink*] I never had anything against you, Baron. But my character is like Lermontov's [*In a low voice*] I even rather resemble Lermontov, they say. . . .

> *Takes a scent-bottle from his pocket, and scents his hands.*

TUZENBACH. I've sent in my resignation. Basta! I've been thinking about it for five years, and at last made up my mind. I shall work.

SOLENI. [*Declaims*] " Do not be angry, Aleko . . . forget, forget, thy dreams of yore. . . ."

> *While he is speaking* ANDREY *enters quietly with a book, and sits by the table.*

TUZENBACH. I shall work.

CHEBUTIKIN. [*Going with* IRINA *into the dining-room*] And the food was also real Caucasian onion soup, and, for a roast, some chehartma.

SOLENI. Cheremsha* isn't meat at all, but a plant something like an onion.

CHEBUTIKIN. No, my angel. Chehartma isn't onion, but roast mutton.

SOLENI. And I tell you, cheremsha—is a sort of onion.

CHEBUTIKIN. And I tell you, chehartma—is mutton.

SOLENI. And I tell you, cheremsha—is a sort of onion.

CHEBUTIKIN. What's the use of arguing! You've never been in the Caucasus, and never ate any chehartma.

SOLENI. I never ate it, because I hate it. It smells like garlic.

* A variety of garlic.

ANDREY. [*Imploring*] Please, please ! I ask you !

TUZENBACH. When are the entertainers coming ?

IRINA. They promised for about nine ; that is, quite soon.

TUZENBACH. [*Embraces* ANDREY]

" Oh my house, my house, my new-built house."

ANDREY. [*Dances and sings*]

" Newly-built of maple-wood."

CHEBUTIKIN. [*Dances*]

" Its walls are like a sieve ! " [*Laughter.*

TUZENBACH. [*Kisses* ANDREY] Hang it all, let's drink. Andrey, old boy, let's drink with you. And I'll go with you, Andrey, to the University of Moscow.

SOLENI. Which one ? There are two universities in Moscow.

ANDREY. There's one university in Moscow.

SOLENI. Two, I tell you.

ANDREY. Don't care if there are three. So much the better.

SOLENI. There are two universities in Moscow ! [*There are murmurs and " hushes "*] There are two universities in Moscow, the old one and the new one. And if you don't like to listen, if my words annoy you, then I need not speak. I can even go into another room. . . . [*Exit.*

TUZENBACH. Bravo, bravo ! [*Laughs*] Come on, now. I'm going to play. Funny man, Soleni. . . .

[*Goes to the piano and plays a waltz.*

MASHA. [*Dancing solo*] The Baron's drunk, the Baron's drunk, the Baron's drunk !

NATASHA *comes in.*

NATASHA. [*To* CHEBUTIKIN] Ivan Romanovitch !

Says something to CHEBUTIKIN, *then goes out quietly ;* CHEBUTIKIN *touches* TUZENBACH *on the shoulder and whispers something to him.*

IRINA. What is it ?

CHEBUTIKIN. Time for us to go. Good-bye.

TUZENBACH. Good-night. It's time we went.

IRINA. But, really, the entertainers ?

ANDREY. [*In confusion*] There won't be any entertainers. You see, dear, Natasha says that Bobby isn't quite well, and so. . . . In a word, I don't care, and it's absolutely all one to me.

IRINA. [*Shrugging her shoulders*] Bobby ill !

MASHA. What is she thinking of ! Well, if they are sent home, I suppose they must go. [*To* IRINA] Bobby's all right, it's she herself. . . . Here ! [*Taps her forehead*] Little bourgeoise !

> ANDREY *goes to his room through the right-hand door,* CHEBUTIKIN *follows him. In the dining-room they are saying good-bye.*

FEDOTIK. What a shame ! I was expecting to spend the evening here, but of course, if the little baby is ill . . . I'll bring him some toys to-morrow.

RODE. [*Loudly*] I slept late after dinner to-day because I thought I was going to dance all night. It's only nine o'clock now !

MASHA. Let's go into the street, we can talk there. Then we can settle things.

> *Good-byes and good nights are heard.* TUZENBACH'S *merry laughter is heard.* [*All go out*] ANFISA AND *the maid clear the table, and put out the lights.* [*The nurse sings*] ANDREY, *wearing an overcoat and a hat, and* CHEBUTIKIN *enter silently.*

CHEBUTIKIN. I never managed to get married because my life flashed by like lightning, and because I was madly in love with your mother, who was married.

ANDREY. One shouldn't marry. One shouldn't, because it's dull.

CHEBUTIKIN. So there I am, in my loneliness. Say what you will, loneliness is a terrible thing, old fellow. . . . Though really . . . of course, it absolutely doesn't matter !

ANDREY. Let's be quicker.

CHEBUTIKIN. What are you in such a hurry for ? We shall be in time.

ANDREY. I'm afraid my wife may stop me.

CHEBUTIKIN. Ah !

ANDREY. I shan't play to-night, I shall only sit and look on. I don't feel very well. . . . What am I to do for my asthma, Ivan Romanovitch ?

CHEBUTIKIN. Don't ask me ! I don't remember, old fellow, I don't know.

ANDREY. Let's go through the kitchen.   [*They go out.*
     *A bell rings, then a second time ; voices and laughter
     are heard.*

IRINA. [*Enters*] What's that ?

ANFISA. [*Whispers*] The entertainers !   [*Bell.*

IRINA. Tell them there's nobody at home, nurse. They must excuse us.

     ANFISA *goes out.* IRINA *walks about the room deep
     in thought ; she is excited.* SOLENI *enters.*

SOLENI. [*In surprise*] There's nobody here. . . . Where are they all ?

IRINA. They've gone home.

SOLENI. How strange. Are you here alone ?

IRINA. Yes, alone. [*A pause*] Good-bye.

SOLENI. Just now I behaved tactlessly, with insufficient reserve. But you are not like all the others, you are noble and pure, you can see the truth. . . . You alone can understand me. I love you, deeply, beyond measure, I love you.

IRINA. Good-bye! Go away.

SOLENI. I cannot live without you. [*Follows her*] Oh, my happiness! [*Through his tears*] Oh, joy! Wonderful, marvellous, glorious eyes, such as I have never seen before. . . .

IRINA. [*Coldly*] Stop it, Vassili Vassilevitch!

SOLENI. This is the first time I speak to you of love, and it is as if I am no longer on the earth, but on another planet. [*Wipes his forehead*] Well, never mind. I can't make you love me by force, of course . . . but I don't intend to have any more-favoured rivals. . . . No . . . I swear to you by all the saints, I shall kill my rival. . . . Oh, beautiful one!

> NATASHA *enters with a candle; she looks in through one door, then through another, and goes past the door leading to her husband's room.*

NATASHA. Here's Andrey. Let him go on reading. Excuse me, Vassili Vassilevitch, I did not know you were here; I am engaged in domesticities.

SOLENI. It's all the same to me. Good-bye! [*Exit.*

NATASHA. You're so tired, my poor dear girl! [*Kisses* IRINA] If you only went to bed earlier.

IRINA. Is Bobby asleep?

NATASHA. Yes, but restlessly. By the way, dear, I wanted to tell you, but either you weren't at home, or I was busy . . . I think Bobby's present nursery is cold and damp. And your room would be so nice for the child. My dear, darling girl, do change over to Olga's for a bit!

IRINA. [*Not understanding*] Where?

> *The bells of a troika are heard as it drives up to the house.*

NATASHA. You and Olga can share a room, for the time being, and Bobby can have yours. He's such a darling; to-day I said to him, "Bobby, you're mine! Mine!"

K

And he looked at me with his dear little eyes. [*A bell rings*]
It must be Olga. How late she is ! [*The maid enters and
whispers to* NATASHA] Protopopov ? What a queer man to
do such a thing. Protopopov's come and wants me to go for
a drive with him in his troika. [*Laughs*] How funny these
men are. . . . [*A bell rings*] Somebody has come. Suppose
I did go and have half an hour's drive. . . . [*To the maid*]
Say I shan't be long. [*Bell rings*] Somebody's ringing,
it must be Olga.   [*Exit*.

> *The maid runs out ;* IRINA *sits deep in thought ;*
> KULIGIN *and* OLGA *enter, followed by* VERSHININ.

KULIGIN. Well, there you are. And you said there was
going to be a party.

VERSHININ. It's queer ; I went away not long ago, half
an hour ago, and they were expecting entertainers.

IRINA. They've all gone.

KULIGIN. Has Masha gone too ? Where has she gone ?
And what's Protopopov waiting for downstairs in his troika ?
Whom is he expecting ?

IRINA. Don't ask questions . . . I'm tired.

KULIGIN. Oh, you're all whimsies. . . .

OLGA. My committee meeting is only just over. I'm
tired out. Our chairwoman is ill, so I had to take her place.
My head, my head is aching. . . . [*Sits*] Andrey lost 200
roubles at cards yesterday . . . the whole town is talking
about it. . . .

KULIGIN. Yes, my meeting tired me too.   [*Sits*.

VERSHININ. My wife took it into her head to frighten me
just now by nearly poisoning herself. It's all right now,
and I'm glad ; I can rest now. . . . But perhaps we ought
to go away ? Well, my best wishes, Feodor Ilitch, let's go
somewhere together ! I can't, I absolutely can't stop at
home. . . . Come on '

KULIGIN. I'm tired. I won't go. [*Gets up*] I'm tired·
Has my wife gone home ?

IRINA. I suppose so.

KULIGIN. [*Kisses* IRINA's *hand*] Good-bye, I'm going to
rest all day to-morrow and the day after. Best wishes !
[*Going*] I should like some tea. I was looking forward to
spending the whole evening in pleasant company and—*o,
fallacem hominum spem !* . . . Accusative case after an inter-
jection. . . .

VERSHININ. Then I'll go somewhere by myself.

[*Exit with* KULIGIN, *whistling.*

OLGA. I've such a headache . . . Andrey has been losing
money. . . . The whole town is talking. . . . I'll go and
lie down. [*Going*] I'm free to-morrow. . . . Oh, my God,
what a mercy ! I'm free to-morrow, I'm free the day after.
. . . Oh my head, my headl. . . .   [*Exit.*

IRINA. [*alone*] They've all gone. Nobody's left.

*A concertina is being played in the street. The nurse
sings.*

NATASHA. [*in fur coat and cap, steps across the dining-room,
followed by the maid*] I'll be back in half an hour. I'm only
going for a little drive.   ..   [*Exit.*

IRINA. [*Alone in her misery*] To Moscow ! Moscow !
Moscow !

Curtain.

ACT THREE

The room shared by OLGA *and* IRINA. *Beds, screened off, on the right and left. It is past 2 a.m. Behind the stage a fire-alarm is ringing ; it has apparently been going for some time. Nobody in the house has gone to bed yet.* MASHA *is lying on a sofa dressed, as usual, in black. Enter* OLGA *and* ANFISA.

ANFISA. Now they are downstairs, sitting under the stairs. I said to them, " Won't you come up," I said, " You can't go on like this," and they simply cried, " We don't know where father is." They said, " He may be burnt up by now." What an idea ! And in the yard there are some people . . . also undressed.

OLGA. [*Takes a dress out of the cupboard*] Take this grey dress. . . . And this . . . . and the blouse as well. . . . Take the skirt, too, nurse. . . . My God ! How awful it is ! The whole of the Kirsanovsky Road seems to have burned down. Take this . . . and this. . . . [*Throws clothes into her hands*] The poor Vershinins are so frightened. . . . Their house was nearly burnt. They ought to come here for the night. . . . They shouldn't be allowed to go home. . . . Poor Fedotik is completely burnt out, there's nothing left. . . .

ANFISA. Couldn't you call Ferapont, Olga dear. I can hardly manage. . . .

OLGA. [*Rings*] They'll never answer. . . . [*At the door*] Come here, whoever there is ! [*Through the open door can be*

148

seen a window, red with flame : a fire-engine is heard passing the house] How awful this is. And how I'm sick of it ! [FERAPONT *enters*] Take these things down. . . . The Kolotilin girls are down below . . . and let them have them. This, too. . . .

FERAPONT. Yes'm. In the year twelve Moscow was burning too. Oh, my God ! The Frenchmen were surprised.

OLGA. Go on, go on. . . .

FERAPONT. Yes'm.   [*Exit.*

OLGA. Nurse, dear, let them have everything. We don't want anything. Give it all to them, nurse. . . . I'm tired, I can hardly keep on my legs. . . . The Vershinins mustn't be allowed to go home. . . . The girls can sleep in the drawing-room, and Alexander Ignateyevitch can go downstairs to the Baron's flat . . . Fedotik can go there, too, or else into our dining-room. . . . The doctor is drunk, beastly drunk, as if on purpose, so nobody can go to him. Vershinin's wife, too, may go into the drawing-room.

ANFISA. [*Tired*] Olga, dear girl, don't dismiss me ! Don't dismiss me !

OLGA. You're talking nonsense, nurse. Nobody is dismissing you.

ANFISA. [*Puts* OLGA'S *head against her bosom*] My dear, precious girl, I'm working, I'm toiling away . . . I'm growing weak, and they'll all say go away ! And where shall I go ? Where ? I'm eighty. Eighty-one years old. . . .

OLGA. You sit down, nurse dear. . . . You're tired, poor dear. . . . [*Makes her sit down*] Rest, dear. You're so pale !

NATASHA *comes in.*

NATASHA. They are saying that a committee to assist the

sufferers from the fire must be formed at once. What do you think of that ? It's a beautiful idea. Of course the poor ought to be helped, it's the duty of the rich. Bobby and little Sophy are sleeping, sleeping as if nothing at all was the matter. There's such a lot of people here, the place is full of them, wherever you go. There's influenza in the town now. I'm afraid the children may catch it.

OLGA. [*Not attending*] In this room we can't see the fire, it's quiet here. . . .

NATASHA. Yes . . . I suppose I'm all untidy. [*Before the looking-glass*] They say I'm growing stout . . . it isn't true ! Certainly it isn't ! Masha's asleep ; the poor thing is tired out. . . . [*Coldly, to* ANFISA] Don't dare to be seated in my presence ! Get up ! Out of this ! [*Exit* ANFISA ; *a pause*] I don't understand what makes you keep on that old woman !

OLGA. [*Confusedly*] Excuse me, I don't understand either. . . .

NATASHA. She's no good here. She comes from the country, she ought to live there. . . . Spoiling her, I call it ! I like order in the house ! We don't want any unnecessary people here. [*Strokes her cheek*] You're tired, poor thing ! Our head mistress is tired ! And when my little Sophie grows up and goes to school I shall be so afraid of you.

OLGA. I shan't be head mistress.

NATASHA. They'll appoint you, Olga. It's settled.

OLGA. I'll refuse the post. I can't . . . I'm not strong enough. . . . [*Drinks water*] You were so rude to nurse just now . . . I'm sorry. I can't stand it . . . everything seems dark in front of me. . . .

NATASHA. [*Excited*] Forgive me, Olga, forgive me . . . I didn't want to annoy you.

MASHA *gets up, takes a pillow and goes out angrily.*

OLGA. Remember, dear . . . we have been brought up, in an unusual way, perhaps, but I can't bear this. Such behaviour has a bad effect on me, I get ill . . . I simply lose heart !

NATASHA. Forgive me, forgive me. . . .   [*Kisses her.*

OLGA. Even the least bit of rudeness, the slightest impoliteness, upsets me.

NATASHA. I often say too much, it's true, but you must agree, dear, that she could just as well live in the country.

OLGA. She has been with us for thirty years.

NATASHA. But she can't do any work now. Either I don't understand, or you don't want to understand me. She's no good for work, she can only sleep or sit about.

OLGA. And let her sit about.

NATASHA. [*Surprised*] What do you mean ? She's only a servant. [*Crying*] I don't understand you, Olga. I've got a nurse, a wet-nurse, we've a cook, a housemaid . . . what do we want that old woman for as well ? What good is she ?   [*Fire-alarm behind the stage.*

OLGA. I've grown ten years older to-night.

NATASHA. We must come to an agreement, Olga. Your place is the school, mine—the home. You devote yourself to teaching, I, to the household. And if I talk about servants, then I do know what I am talking about ; I do know what I am talking about. . . . And to-morrow there's to be no more of that old thief, that old hag . . . [*Stamping*] that witch ! And don't you dare to annoy me ! Don't you dare ! [*Stopping short*] Really, if you don't move downstairs, we shall always be quarrelling. This is awful.

    Enter KULIGIN.

KULIGIN. Where's Masha ? It's time we went home.

The fire seems to be going down. [*Stretches himself*] Only one block has burnt down, but there was such a wind that it seems at first the whole town was going to burn. [*Sits*] I'm tired out. My dear Olga . . . I often think that if it hadn't been for Masha, I should have married you. You are awfully nice. . . . I am absolutely tired out.   [*Listens.*

OLGA. What is it ?

KULIGIN. The doctor, of course, has been drinking hard ; he's terribly drunk. He might have done it on purpose ! [*Gets up*] He seems to be coming here. . . . Do you hear him ? Yes, here. . . . [*Laughs*] What a man . . . really . . . I'll hide myself. [*Goes to the cupboard and stands in the corner*] What a rogue.

OLGA. He hadn't touched a drop for two years, and now he suddenly goes and get's drunk. . . . .

          [*Retires with* NATASHA *to the back of the room.*
          CHEBUTIKIN *enters ; apparently sober, he stops, looks round, then goes to the wash-stand and begins to wash his hands.*

CHEBUTIKIN. [*Angrily*] Devil take them all . . . take them all. . . . They think I'm a doctor and can cure everything, and I know absolutely nothing, I've forgotten all I ever knew, I remember nothing, absolutely nothing. [OLGA *and* NATASHA *go out, unnoticed by him*] Devil take it. Last Wednesday I attended a woman in Zasip—and she died, and it's my fault that she died. Yes . . . I used to know a certain amount five-and-twenty years ago, but I don't remember anything now. Nothing. Perhaps I'm not really a man, and am only pretending that I've got arms and legs and a head ; perhaps I don't exist at all, and only imagine that I walk, and eat, and sleep. [*Cries*] Oh, if only I didn't exist ! [*Stops crying ; angrily*] The devil only knows. . . . Day before yesterday they were talking in the

club ; they said, Shakespeare, Voltaire . . . I'd never read,
never read at all, and I put on an expression as if I had read.
And so did the others. Oh, how beastly ! How petty !
And then I remembered the woman I killed on Wednesday
. . . and I couldn't get her out of my mind, and everything
in my mind became crooked, nasty, wretched. . . . So I
went and drank. . . .

> IRINA, VERSHININ *and* TUZENBACH *enter ;* TUZEN-
> BACH *is wearing new and fashionable civilian
> clothes.*

IRINA. Let's sit down here. Nobody will come in
here.

VERSHININ. The whole town would have been destroyed
if it hadn't been for the soldiers. Good men ! [*Rubs his
hands appreciatively*] Splendid people ! Oh, what a fine
lot !

KULIGIN. [*Coming up to him*] What's the time ?

TUZENBACH. It's past three now. It's dawning.

IRINA. They are all sitting in the dining-room, nobody
is going. And that Soleni of yours is sitting there. . . .
[*To* CHEBUTIKIN] Hadn't you better be going to sleep,
doctor ?

CHEBUTIKIN. It's all right . . . thank you. . . .
                                        [*Combs his beard.*

KULIGIN. [*Laughs*] Speaking's a bit difficult, eh, Ivan
Romanovitch ! [*Pats him on the shoulder*] Good man ! *In
vino veritas*, the ancients used to say.

TUZENBACH. They keep on asking me to get up a concert
in aid of the sufferers.

IRINA. As if one could do anything. . . .

TUZENBACH. It might be arranged, if necessary. In my
opinion Maria Sergeyevna is an excellent pianist.

KULIGIN. Yes, excellent !

IRINA. She's forgotten everything. She has'nt played for three years . . . or four.

TUZENBACH. In this town absolutely nobody understands music, not a soul except myself, but I do understand it, and assure you on my word of honour that Maria Sergeyevna plays excellently, almost with genius.

KULIGIN. You are right, Baron, I'm awfully fond of Masha. She's very fine.

TUZENBACH. To be able to play so admirably and to realize at the same time that nobody, nobody can understand you!

KULIGIN. [*Sighs*] Yes. . . . But will it be quite all right for her to take part in a concert? [*Pause*] You see, I don't know anything about it. Perhaps it will even be all to the good. Although I must admit that our Director is a good man, a very good man even, a very clever man, still he has such views. . . . Of course it isn't his business but still, if you wish it, perhaps I'd better talk to him.

> CHEBUTIKIN *takes a porcelain clock into his hands and examines it.*

VERSHININ. I got so dirty while the fire was on, I don't look like anybody on earth. [*Pause*] Yesterday I happened to hear, casually, that they want to transfer our brigade to some distant place. Some said to Poland, others, to Chita.

TUZENBACH. I heard so, too. Well, if it is so, the town will be quite empty.

IRINA. And we'll go away, too!

CHEBUTIKIN. [*Drops the clock which breaks to pieces*] To smithereens!

> *A pause; everybody is pained and confused.*

KULIGIN. [*Gathering up the pieces*] To smash such a

valuable object—oh, Ivan Romanovitch, Ivan Romanovitch!
A very bad mark for your misbehaviour!

IRINA. That clock used to belong to our mother.

CHEBUTIKIN. Perhaps. . . . To your mother, your mother.
Perhaps I didn't break it; it only looks as if I broke
it. Perhaps we only think that we exist, when really
we don't. I don't know anything, nobody knows anything. [*At the door*] What are you looking at ? Natasha
has a little romance with Protopopov, and you don't see
it. . . . There you sit and see nothing, and Natasha has
a little romance with Protopovov. . . . [*Sings*] Won't you
please accept this date. . . .   [*Exit.*

VERSHININ. Yes. [*Laughs*] How strange everything really
is ! [*Pause*] When the fire broke out, I hurried off home ;
when I get there I see the house is whole, uninjured, and in
no danger, but my two girls are standing by the door in just
their underclothes, their mother isn't there, the crowd is
excited, horses and dogs are running about, and the girls'
faces are so agitated, terrified, beseeching, and I don't know
what else. My heart was pained when I saw those faces.
My God, I thought, what these girls will have to put up
with if they live long ! I caught them up and ran, and still
kept on thinking the one thing : what they will have to live
through in this world ! [*Fire-alarm ; a pause*] I come here
and find their mother shouting and angry. [MASHA *enters
with a pillow and sits on the sofa*] And when my girls were
standing by the door in just their underclothes, and the
street was red from the fire, there was a dreadful noise, and
I thought that something of the sort used to happen many
years ago when an enemy made a sudden attack, and looted,
and burned. . . . And at the same time what a difference
there really is between the present and the past ! And when

a little more time has gone by, in two or three hundred years perhaps, people will look at our present life with just the same fear, and the same contempt, and the whole past will seem clumsy and dull, and very uncomfortable, and strange.   Oh, indeed, what a life there will be, what a life ! [*Laughs*] Forgive me, I've dropped into philosophy again. Please let me continue.   I do awfully want to philosophize, it's just how I feel at present. [*Pause*] As if they are all asleep.   As I was saying :   what a life there will be !   Only just imagine. . . . There are only three persons like your-selves in the town just now, but in future generations there will be more and more, and still more, and the time will come when everything will change and become as you would have it, people will live as you do, and then you too will go out of date ;   people will be born who are better than you. . . [*Laughs*] Yes, to-day I am quite exceptionally in the vein. I am devilishly keen on living. . . .   [*Sings.*

> " The power of love all ages know,
>
>   From its assaults great good does grow."

                                                                    [*Laughs*

MASHA. Trum-tum-tum . . .

VERSHININ. Tum-tum . . .

MASHA. Tra-ra-ra ?

VERSHININ. Tra-ta-ta.   [*Laughs.*

        Enter FEDOTIK.

FEDOTIK. [*Dancing*] I'm burnt out, I'm burnt out ! Down to the ground !   [*Laughter.*

IRINA. I don't see anything funny about it.   Is every-thing burnt ?

FEDOTIK. [*Laughs*] Absolutely.   Nothing left at all. The guitar's burnt, and the photographs are burnt, and all my correspondence. . . . And I was going to make you a present of a note-book, and that's burnt too.

SOLENI *comes in.*

IRINA. No, you can't come here, Vassili Vassilevitch. Please go away.

SOLENI. Why can the Baron come here and I can't?

VERSHININ. We really must go. How's the fire?

SOLENI. They say it's going down. No, I absolutely don't see why the Baron can, and I can't?

[*Scents his hands.*

VERSHININ. Trum-tum-tum.

MASHA. Trum-tum.

VERSHININ. [*Laughs to* SOLENI] Let's go into the dining-room.

SOLENI. Very well, we'll make a note of it. "If I should try to make this clear, the geese would be annoyed, I fear." [*Looks at* TUZENBACH] There, there, there. . . .

[*Goes out with* VERSHININ *and* FEDOTIK.

IRINA. How Soleni smelt of tobacco. . . . [*In surprise*] The Baron's asleep! Baron! Baron!

TUZENBACH. [*Waking*] I am tired, I must say. . . . The brickworks. . . . No, I'm not wandering, I mean it; I'm going to start work soon at the brickworks . . . I've already talked it over. [*Tenderly, to* IRINA] You're so pale, and beautiful, and charming. . . . Your paleness seems to shine through the dark air as if it was a light. . . . You are sad, displeased with life. . . . Oh, come with me, let's go and work together!

MASHA. Nicolai Lvovitch, go away from here.

TUZENBACH. [*Laughs*] Are you here? I didn't see you. [*Kisses* IRINA'S *hand*] Good-bye, I'll go . . . I look at you now and I remember, as if it was long ago, your name-day, when you, cheerfully and merrily, were talking about the joys of labour. . . . And how happy life seemed to me, then! What has happened to it now? [*Kisses her hand*]

There are tears in your eyes. Go to bed now ; it is already
day . . . the morning begins. . . . If only I was allowed
to give my life for you !

MASHA. Nicolai Lvovitch, go away ! What business . . .

TUZENBACH. I'm off.   [*Exit.*

MASHA. [*Lies down*] Are you asleep, Feodor ?

KULIGIN. Eh ?

MASHA. Shouldn't you go home.

KULIGIN. My dear Masha, my darling Masha. . . .

IRINA. She's tired out. You might let her rest, Fedia.

KULIGIN. I'll go at once. My wife's a good, splendid . . .
I love you, my only one. . . .

MASHA. [*Angrily*] Amo, amas, amat, amamus, amatis,
amant.

KULIGIN. [*Laughs*] No, she really is wonderful. I've
been your husband seven years, and it seems as if I was
only married yesterday. On my word. No, you really are
a wonderful woman. I'm satisfied, I'm satisfied, I'm
satisfied !

MASHA. I'm bored, I'm bored, I'm bored. . . . [*Sits up*]
But I can't get it out of my head. . . . It's simply disgraceful. It has been gnawing away at me . . . I can't
keep silent. I mean about Andrey. . . . He has mortgaged
this house with the bank, and his wife has got all the money ;
but the house doesn't belong to him alone, but to the four
of us ! He ought to know that, if he's an honourable
man.

KULIGIN. What's the use, Masha ? Andrey is in debt all
round ; well, let him do as he pleases.

MASHA. It's disgraceful, anyway.   [*Lies down.*

KULIGIN. You and I are not poor. I work, take my
classes, give private lessons . . . I am a plain, honest man
. . . Omnia mea mecum porto, as they say.

MASHA. I don't want anything, but the unfairness of it
disgusts me. [*Pause*] You go, Feodor.

KULIGIN. [*Kisses her*] You're tired, just rest for half an
hour, and I'll sit and wait for you. Sleep. . . . [*Going*]
I'm satisfied, I'm satisfied, I'm satisfied. [*Exit.*

IRINA. Yes, really, our Andrey has grown smaller; how
he's snuffed out and aged with that woman! He used to
want to be a professor, and yesterday he was boasting that
at last he had been made a member of the district council.
He is a member, and Protopopov is chairman. . . . The
whole town talks and laughs about it, and he alone knows
and sees nothing. . . . And now everybody's gone to look
at the fire, but he sits alone in his room and pays no attention, only just plays on his fiddle. [*Nervily*] Oh, it's awful,
awful, awful. [*Weeps*] I can't, I can't bear it any longer!
. . . I can't, I can't! . . . [OLGA *comes in and clears up
at her little table.* IRINA *is sobbing loudly*] Throw me out,
throw me out, I can't bear any more!

OLGA. [*Alarmed*] What is it, what is it? Dear!

IRINA! [*Sobbing*] Where? Where has everything gone?
Where is it all? Oh my God, my God! I've forgotten
everything, everything . . . I don't remember what is the
Italian for window or, well, for ceiling . . . I forget everything, every day I forget it, and life passes and will never
return, and we'll never go away to Moscow . . . I see that
we'll never go. . . .

OLGA. Dear, dear. . . .

IRINA. [*Controlling herself*] Oh, I am unhappy . . . I
can't work, I shan't work. Enough, enough! I used to
be a telegraphist, now I work at the town council offices,
and I have nothing but hate and contempt for all they give
me to do . . . I am already twenty-three, I have already
been at work for a long while, and my brain has dried up.

and I've grown thinner, plainer, older, and there is no relief of any sort, and time goes and it seems all the while as if I am going away from the real, the beautiful life, farther and farther away, down some precipice. I'm in despair and I can't understand how it is that I am still alive, that I haven't killed myself.

OLGA. Don't cry, dear girl, don't cry . . . I suffer, too.

IRINA. I'm not crying, not crying. . . . Enough. . . . Look, I'm not crying any more. Enough . . . enough!

OLGA. Dear, I tell you as a sister and a friend, if you want my advice, marry the Baron. [IRINA *cries softly*] You respect him, you think highly of him. . . . It is true that he is not handsome, but he is so honourable and clean . . . people don't marry from love, but in order to do one's duty. I think so, at any rate, and I'd marry without being in love. Whoever he was, I should marry him, so long as he was a decent man. Even if he was old. . . .

IRINA. I was always waiting until we should be settled in Moscow, there I should meet my true love; I used to think about him, and love him. . . . But it's all turned out to be nonsense, all nonsense. . . .

OLGA. [*Embraces her sister*] My dear, beautiful sister, I understand everything; when Baron Nicolai Lvovitch left the army and came to us in evening dress,* he seemed so bad-looking to me that I even started crying. . . . He asked, " What are you crying for ? " How could I tell him ! But if God brought him to marry you, I should be happy. That would be different, quite different.

NATASHA *with a candle walks across the stage from right to left without saying anything.*

MASHA. [*Sitting up*] She walks as if she's set something on fire.

* *I.e.* in the correct dress for making a proposal of marriage.

OLGA. Masha, you're silly, you're the silliest of the family. Please forgive me for saying so.   [*Pause.*

MASHA. I want to make a confession, dear sisters. My soul is in pain. I will confess to you, and never again to anybody . . . I'll tell you this minute. [*Softly*] It's my secret but you must know everything . . . I can't be silent. . . . [*Pause*] I love, I love . . . I love that man. . . . You saw him only just now. . . . Why don't I say it . . . in one word. I love Vershinin.

OLGA. [*Goes behind her screen*] Stop that, I don't hear you in any case.

MASHA. What am I to do ? [*Takes her head in her hands*] First he seemed queer to me, then I was sorry for him . . . then I fell in love with him . . . fell in love with his voice, his words, his misfortunes, his two daughters.

OLGA. [*Behind the screen*] I'm not listening. You may talk any nonsense you like, it will be all the same, I shan't hear.

MASHA. Oh, Olga, you are foolish. I am in love—that means that is to be my fate. It means that is to be my lot. . . . And he loves me. . . . It is all awful. Yes ; it isn't good, is it ? [*Takes* IRINA's *hand and draws her to her*] Oh, my dear. . . . How are we going to live through our lives, what is to become of us. . . . When you read a novel it all seems so old and easy, but when you fall in love yourself, then you learn that nobody knows anything, and each must decide for himself. . . . My dear ones, my sisters . . . I've confessed, now I shall keep silence. . . . Like the lunatics in Gogol's story, I'm going to be silent . . . silent . . .

ANDREY *enters, followed by* FERAPONT.

ANDREY. [*Angrily*] What do you want ? I don't understand.

162   THE THREE SISTERS

FERAPONT. [*At the door, impatiently*] I've already told
you ten times, Andrey Sergeyevitch.

ANDREY. In the first place I'm not Andrey Sergeyevitch,
but sir.*

FERAPONT. The firemen, sir, ask if they can go across your
garden to the river.   Else they go right round, right round ;
it's a nuisance.

ANDREY. All right.   Tell them it's all right. [*Exit* FERA-
PONT] I'm tired of them.   Where is Olga ? [OLGA *comes
out from behind the screen*] I came to you for the key of the
cupboard.   I lost my own.   You've got a little key.
[Olga *gives him the key ;* IRINA *goes behind the screen ; pause*]
What a huge fire !   It's going down now.   Hang it all, that
Ferapont made me so angry that I talked nonsense to him.
. . . Sir, indeed. . . . [*A pause*] Why are you so silent,
OLGA ? [*Pause*] It's time you stopped all that nonsense and
behaved as if you were properly alive. . . . You are here,
Masha.   Irina is here, well, since we're all here, let's come to
a complete understanding, once and for all.   What have
you against me ?   What is it ?

OLGA. Please don't, Andrey dear.   We'll talk to-morrow.
[*Excited*] What an awful night !

ANDREY. [*Much confused*] Don't excite yourself.   I ask
you in perfect calmness ; what have you against me ?   Tell
me straight.

VERSHININ'S VOICE. Trum-tum-tum !

MASHA. [*Stands ; loudly*] Tra-ta-ta ! [*To* OLGA] Good-
bye, Olga, God bless you. [*Goes behind screen and kisses*
IRINA] Sleep well. . . . Good-bye, Andrey.   Go away now,
they're tired . . . you can explain to-morrow. . . .

[*Exit.*

* Quite literally, " your high honour," to correspond to Andrey's
rank as a civil servant.

ANDREY. I'll only say this and go. Just now. . . . In the first place, you've got something against Natasha, my wife; I've noticed it since the very day of my marriage. Natasha is a beautiful and honest creature, straight and honourable—that's my opinion. I love and respect my wife; understand it, I respect her, and I insist that others should respect her too. I repeat, she's an honest and honourable person, and all your disapproval is simply silly . . . [*Pause*] In the second place, you seem to be annoyed because I am not a professor, and am not engaged in study. But I work for the zemstvo, I am a member of the district council, and I consider my service as worthy and as high as the service of science. I am a member of the district council, and I am proud of it, if you want to know. . . . [*Pause*] In the third place, I have still this to say . . . that I have mortgaged the house without obtaining your permission. . . . For that I am to blame, and ask to be forgiven. My debts led me into doing it . . . thirty-five thousand . . . I do not play at cards any more, I stopped long ago, but the chief thing I have to say in my defence is that you girls receive a pension, and I don't . . . my wages, so to speak. . . .   [*Pause.*

KULIGIN. [*At the door*] Is Masha there? [*Excitedly*] Where is she? It's queer. . . .   [*Exit.*

ANDREY. They don't hear. Natasha is a splendid, honest person. [*Walks about in silence, then stops*] When I married I thought we should be happy . . . all of us. . . . But, my God. . . . [*Weeps*] My dear, dear sisters, don't believe me, don't believe me. . . .   [*Exit.*

    Fire-alarm. The stage is clear.

IRINA. [*behind the screen*] Olga, who's knocking on the floor?

OLGA. It's doctor Ivan Romanovitch. He's dry.

IRINA. What a restless night ! [*Pause*] Olga ! [*Looks out*] Did you hear ? They are taking the brigade away from us ; it's going to be transferred to some place far away.

OLGA. It's only a rumour.

IRINA. Then we shall be left alone. . . . Olga !

OLGA. Well ?

IRINA. My dear, darling sister, I esteem, I highly value the Baron, he's a splendid man ; I'll marry him, I'll consent, only let's go to Moscow ! I implore you, let's go ! There's nothing better than Moscow on earth ! Let's go, Olga, let's go !

Curtain.

ACT FOUR

The old garden at the house of the PROSOROVS. *There is a long avenue of firs, at the end of which the river can be seen. There is a forest on the far side of the river. On the right is the terrace of the house : bottles and tumblers are on a table here ; it is evident that champagne has just been drunk. It is midday. Every now and again passers-by walk across the garden, from the road to the river ; five soldiers go past rapidly.* CHEBUTIKIN, *in a comfortable frame of mind which does not desert him throughout the act, sits in an armchair in the garden, waiting to be called. He wears a peaked cap and has a stick.* IRINA, KULIGIN *with a cross hanging from his neck and without his moustaches, and* TUZENBACH *are standing on the terrace seeing off* FEDOTIK *and* RODE, *who are coming down into the garden ; both officers are in service uniform.*

TUZENBACH. [*Exchanges kisses with* FEDOTIK] You're a good sort, we got on so well together. [*Exchanges kisses with* RODE] Once again. . . . Good-bye, old man !

IRINA. Au revoir !

FEDOTIK. It isn't au revoir, it's good-bye ; we'll never meet again !

KULIGIN. Who knows ! [*Wipes his eyes ; smiles*] Here I've started crying !

IRINA. We'll meet again sometime.

FEDOTIK. After ten years—or fifteen ? We'll hardly

know one another then ; we'll say, " How do you do ? " coldly. . . . [*Takes a snapshot*] Keep still. . . . Once more, for the last time.

RODE. [*Embracing* TUZENBACH] We shan't meet again. . . . [*Kisses* IRINA's *hand*] Thank you for everything, for everything !

FEDOTIK. [*Grieved*] Don't be in such a hurry !

TUZENBACH. We shall meet again, if God wills it. Write to us. Be sure to write.

RODE. [*Looking round the garden*] Good-bye, trees ! [*Shouts*] Yo-ho ! [*Pause*] Good-bye, echo !

KULIGIN. Best wishes. Go and get yourselves wives there in Poland. . . . Your Polish wife will clasp you and call you " kochanku ! " *   [*Laughs.*

FEDOTIK. [*Looking at the time*] There's less than an hour left. Soleni is the only one of our battery who is going on the barge ; the rest of us are going with the main body. Three batteries are leaving to-day, another three to-morrow, and then the town will be quiet and peaceful.

TUZENBACH. And terribly dull.

RODE. And where is Maria Sergeyevna ?

KULIGIN. Masha is in the garden.

FEDOTIK. We'd like to say good-bye to her.

RODE. Good-bye, I must go, or else I'll start weeping. . . . [*Quickly embraces* KULIGIN *and* TUZENBACH, *and kisses* IRINA's *hand*] We've been so happy here. . . .

FEDOTIK. [*To* KULIGIN] Here's a keepsake for you . . . a note-book with a pencil. . . . We'll go to the river from here. . . .   [*They go aside and both look round.*

RODE. [*Shouts*] Yo-ho !

KULIGIN. [*Shouts*] Good-bye.

* Darling

At the back of the stage FEDOTIK *and* RODE *meet*
MASHA; *they say good-bye and go out with her.*

IRINA. They've gone. . . .

[*Sits on the bottom step of the terrace.*

CHEBUTIKIN. And they forgot to say good-bye to
me.

IRINA. But why is that ?

CHEBUTIKIN. I just forgot, somehow. Though I'll soon
see them again, I'm going to-morrow. Yes . . . just one
day left. I shall be retired in a year, then I'll come here
again and finish my life near you. I've only one year before
I get my pension. . . . [*Puts one newspaper into his pocket
and takes another out*] I'll come here to you and change my
life radically . . . I'll be so quiet . . . so agree . . . agree-
able, respectable. . . .

IRINA. Yes, you ought to change your life, dear man,
somehow or other.

CHEBUTIKIN. Yes, I feel it.   [*Sings softly.*
" Tarara-boom-deay. . . ."

KULIGIN. We won't reform Ivan Romanovitch ! We
won't reform him !

CHEBUTIKIN. If only I was apprenticed to you ! Then I'd
reform.

IRINA. Feodor has shaved his moustache ! I can't bear
to look at him.

KULIGIN. Well, what about it ?

CHEBUTIKIN. I could tell you what your face looks like
now, but it wouldn't be polite.

KULIGIN. Well ! It's the custom, it's *modus vivendi.*
Our Director is clean-shaven, and so I too, when I received
my inspectorship, I had my moustaches removed. Nobody
likes it, but it's all one to me. I'm satisfied. Whether I've
got moustaches or not, I'm satisfied. . . .   [*Sits.*

At the back of the stage ANDREY *is wheeling a perambulator containing a sleeping infant.*

IRINA. Ivan Romanovitch, be a darling. I'm awfully worried. You were out on the boulevard last night; tell me, what happened ?

CHEBUTIKIN. What happened ? Nothing. Quite a trifling matter. [*Reads paper*] Of no importance !

KULIGIN. They say that Soleni and the Baron met yesterday on the boulevard near the theatre. . . .

TUZENBACH. Stop ! What right . . .

[*Waves his hand and goes into the house.*

KULIGIN. Near the theatre . . . Soleni started behaving offensively to the Baron, who lost his temper and said something nasty. . . .

CHEBUTIKIN. I don't know. It's all bunkum.

KULIGIN. At some seminary or other a master wrote " bunkum " on an essay, and the student couldn't make the letters out—thought it was a Latin word " luckum." [*Laughs*] Awfully funny, that. They say that Soleni is in love with Irina and hates the Baron. . . . That's quite natural. Irina is a very nice girl. She's even like Masha, she's so thoughtful. . . . Only, Irina, your character is gentler. Though Masha's character, too, is a very good one. I'm very fond of Masha.

[*Shouts of " Yo-ho ! " are heard behind the stage.*

IRINA. [*Shudders*] Everything seems to frighten me to-day. [*Pause*] I've got everything ready, and I send my things off after dinner. The Baron and I will be married to-morrow, and to-morrow we go away to the brickworks, and the next day I go to the school, and the new life begins. God will help me ! When I took my examination for the teacher's post, I actually wept for joy and gratitude. . . . [*Pause*] The cart will be here in a minute for my things. . . .

KULIGIN. Somehow or other, all this doesn't seem at all serious. As if it was all ideas, and nothing really serious. Still, with all my soul I wish you happiness.

CHEBUTIKIN. [*With deep feeling*] My splendid . . . my dear, precious girl. . . . You've gone on far ahead, I won't catch up with you. I'm left behind like a migrant bird grown old, and unable to fly. Fly, my dear, fly, and God be with you ! [*Pause*] It's a pity you shaved your moustaches, Feodor Ilitch.

KULIGIN. Oh, drop it ! [*Sighs*] To-day the soldiers will be gone, and everything will go on as in the old days. Say what you will, Masha is a good, honest woman. I love her very much, and thank my fate for her. People have such different fates. There's a Kosirev who works in the excise department here. He was at school with me ; he was expelled from the fifth class of the High School for being entirely unable to understand *ut consecutivum*. He's awfully hard up now and in very poor health, and when I meet him I say to him, "How do you do, *ut consecutivum*." " Yes," he said, " precisely *consecutivum* . . ." and coughs. But I've been successful all my life, I'm happy, and I even have a Stanislaus Cross, of the second class, and now I myself teach others that *ut consecutivum*. Of course, I'm a clever man, much cleverer than many, but happiness doesn't only lie in that. . . .

> " *The Maiden's Prayer* " *is being played on the piano in the house.*

IRINA. To-morrow night I shan't hear that " Maiden's Prayer " any more, and I shan't be meeting Protopopov. . . . [*Pause*] Protopopov is sitting there in the drawing-room ; and he came to-day. . .

KULIGIN. Hasn't the head-mistress come yet ?

IRINA. No. She has been sent for. If you only knew

how difficult it is for me to live alone, without Olga. . . .
She lives at the High School ; she, a head-mistress, busy all
day with her affairs and I'm alone, bored, with nothing to
do, and hate the room I live in. . . . I've made up my
mind : if I can't live in Moscow, then it must come to this.
It's fate.   It can't be helped.   It's all the will of God, that's
the truth.   Nicolai Lvovitch made me a proposal. . . .
Well ?   I thought it over and made up my mind.   He's a
good man . . . it's quite remarkable how good he is. . . .
And suddenly my soul put out wings, I became happy, and
light-hearted, and once again the desire for work, work,
came over me. . . . Only something happened yesterday,
some secret dread has been hanging over me. . . .

CHEBUTIKIN. Luckum. Rubbish.

NATASHA. [*At the window*] The head-mistress.

KULIGIN. The head-mistress has come. Let's go.

[*Exit with* IRINA *into the house.*

CHEBUTIKIN. " It is my washing day. . . . Tara-ra . . .
boom-deay."

MASHA *approaches,* ANDREY *is wheeling a perambulator at the back.*

MASHA. Here you are, sitting here, doing nothing.

CHEBUTIKIN. What then ?

MASHA. [*Sits*] Nothing. . . . [*Pause*] Did you love my
mother ?

CHEBUTIKIN. Very much.

MASHA. And did she love you ?

CHEBUTIKIN. [*After a pause*] I don't remember that.

MASHA. Is my man here ? When our cook Martha used
to ask about her gendarme, she used to say my man. Is
he here ?

CHEBUTIKIN. Not yet.

MASHA. When you take your happiness in little bits, in

snatches, and then lose it, as I have done, you gradually get coarser, more bitter. [*Points to her bosom*] I'm boiling in here. . . . [*Looks at* ANDREY *with the perambulator*] There's our brother Andrey. . . . All our hopes in him have gone. There was once a great bell, a thousand persons were hoisting it, much money and labour had been spent on it, when it suddenly fell and was broken. Suddenly, for no particular reason. . . . Andrey is like that. . . .

ANDREY. When are they going to stop making such a noise in the house ? It's awful.

CHEBUTIKIN. They won't be much longer. [*Looks at his watch*] My watch is very old-fashioned, it strikes the hours. . . . [*Winds the watch and makes it strike*] The first, second, and fifth batteries are to leave at one o'clock precisely. [*Pause*] And I go to-morrow.

ANDREY. For good ?

CHEBUTIKIN. I don't know. Perhaps I'll return in a year The devil only knows . . . it's all one. . . .

       [*Somewhere a harp and violin are being played.*

ANDREY. The town will grow empty. It will be as if they put a cover over it. [*Pause*] Something happened yesterday by the theatre. The whole town knows of it, but I don't.

CHEBUTIKIN. Nothing. A silly little affair. Soleni started irritating the Baron, who lost his temper and insulted him, and so at last Soleni had to challenge him. [*Looks at his watch*] It's about time, I think. . . . At half-past twelve, in the public wood, that one you can see from here across the river. . . . Piff-paff. [*Laughs*] Soleni thinks he's Lermontov, and even writes verses. That's all very well, but this is his third duel.

MASHA. Whose ?

CHEBUTIKIN. Soleni's.

MASHA. And the Baron?

CHEBUTIKIN. What about the Baron?   [*Plause.*

MASHA. Everything's all muddled up in my head. . . .
But I say it ought not to be allowed.   He might wound the
Baron or even kill him.

CHEBUTIKIN. The Baron is a good man, but one Baron
more or less—what difference does it make? It's all the
same! [*Beyond the garden somebody shouts "Co-ee! Hallo!"*]
You wait.   That's Skvortsov shouting; one of the seconds.
He's in a boat.   [*Pause.*

ANDREY. In my opinion it's simply immoral to fight in a
duel, or to be present, even in the quality of a doctor.

CHEBUTIKIN. It only seems so. . . . We don't exist,
there's nothing on earth, we don't really live, it only seems
that we live.   Does it matter, anyway!

MASHA. You talk and talk the whole day long. . . .
[*Going*] You live in a climate like this, where it might snow
any moment, and there you talk. . . . [*Stops*] I won't go
into the house, I can't go there. . . . Tell me when Vershinin comes. . . . [*Goes along the avenue*] The migrant
birds are already on the wing. . . . [*Looks up*] Swans or
geese.   My dear, happy things. . . .   [*Exit.*

ANDREY. Our house will be empty.   The officers will go
away, you are going, my sister is getting married, and I alone
will remain in the house.

CHEBUTIKIN. And your wife?

FERAPONT *enters with some documents.*

ANDREY. A wife's a wife.   She's honest, well-bred, yes,
and kind, but with all that there is still something about
her that degenerates her into a petty, blind, even in some
respects misshapen animal.   In any case, she isn't a man:
I tell you as a friend, as the only man to whom I can lay
bare my soul.   I love Natasha, it's true, but sometimes she

seems extraordinarily vulgar, and then I lose myself
and can't understand why I love her so much, or, at any
rate, used to love her. . . .

CHEBUTIKIN. [*Rises*] I'm going away to-morrow, old
chap, and perhaps we'll never meet again, so here's my
advice. Put on your cap, take a stick in your hand, go . . .
go on and on, without looking round. And the farther
you go, the better.

> SOLENI *goes across the back of the stage with two*
> *officers ; he catches sight of* CHEBUTIKIN, *and turns*
> *to him, the officers go on.*

SOLENI. Doctor, it's time. It's half-past twelve already.
[*Shakes hands with* ANDREY.

CHEBUTIKIN. Half a minute. I'm tired of the lot of you.
[*To* ANDREY) If anybody asks for me, say I'll be back soon.
. . . [*Sighs*] Oh, oh, oh !

SOLENI. " He didn't have the time to sigh. The bear sat
on him heavily." [*Goes up to him*] What are you groaning
about, old man ?

CHEBUTIKIN. Stop it !

SOLENI. How's your health ?

CHEBUTIKIN. [*Angry*] Mind your own business.

SOLENI. The old man is unnecessarily excited. I won't
go far, I'll only just bring him down like a snipe. [*Takes
out his scent-bottle and scents his hands*] I've poured out a
whole bottle of scent to-day and they still smell . . . of a
dead body. [*Pause*] Yes. . . . You remember the poem
> " But he, the rebel seeks the storm,
> As if the storm will bring him rest . . ." ?

CHEBUTIKIN. Yes.
> " He didn't have the time to sigh,
> The bear sat on him heavily."

[*Exit* with SOLENI.

Shouts are heard. ANDREY *and* FERAPONT *come in.*

FERAPONT. Documents to sign. . . .

ANDREY. [*Irritated*] Go away! Leave me! Please!
[*Goes away with the perambulator.*

FERAPONT. That's what documents are for, to be signed.
[*Retires to back of stage.*

Enter IRINA, *with* TUZENBACH *in a straw hat;* KULI-
GIN *walks across the stage, shouting " Co-ee, Masha,
co-ee ! "*

TUZENBACH. He seems to be the only man in the town
who is glad that the soldiers are going.

IRINA. One can understand that. [*Pause*] The town will
be empty.

TUZENBACH. My dear, I shall return soon.

IRINA. Where are you going?

TUZENBACH. I must go into the town and then . . . see
the others off.

IRINA. It's not true . . . Nicolai, why are you so absent-
minded to-day? [*Pause*] What took place by the theatre
yesterday?

TUZENBACH. [*Making a movement of impatience*] In an
hour's time I shall return and be with you again. [*Kisses
her hands*] My darling . . . [*Looking her closely in the face*]
it's five years now since I fell in love with you, and still I
can't get used to it, and you seem to me to grow more and
more beautiful. What lovely, wonderful hair! What eyes!
I'm going to take you away to-morrow. We shall work,
we shall be rich, my dreams will come true. You will be
happy. There's only one thing, one thing only: you don't
love me!

IRINA. It isn't in my power! I shall be your wife, I shall
be true to you, and obedient to you, but I can't love you.
What can I do! [*Cries*] I have never been in love in my

life. Oh, I used to think so much of love, I have been
thinking about it for so long by day and by night, but my
soul is like an expensive piano which is locked and the key
lost. [*Pause*] You seem so unhappy.

TUZENBACH. I didn't sleep all night. There is nothing
in my life so awful as to be able to frighten me, only that lost
key torments my soul and does not let me sleep. Say
something to me [*Pause*] say something to me. . . .

IRINA. What can I say, what ?

TUZENBACH. Anything.

IRINA. Don't ! don't !   [*Pause.*

TUZENBACH. It is curious how silly trivial little things,
sometimes for no apparent reason, become significant. At
first you laugh at these things, you think they are of no
importance, you go on and you feel that you haven't got
the strength to stop yourself. Oh don't let's talk about it !
I am happy. It is as if for the first time in my life I see
these firs, maples, beeches, and they all look at me in-
quisitively and wait. What beautiful trees and how beautiful, when one comes to think of it, life must be near them !
[*A shout of Co-ee ! in the distance*] It's time I went. . . .
There's a tree which has dried up but it still sways in the
breeze with the others. And so it seems to me that if I die, I
shall still take part in life in one way or another. Good-bye,
dear. . . . [*Kisses her hands*] The papers which you gave
me are on my table under the calendar.

IRINA. I am coming with you.

TUZENBACH. [*Nervously*] No, no ! [*He goes quickly and
stops in the avenue*] Irina !

IRINA. What is it ?

TUZENBACH. [*Not knowing what to say*] I haven't had any
coffee to-day. Tell them to make me some. . . .

                                        [*He goes out quickly.*

IRINA *stands deep in thought. Then she goes to the back of the stage and sits on a swing.* ANDREY *comes in with the perambulator and* FERAPONT *also appears.*

FERAPONT. Andrey Sergeyevitch, it isn't as if the documents were mine, they are the government's. I didn't make them.

ANDREY. Oh, what has become of my past and where is it? I used to be young, happy, clever, I used to be able to think and frame clever ideas, the present and the future seemed to me full of hope. Why do we, almost before we have begun to live, become dull, grey, uninteresting, lazy, apathetic, useless, unhappy. . . . This town has already been in existence for two hundred years and it has a hundred thousand inhabitants, not one of whom is in any way different from the others. There has never been, now or at any other time, a single leader of men, a single scholar, an artist, a man of even the slightest enimence who might arouse envy or a passionate desire to be imitated. They only eat, drink, sleep, and then they die . . . more people are born and also eat, drink, sleep, and so as not to go silly from boredom, they try to make life many-sided with their beastly backbiting, vodka, cards, and litigation. The wives deceive their husbands, and the husbands lie, and pretend they see nothing and hear nothing, and the evil influence irresistibly oppresses the children and the divine spark in them is extinguished, and they become just as pitiful corpses and just as much like one another as their fathers and mothers. . . . [*Angrily to* FERAPONT] What do you want ?

FERAPONT. What ? Documents want signing.

ANDREY. I'm tired of you.

FERAPONT. [*Handing him papers*] The hall-porter from the law courts was saying just now that in the winter

there were two hundred degrees of frost in Petersburg.

ANDREY. The present is beastly, but when I think of the
future, how good it is ! I feel so light, so free ; there is a
light in the distance, I see freedom. I see myself and my
children freeing ourselves from vanities, from kvass, from
goose baked with cabbage, from after-dinner naps, from
base idleness. . . .

FERAPONT. He was saying that two thousand people were
frozen to death. The people were frightened, he said. In
Petersburg or Moscow, I don't remember which.

ANDREY. [*Overcome by a tender emotion*] My dear sisters,
my beautiful sisters ! [*Crying*] Masha, my sister. . . .

NATASHA. [*At the window*] Who's talking so loudly out
here ? Is that you, Andrey ? You'll wake little Sophie.
*Il ne faut pas faire du bruit, la Sophie est dormée deja. Vous
êtes un ours.* [*Angrily*] If you want to talk, then give the
perambulator and the baby to somebody else. Ferapont,
take the perambulator !

FERAPONT. Yes'm. [*Takes the perambulator.*

ANDREY. [*Confused*] I'm speaking quietly.

NATASHA. [*At the window, nursing her boy*] Bobby !
Naughty Bobby ! Bad little Bobby !

ANDREY. [*Looking through the papers*] All right, I'll look
them over and sign if necessary, and you can take them
back to the offices. . . .

> *Goes into house reading papers ;* FERAPONT *takes the
> perambulator to the back of the garden.*

NATASHA. [*At the window*] Bobby, what's your mother's
name ? Dear, dear ! And who's this ? That's Aunt
Olga. Say to your aunt, " How do you do, Olga ! "

> *Two wandering musicians, a man and a girl, are play-
> ing on a violin and a harp.* VERSHININ, OLGA, *and*

M

ANFISA *come out of the house and listen for a minute in silence ;* IRINA *comes up to them.*

OLGA. Our garden might be a public thoroughfare, from the way people walk and ride across it. Nurse, give those musicians something !

ANFISA. [*Gives money to the musicians*] Go away with God's blessing on you. [*The musicians bow and go away*] A bitter sort of people. You don't play on a full stomach. [*To* IRINA] How do you do, Arisha ! [*Kisses her*] Well, little girl, here I am, still alive ! Still alive ! In the High School, together with little Olga, in her official apartments . . . so the Lord has appointed for my old age. Sinful woman that I am, I've never lived like that in my life before. . . . A large flat, government property, and I've a whole room and bed to myself. All government property. I wake up at nights and, oh God, and Holy Mother, there isn't a happier person than I !

VERSHININ. [*Looks at his watch*] We are going soon, Olga Sergeyevna. It's time for me to go. [*Pause*] I wish you every . . . every. . . . Where's Maria Sergeyevna ?

IRINA. She's somewhere in the garden. I'll go and look for her.

VERSHININ. If you'll be so kind. I haven't time.

ANFISA. I'll go and look, too. [*Shouts*] Little Masha, co-ee ! [*Goes out with* IRINA *down into the garden*] Co-ee, co-ee !

VERSHININ. Everything comes to an end. And so we, too, must part. [*Looks at his watch*] The town gave us a sort of farewell breakfast, we had champagne to drink and the mayor made a speech, and I ate and listened, but my soul was here all the time. . . . [*Looks round the garden*] I'm so used to you now.

OLGA. Shall we ever meet again ?

VERSHININ. Probably not. [*Pause*] My wife and both my

daughters will stay here another two months. If anything happens, or if anything has to be done . . .

OLGA. Yes, yes, of course. You need not worry. [*Pause*] To-morrow there won't be a single soldier left in the town, it will all be a memory, and, of course, for us a new life will begin. . . . [*Pause*] None of our plans are coming right. I didn't want to be a head-mistress, but they made me one, all the same. It means there's no chance of Moscow. . . .

VERSHININ. Well . . . thank you for everything. Forgive me if I've . . . I've said such an awful lot—forgive me for that too, don't think badly of me.

OLGA. [*Wipes her eyes*] Why isn't Masha coming . . . .

VERSHININ. What else can I say in parting ? Can I philosophize about anything ? [*Laughs*] Life is heavy. To many of us it seems dull and hopeless, but still, it must be acknowledged that it is getting lighter and clearer, and it seems that the time is not far off when it will be quite clear. [*Looks at his watch*] It's time I went ! Mankind used to be absorbed in wars, and all its existence was filled with campaigns, attacks, defeats, now we've outlived all that, leaving after us a great waste place, which there is nothing to fill with at present ; but mankind is looking for something, and will certainly find it. Oh, if it only happened more quickly. [*Pause*] If only education could be added to industry, and industry to education. [*Looks at his watch*] It's time I went. . . .

OLGA. Here she comes.

Enter MASHA.

VERSHININ. I came to say good-bye. . . .

OLGA *steps aside a little, so as not to be in their way.*

MASHA. [*Looking him in the face*] Good-bye. . . .

[*Prolonged kiss.*

OLGA. Don't, don't,   [MASHA *is crying bitterly,*

VERSHININ. Write to me. . . . Don't forget! Let me go. . . . It's time. Take her, Olga Sergeyevna . . . it's time . . . I'm late . . .

> *He kisses* OLGA'S *hand in evident emotion, then embraces* MASHA *once more and goes out quickly.*

OLGA. Don't, Masha! Stop, dear. . . . [KULIGIN *enters.*

KULIGIN. [*Confused*] Never mind, let her cry, let her. . . . My dear Masha, my good Masha. . . . You're my wife, and I'm happy, whatever happens . . . I'm not complaining, I don't reproach you at all. . . . Olga is a witness to it. . . . Let's begin to live again as we used to, and not by a single word, or hint . . .

MASHA. [*Restraining her sobs*]

> " There stands a green oak by the sea,
>   And a chain of bright gold is around it. . . .
>   And a chain of bright gold is around it. . . ."

I'm going off my head. . . " There stands . . . a green oak . . . by the sea." . . .

OLGA. Don't, Masha, don't . . . give her some water. . . .

MASHA. I'm not crying any more.

KULIGIN. She's not crying any more . . . she's a good . . .

> [*A shot is heard from a distance.*

MASHA. " There stands a green oak by the sea,
>   And a chain of bright gold is around it. . . .
>   An oak of green gold. . . ."

I'm mixing it up. . . . [*Drinks some water*] Life is dull . . . I don't want anything more now . . . I'll be all right in a moment. . . . It doesn't matter. . . . What do those lines mean? Why do they run in my head? My thoughts are all tangled.

IRINA *enters.*

OLGA. Be quiet, Masha. There's a good girl. . . . Let's go in.

MASHA. [*Angrily*] I shan't go in there. [*Sobs, but controls herself at once*] I'm not going to go into the house, I won't go. . . .

IRINA. Let's sit here together and say nothing. I'm going away to-morrow. . . .   [*Pause.*

KULIGIN. Yesterday I took away these whiskers and this beard from a boy in the third class. . . . [*He puts on the whiskers and beard*] Don't I look like the German master. . . . [*Laughs*] Don't I ? The boys are amusing.

MASHA. You really do look like that German of yours.

OLGA. [*Laughs*] Yes.   [MASHA *weeps.*

IRINA. Don't, Masha !

KULIGIN. It's a very good likeness. . . .

    Enter NATASHA.

NATASHA. [*To the maid*] What ? Mihail Ivanitch Protopopov will sit with little Sophie, and Andrey Sergeye-vitch can take little Bobby out. Children are such a bother. . . . [*To* IRINA] Irina, it's such a pity you're going away to-morrow. Do stop just another week. [*Sees* KULIGIN *and screams ; he laughs and takes off his beard and whiskers*] How you frightened me ! [*To* IRINA] I've grown used to you and do you think it will be easy for me to part from you ? I'm going to have Andrey and his violin put into your room —let him fiddle away in there !—and we'll put little Sophie into his room. The beautiful, lovely child ! What a little girlie ! To-day she looked at me with such pretty eyes and said " Mamma ! "

KULIGIN. A beautiful child, it's quite true.

NATASHA. That means I shall have the place to myself

to-morrow. [*Sighs*] In the first place I shall have that avenue of fir-trees cut down, then that maple. It's so ugly at nights. . . . [*To* IRINA] That belt doesn't suit you at all, dear. . . . It's an error of taste. And I'll give orders to have lots and lots of little flowers planted here, and they'll smell. . . . [*Severely*] Why is there a fork lying about here on the seat ? [*Going towards the house, to the maid*] Why is there a fork lying about here on the seat, I say ? [*Shouts*] Don't you dare to answer me !

KULIGIN. Temper ! temper !

[*A march is played off ; they all listen.*

OLGA. They're going.

CHEBUTIKIN *comes in.*

MASHA. They're going. Well, well. . . . *Bon voyage!* [*To her husband*] We must be going home. . . . Where's my coat and hat ?

KULIGIN. I took them in . . . I'll bring them, in a moment.

OLGA. Yes, now we can all go home. It's time.

CHEBUTIKIN. Olga Sergeyevna !

OLGA. What is it ? [*Pause*] What is it ?

CHEBUTIKIN. Nothing . . . I don't know how to tell you. . . . [*Whispers to her.*

OLGA. [*Frightened*] It can't be true !

CHEBUTIKIN. Yes . . . such a story . . . I'm tired out, exhausted, I won't say any more. . . . [*Sadly*] Still, it's all the same !

MASHA. What's happened ?

OLGA. [*Embraces* IRINA] This is a terrible day . . . I don't know how to tell you, dear. . . .

IRINA. What is it ? Tell me quickly, what is it ? For God's sake !   [*Cries.*

CHEBUTIKIN. The Baron was killed in the duel just now.

IRINA. [*Cries softly*] I knew it, I knew it. . . .

CHEBUTIKIN. [*Sits on a bench at the back of the stage*] I'm tired. . . . [*Takes a paper from his pocket*] Let 'em cry. . . . [*Sings softly*] "Tarara-boom-deay, it is my washing day. . . ." Isn't it all the same !

> The three sisters are standing, pressing against one
> another.

MASHA. Oh, how the music plays ! They are leaving us, one has quite left us, quite and for ever. We remain alone, to begin our life over again. We must live . . . we must live. . . .

IRINA. [*Puts her head on* OLGA's *bosom*] There will come a time when everybody will know why, for what purpose, there is all this suffering, and there will be no more mysteries. But now we must live . . . we must work, just work ! To-morrow, I'll go away alone, and I'll teach and give my whole life to those who, perhaps, need it. It's autumn now, soon it will be winter, the snow will cover everything, and I shall be working, working. . . .

OLGA. [*Embraces both her sisters*] The bands are playing so gaily, so bravely, and one does so want to live ! Oh, my God ! Time will pass on, and we shall depart for ever, we shall be forgotten ; they will forget our faces, voices, and even how many there were of us, but our sufferings will turn into joy for those who will live after us, happiness and peace will reign on earth, and people will remember with kindly words, and bless those who are living now. Oh dear sisters, our life is not yet at an end. Let us live. The music is so gay, so joyful, and, it seems that in a little while we shall know why we are living, why we are suffering. . . . If we could only know, if we could only know !

> The music has been growing softer and softer ; KULIGIN,
> smiling happily, brings out the hat and coat ;

ANDREY *wheels out the perambulator in which* BOBBY *is sitting.*

CHEBUTIKIN. [*Sings softly*] " Tara . . . ra-boom-deay. . . . It is my washing-day." . . . [*Reads a paper*] It's all the same ! It's all the same !

OLGA. If only we could know, if only we could know !

Curtain.

UNCLE VANYA
SCENES FROM COUNTRY LIFE
IN FOUR ACTS

CHARACTERS

ALEXANDER SEREBRAKOFF, *a retired professor.*

HELENA, *his wife, twenty-seven years old.*

SONIA, *his daughter by a former marriage.*

MME. VOITSKAYA, *widow of a privy councillor, and mother of Serebrakoff's first wife.*

IVAN (VANYA) VOITSKI, *her son.*

MICHAEL ASTROFF, *a doctor.*

ILIA (WAFFLES) TELEGIN, *an impoverished landowner.*

MARINA, *an old nurse.*

A WORKMAN.

The scene is laid on SEREBRAKOFF'S *country place.*

ACT ONE

A country house on a terrace. In front of it a garden. In an avenue of trees, under an old poplar, stands a table set for tea, with a samovar, etc. Some benches and chairs stand near the table. On one of them is lying a guitar. A hammock is swung near the table. It is three o'clock in the afternoon of a cloudy day.

MARINA, *a quiet, grey-haired, little old woman, is sitting at the table knitting a stocking.*

ASTROFF *is walking up and down near her.*

MARINA. [*Pouring some tea into a glass*] Take a little tea, my son.

ASTROFF. [*Takes the glass from her unwillingly*] Somehow, I don't seem to want any.

MARINA. Then will you have a little vodka instead ?

ASTROFF. No, I don't drink vodka every day, and besides, it is too hot now. [*A pause*] Tell me, nurse, how long have we known each other ?

MARINA. [*Thoughtfully*] Let me see, how long is it ? Lord—help me to remember. You first came here, into our parts—let me think—when was it ? Sonia's mother was still alive—it was two winters before she died ; that was eleven years ago—[*thoughtfully*] perhaps more.

ASTROFF. Have I changed much since then ?

MARINA. Oh, yes. You were handsome and young then, and now you are an old man and not handsome any more. You drink, too.

ASTROFF. Yes, ten years have made me another man.

And why ? Because I am overworked. Nurse, I am on my
feet from dawn till dusk. I know no rest; at night I
tremble under my blankets for fear of being dragged out to
visit someone who is sick; I have toiled without repose
or a day's freedom since I have known you; could I help
growing old ? And then, existence is tedious, anyway;
it is a senseless, dirty business, this life, and goes heavily.
Everyone about here is silly, and after living with them
for two or three years one grows silly oneself. It is
inevitable. [*Twisting his moustache*] See what a long
moustache I have grown. A foolish, long moustache.
Yes, I am as silly as the rest, nurse, but not as stupid; no,
I have not grown stupid. Thank God, my brain is not
addled yet, though my feelings have grown numb. I
ask nothing, I need nothing, I love no one, unless it is
yourself alone. [*He kisses her head*] I had a nurse just
like you when I was a child.

MARINA.   Don't you want a bite of something to eat ?

ASTROFF.   No. During the third week of Lent I went
to the epidemic at Malitskoi. It was eruptive typhoid.
The peasants were all lying side by side in their huts, and
the calves and pigs were running about the floor among the
sick. Such dirt there was, and smoke! Unspeakable!
I slaved among those people all day, not a crumb passed
my lips, but when I got home there was still no rest for me ;
a switchman was carried in from the railroad; I laid him
on the operating table and he went and died in my arms
under chloroform, and then my feelings that should have
been deadened awoke again, my conscience tortured me
as if I had killed the man.   I sat down and closed my eyes—
like this—and thought : will our descendants two hundred
years from now, for whom we are breaking the road,
remember to give us a kind word ?   No, nurse, they will
forget.

MARINA.   Man is forgetful, but God remembers.

ACT ONE 189

ASTROFF. Thank you for that. You have spoken the truth.

> Enter VOITSKI *from the house. He has been asleep after dinner and looks rather dishevelled. He sits down on the bench and straightens his collar.*

VOITSKI. H'm. Yes. [*A pause*] Yes.

ASTROFF. Have you been asleep ?

VOITSKI. Yes, very much so. [*He yawns*] Ever since the Professor and his wife have come, our daily life seems to have jumped the track. I sleep at the wrong time, drink wine, and eat all sorts of messes for luncheon and dinner. It isn't wholesome. Sonia and I used to work together and never had an idle moment, but now Sonia works alone and I only eat and drink and sleep. Something is wrong.

MARINA. [*Shaking her head*] Such a confusion in the house ! The Professor gets up at twelve, the samovar is kept boiling all the morning, and everything has to wait for him. Before they came we used to have dinner at one o'clock, like everybody else, but now we have it at seven. The Professor sits up all night writing and reading, and suddenly, at two o'clock, there goes the bell ! Heavens, what is that ? The Professor wants some tea ! Wake the servants, light the samovar ! Lord what disorder !

ASTROFF. Will they be here long ?

VOITSKI. A hundred years ! The Professor has decided to make his home here.

MARINA. Look at this now ! The samovar has been on the table for two hours, and they are all out walking !

VOITSKI. All right, don't get excited ; here they come.

> *Voices are heard approaching.* SEREBRAKOFF, HELENA, SONIA, *and* TELEGIN *come in from the depths of the garden, returning from their walk.*

SEREBRAKOFF. Superb ! Superb ! What beautiful views !

TELEGIN. They are wonderful, your Excellency.

Sonia.   To-morrow we shall go into the woods, shall we, papa ?

Voitski.   Ladies and gentlemen, tea is ready.

Serebrakoff.   Won't you please be good enough to send my tea into the library ?   I still have some work to finish.

Sonia.   I am sure you will love the woods.

> Helena, Serebrakoff, *and* Sonia *go into the house.*
> Telegin *sits down at the table beside* Marina.

Voitski.   There goes our learned scholar on a hot, sultry day like this, in his overcoat and goloshes and carrying an umbrella !

Astroff.   He is trying to take good care of his health.

Voitski.   How lovely she is !   How lovely !   I have never in my life seen a more beautiful woman.

Telegin.   Do you know, Marina, that as I walk in the fields or in the shady garden, as I look at this table here, my heart swells with unbounded happiness.   The weather is enchanting, the birds are singing, we are all living in peace and contentment—what more could the soul desire ?

> [*Takes a glass of tea.*

Voitski.   [*Dreaming*] Such eyes—a glorious woman !

Astroff.   Come, Ivan, tell us something.

Voitski.   [*Indolently*] What shall I tell you ?

Astroff.   Haven't you any news for us ?

Voitski.   No, it is all stale.   I am just the same as usual, or perhaps worse, because I have become lazy.   I don't do anything now but croak like an old raven.   My mother, the old magpie, is still chattering about the emancipation of woman, with one eye on her grave and the other on her learned books, in which she is always looking for the dawn of a new life.

Astroff.   And the Professor ?

Voitski.   The Professor sits in his library from morning till night, as usual—

" Straining the mind, wrinkling the brow,
 We write, write, write,
 Without respite
 Or hope of praise in the future or now."

Poor paper ! He ought to write his autobiography ; he
would make a really splendid subject for a book ! Imagine
it, the life of a retired professor, as stale as a piece of hard-
tack, tortured by gout, headaches, and rheumatism, his
liver bursting with jealousy and envy, living on the estate
of his first wife, although he hates it, because he can't afford
to live in town. He is everlastingly whining about his
hard lot, though, as a matter of fact, he is extraordinarily
lucky. He is the son of a common deacon and has attained
the professor's chair, become the son-in-law of a senator, is
called " your Excellency," and so on. But I'll tell you
something ; the man has been writing on art for twenty-five
years, and he doesn't know the very first thing about it.
For twenty-five years he has been chewing on other men's
thoughts about realism, naturalism, and all such foolishness ;
for twenty-five years he has been reading and writing
things that clever men have long known and stupid ones
are not interested in ; for twenty-five years he has been
making his imaginary mountains out of molehills. And
just think of the man's self-conceit and presumption
all this time ! For twenty-five years he has been masquer-
ading in false clothes and has now retired, absolutely
unknown to any living soul ; and yet see him ! stalking
across the earth like a demi-god !

ASTROFF. I believe you envy him.

VOITSKI. Yes, I do. Look at the success he has had
with women ! Don Juan himself was not more favoured.
His first wife, who was my sister, was a beautiful, gentle
being, as pure as the blue heaven there above us, noble,
great-hearted, with more admirers than he has pupils,
and she loved him as only beings of angelic purity can love

those who are as pure and beautiful as themselves. His mother-in-law, my mother, adores him to this day, and he still inspires a sort of worshipful awe in her. His second wife is, as you see, a brilliant beauty ; she married him in his old age and has surrendered all the glory of her beauty and freedom to him. Why ? What for ?

ASTROFF.   Is she faithful to him ?

VOITSKI.   Yes, unfortunately she is.

ASTROFF.   Why " unfortunately " ?

VOITSKI.   Because such fidelity is false and unnatural, root and branch. It sounds well, but there is no logic in it.   It is thought immoral for a woman to deceive an old husband whom she hates, but quite moral for her to strangle her poor youth in her breast and banish every vital desire from her heart.

TELEGIN.   [*In a tearful voice*] Vanya, I don't like to hear you talk so. Listen, Vanya ; everyone who betrays husband or wife is faithless, and could also betray his country.

VOITSKI.   [*Crossly*] Turn off the tap, Waffles.

TELEGIN.   No, allow me, Vanya. My wife ran away with a lover on the day after our wedding, because my exterior was unprepossessing. I have never failed in my duty since then.   I love her and am true to her to this day. I help her all I can and have given my fortune to educate the daughter of herself and her lover. I have forfeited my happiness, but I have kept my pride. And she ? Her youth has fled, her beauty has faded according to the laws of nature, and her lover is dead. What has she kept ?

>   HELENA *and* SONIA *come in ; after them comes* MME.
>   VOITSKAYA *carrying a book. She sits down and begins to read. Someone hands her a glass of tea which she drinks without looking up.*

SONIA.   [*Hurriedly, to the nurse*] There are some peasants

waiting out there. Go and see what they want. I shall
pour the tea.   [*Pours out some glasses of tea.*

  MARINA *goes out.* HELENA *takes a glass and sits
   drinking in the hammock.*

ASTROFF. I have come to see your husband. You wrote
me that he had rheumatism and I know not what else, and
that he was very ill, but he appears to be as lively as a
cricket.

HELENA. He had a fit of the blues yesterday evening and
complained of pains in his legs, but he seems all right again
to-day.

ASTROFF. And I galloped over here twenty miles at
breakneck speed! No matter, though, it is not the first
time. Once here, however, I am going to stay until
to-morrow, and at any rate sleep *quantum satis.*

SONIA. Oh, splendid! You so seldom spend the night
with us. Have you had dinner yet?

ASTROFF. No.

SONIA. Good. So you will have it with us. We dine
at seven now. [*Drinks her tea*] This tea is cold!

TELEGIN. Yes, the samovar has grown cold.

HELENA. Don't mind, Monsieur Ivan, we will drink
cold tea, then.

TELEGIN. I beg your pardon, my name is not Ivan, but
Ilia, ma'am—Ilia Telegin, or Waffles, as I am sometimes
called on account of my pock-marked face. I am Sonia's
godfather, and his Excellency, your husband, knows me
very well. I now live with you, ma'am, on this estate, and
perhaps you will be so good as to notice that I dine with
you every day.

SONIA. He is our great help, our right-hand man.
[*Tenderly*] Dear godfather, let me pour you some tea.

MME. VOITSKAYA. Oh! Oh!

SONIA. What is it, grandmother?

MME. VOITSKAYA. I forgot to tell Alexander—I have

             N

lost my memory—I received a letter to-day from Paul Alexevitch in Kharkoff. He has sent me a new pamphlet.

ASTROFF. Is it interesting?

MME. VOITSKAYA. Yes, but strange. He refutes the very theories which he defended seven years ago. It is appalling!

VOITSKI. There is nothing appalling about it. Drink your tea, mamma.

MME. VOITSKAYA. It seems you never want to listen to what I have to say. Pardon me, Jean, but you have changed so in the last year that I hardly know you. You used to be a man of settled convictions and had an illuminating personality——

VOITSKI. Oh, yes. I had an illuminating personality, which illuminated no one. [A pause] I had an illuminating personality! You couldn't say anything more biting. I am forty-seven years old. Until last year I endeavoured, as you do now, to blind my eyes by your pedantry to the truths of life. But now— Oh, if you only knew! If you knew how I lie awake at night, heartsick and angry, to think how stupidly I have wasted my time when I might have been winning from life everything which my old age now forbids.

SONIA. Uncle Vanya, how dreary!

MME. VOITSKAYA. [To her son] You speak as if your former convictions were somehow to blame, but you yourself, not they, were at fault. You have forgotten that a conviction, in itself, is nothing but a dead letter. You should have done something.

VOITSKI. Done something! Not every man is capable of being a writer perpetuum mobile like your Herr Professor.

MME. VOITSKAYA. What do you mean by that?

SONIA. [Imploringly] Mother! Uncle Vanya! I entreat you!

VOITSKI. I am silent. I apologise and am silent.

[*A pause.*

HELENA. What a fine day! Not too hot.   [*A pause.*

VOITSKI. A fine day to hang oneself.

TELEGIN *tunes the guitar.* MARINA *appears near the house, calling the chickens.*

MARINA. Chick, chick, chick!

SONIA. What did the peasants want, nurse?

MARINA. The same old thing, the same old nonsense. Chick, chick, chick!

SONIA. Why are you calling the chickens?

MARINA. The speckled hen has disappeared with her chicks. I am afraid the crows have got her.

TELEGIN *plays a polka. All listen in silence. Enter* WORKMAN.

WORKMAN. Is the doctor here? [*To* ASTROFF] Excuse me, sir, but I have been sent to fetch you.

ASTROFF. Where are you from?

WORKMAN. The factory.

ASTROFF. [*Annoyed*] Thank you. There is nothing for it, then, but to go. [*Looking around him for his cap*] Damn it, this is annoying!

SONIA. Yes, it is too bad, really. You must come back to dinner from the factory.

ASTROFF. No, I won't be able to do that. It will be too late. Now where, where— [*To the* WORKMAN] Look here, my man, get me a glass of vodka, will you? [*The* WORKMAN *goes out*] Where—where— [*Finds his cap*] One of the characters in Ostroff's plays is a man with a long moustache and short wits, like me. However, let me bid you good-bye, ladies and gentlemen. [*To* HELENA] I should be really delighted if you would come to see me some day with Miss Sonia. My estate is small, but if you are interested in such things I should like to show you a nursery and seedbed whose like you will not find within a thousand miles of here.

My place is surrounded by government forests. The forester is old and always ailing, so I superintend almost all the work myself.

HELENA. I have always heard that you were very fond of the woods. Of course one can do a great deal of good by helping to preserve them, but does not that work interfere with your real calling ?

ASTROFF. God alone knows what a man's real calling is.

HELENA. And do you find it interesting ?

ASTROFF. Yes, very.

VOITSKI. [Sarcastically] Oh, extremely !

HELENA. You are still young, not over thirty-six or seven, I should say, and I suspect that the woods do not interest you as much as you say they do. I should think you would find them monotonous.

SONIA. No, the work is thrilling. Dr. Astroff watches over the old woods and sets out new plantations every year, and he has already received a diploma and a bronze medal. If you will listen to what he can tell you, you will agree with him entirely. He says that forests are the ornaments of the earth, that they teach mankind to understand beauty and attune his mind to lofty sentiments. Forests temper a stern climate, and in countries where the climate is milder, less strength is wasted in the battle with nature, and the people are kind and gentle. The inhabitants of such countries are handsome, tractable, sensitive, graceful in speech and gesture. Their philosophy is joyous, art and science blossom among them, their treatment of women is full of exquisite nobility——

VOITSKI. [Laughing] Bravo ! Bravo ! All that is very pretty, but it is also unconvincing. So, my friend [To ASTROFF] you must let me go on burning firewood in my stoves and building my sheds of planks.

ASTROFF. You can burn peat in your stoves and build

your sheds of stone. Oh, I don't object, of course, to
cutting wood from necessity, but why destroy the forests!
The woods of Russia are trembling under the blows of the
axe. Millions of trees have perished. The homes of the
wild animals and birds have been desolated; the rivers are
shrinking, and many beautiful landscapes are gone for ever.
And why? Because men are too lazy and stupid to stoop
down and pick up their fuel from the ground. [*To* HELENA]
Am I not right, Madame? Who but a stupid barbarian
could burn so much beauty in his stove and destroy that
which he cannot make? Man is endowed with reason
and the power to create, so that he may increase that which
has been given him, but until now he has not created, but
demolished. The forests are disappearing, the rivers are
running dry, the game is exterminated, the climate is
spoiled, and the earth becomes poorer and uglier every
day. [*To* VOITSKI] I read irony in your eye; you do not
take what I am saying seriously, and—and—after all,
it may very well be nonsense. But when I pass peasant-
forests that I have preserved from the axe, or hear the
rustling of the young plantations set out with my own hands,
I feel as if I had had some small share in improving the
climate, and that if mankind is happy a thousand years
from now I will have been a little bit responsible for their
happiness. When I plant a little birch tree and then see
it budding into young green and swaying in the wind, my
heart swells with pride and I— [*Sees the* WORKMAN, *who
is bringing him a glass of vodka on a tray*] however— [*He
drinks*] I must be off. Probably it is all nonsense, anyway.
Good-bye.

> *He goes toward the house.* SONIA *takes his arm and
> goes with him.*

SONIA. When are you coming to see us again?
ASTROFF. I can't say.
SONIA. In a month?

ASTROFF *and* SONIA *go into the house.* HELENA *and*
VOITSKI *walk over to the terrace.*

HELENA. You have behaved shockingly again. Ivan,
what sense was there in teasing your mother and talking
about *perpetuum mobile?* And at breakfast you quarrelled
with Alexander again. Really your behaviour is too
petty.

VOITSKI. But if I hate him?

HELENA. You hate Alexander without reason; he is
like everyone else, and no worse than you are.

VOITSKI. If you could only see your face, your gestures!
Oh, how tedious your life must be.

HELENA. It is tedious, yes, and dreary! You all
abuse my husband and look on me with compassion; you
think, "Poor woman, she is married to an old man."
How well I understand your compassion! As Astroff
said just now, see how you thoughtlessly destroy the forests,
so that there will soon be none left. So you also destroy
mankind, and soon fidelity and purity and self-sacrifice
will have vanished with the woods. Why cannot you look
calmly at a woman unless she is yours? Because, the
doctor was right, you are all possessed by a devil of destruction; you have no mercy on the woods or the birds or on
women or on one another.

VOITSKI. I don't like your philosophy.

HELENA. That doctor has a sensitive, weary face—an
interesting face. Sonia evidently likes him, and she is in
love with him, and I can understand it. This is the third
time he has been here since I have come, and I have not had
a real talk with him yet or made much of him. He thinks I
am disagreeable. Do you know, Ivan, the reason you and
I are such friends? I think it is because we are both lonely
and unfortunate. Yes, unfortunate. Don't look at me
in that way, I don't like it.

VOITSKI. How can I look at you otherwise when I love

you ? You are my joy, my life, and my youth. I know that my chances of being loved in return are infinitely small, do not exist, but I ask nothing of you. Only let me look at you, listen to your voice——

HELENA. Hush, someone will overhear you.

[*They go toward the house.*

VOITSKI. [*Following her*] Let me speak to you of my love, do not drive me away, and this alone will be my greatest happiness !

HELENA. Ah ! This is agony !

> TELEGIN *strikes the strings of his guitar and plays a polka.* MME. VOITSKAYA *writes something on the leaves of her pamphlet.*

The curtain falls.

ACT II

The dining-room of SEREBRAKOFF'S *house. It is night. The tapping of the* WATCHMAN'S *rattle is heard in the garden.* SEREBRAKOFF *is dozing in an arm-chair by an open window and* HELENA *is sitting beside him, also half asleep.*

SEREBRAKOFF. [*Rousing himself*] Who is here? Is it you, Sonia?

HELENA. It is I.

SEREBRAKOFF. Oh, it is you, Nelly. This pain is intolerable.

HELENA. Your shawl has slipped down. [*She wraps up his legs in the shawl*] Let me shut the window.

SEREBRAKOFF. No, leave it open; I am suffocating. I dreamt just now that my left leg belonged to someone else, and it hurt so that I woke. I don't believe this is gout, it is more like rheumatism. What time is it?

HELENA. Half-past twelve. [*A pause.*

SEREBRAKOFF. I want you to look for Batushka's works in the library to-morrow. I think we have him.

HELENA. What is that?

SEREBRAKOFF. Look for Batushka to-morrow morning; we used to have him, I remember. Why do I find it so hard to breathe?

HELENA. You are tired; this is the second night you have had no sleep.

SEREBRAKOFF. They say that Turgenieff got angina of the heart from gout. I am afraid I am getting angina

200

too. Oh, damn this horrible, accursed old age! Ever since I have been old I have been hateful to myself, and, I am sure, hateful to you all as well.

HELENA. You speak as if we were to blame for your being old.

SEREBRAKOFF. I am more hateful to you than to anyone.

> HELENA *gets up and walks away from him, sitting down at a distance.*

SEREBRAKOFF. You are quite right, of course. I am not an idiot; I can understand you. You are young and healthy and beautiful, and longing for life, and I am an old dotard, almost a dead man already. Don't I know it? Of course I see that it is foolish for me to live so long, but wait! I shall soon set you all free. My life cannot drag on much longer.

HELENA. You are overtaxing my powers of endurance. Be quiet, for God's sake!

SEREBRAKOFF. It appears that, thanks to me, everybody's power of endurance is being overtaxed; everybody is miserable, only I am blissfully triumphant. Oh, yes, of course!

HELENA. Be quiet! You are torturing me.

SEREBRAKOFF. I torture everybody. Of course.

HELENA. [*Weeping*] This is unbearable! Tell me, what is it you want me to do?

SEREBRAKOFF. Nothing.

HELENA. Then be quiet, please.

SEREBRAKOFF. It is funny that everybody listens to Ivan and his old idiot of a mother, but the moment I open my lips you all begin to feel ill-treated. You can't even stand the sound of my voice. Even if I am hateful, even if I am a selfish tyrant, haven't I the right to be one at my age? Haven't I deserved it? Haven't I, I ask you, the right to be respected, now that I am old?

HELENA. No one is disputing your rights. [*The window slams in the wind*] The wind is rising, I must shut the window. [*She shuts it*] We shall have rain in a moment. Your rights have never been questioned by anybody.

The WATCHMAN *in the garden sounds his rattle.*

SEREBRAKOFF. I have spent my life working in the interests of learning. I am used to my library and the lecture hall and to the esteem and admiration of my colleagues. Now I suddenly find myself plunged in this wilderness, condemned to see the same stupid people from morning till night and listen to their futile conversation. I want to live; I long for success and fame and the stir of the world, and here I am in exile! Oh, it is dreadful to spend every moment grieving for the lost past, to see the success of others and sit here with nothing to do but to fear death. I cannot stand it! It is more than I can bear. And you will not even forgive me for being old!

HELENA. Wait, have patience; I shall be old myself in four or five years.

SONIA *comes in.*

SONIA. Father, you sent for Dr. Astroff, and now when he comes you refuse to see him. It is not nice to give a man so much trouble for nothing.

SEREBRAKOFF. What do I care about your Astroff? He understands medicine about as well as I understand astronomy.

SONIA. We can't send for the whole medical faculty, can we, to treat your gout?

SEREBRAKOFF. I won't talk to that madman!

SONIA. Do as you please. It's all the same to me.

[*She sits down.*

SEREBRAKOFF. What time is it?

HELENA. One o'clock.

SEREBRAKOFF. It is stifling in here. Sonia, hand me that bottle on the table.

ACT TWO 203

SONIA. Here it is.   [*She hands him a bottle of medicine.*

SEREBRAKOFF. [*Crossly*] No, not that one! Can't you understand me? Can't I ask you to do a thing?

SONIA. Please don't be captious with me. Some people may like it, but you must spare me, if you please, because I don't. Besides, I haven't the time; we are cutting the hay to-morrow and I must get up early.

> VOITSKI *comes in dressed in a long gown and carrying a candle.*

VOITSKI. A thunderstorm is coming up. [*The lightning flashes*] There it is! Go to bed, Helena and Sonia. I have come to take your place.

SEREBRAKOFF. [*Frightened*] No, no, no! Don't leave me alone with him! Oh, don't. He will begin to lecture me.

VOITSKI. But you must give them a little rest. They have not slept for two nights.

SEREBRAKOFF. Then let them go to bed, but you go away too! Thank you. I implore you to go. For the sake of our former friendship do not protest against going. We will talk some other time——

VOITSKI. Our former friendship! Our former——

SONIA. Hush, Uncle Vanya!

SEREBRAKOFF. [*To his wife*] My darling, don't leave me alone with him. He will begin to lecture me.

VOITSKI. This is ridiculous.

> MARINA *comes in carrying a candle.*

SONIA. You must go to bed, nurse, it is late.

MARINA. I haven't cleared away the tea things. Can't go to bed yet.

SEREBRAKOFF. No one can go to bed. They are all worn out, only I enjoy perfect happiness.

MARINA. [*Goes up to* SEREBRAKOFF *and speaks tenderly*] What's the matter, master? Does it hurt? My own legs are aching too, oh, so badly. [*Arranges his shawl about his legs*] You have had this illness such a long time. Sonia's dead mother used to stay awake with you too, and wear herself out for you. She loved you dearly. [*A pause*] Old people want to be pitied as much as young ones, but nobody cares about them somehow. [*She kisses* SEREBRAKOFF'S *shoulder*] Come, master, let me give you some linden-tea and warm your poor feet for you. I shall pray to God for you.

SEREBRAKOFF. [*Touched*] Let us go, Marina.

MARINA. My own feet are aching so badly, oh, so badly ! [*She and* SONIA *lead* SEREBRAKOFF *out*] Sonia's mother used to wear herself out with sorrow and weeping. You were still little and foolish then, Sonia. Come, come, master.

SEREBRAKOFF, SONIA *and* MARINA *go out*.

HELENA. I am absolutely exhausted by him, and can hardly stand.

VOITSKI. You are exhausted by him, and I am exhausted by my own self. I have not slept for three nights.

HELENA. Something is wrong in this house. Your mother hates everything but her pamphlets and the professor ; the professor is vexed, he won't trust me, and fears you ; Sonia is angry with her father, and with me, and hasn't spoken to me for two weeks ; I am at the end of my strength, and have come near bursting into tears at least twenty times to-day. Something is wrong in this house.

VOITSKI. Leave speculating alone.

HELENA. You are cultured and intelligent, Ivan, and you surely understand that the world is not destroyed by villains and conflagrations, but by hate and malice and all this spiteful tattling. It is your duty to make peace, and not to growl at everything.

VOITSKI. Help me first to make peace with myself. My darling !   [*Seizes her hand.*

HELENA. Let go ! [*She drags her hand away*] Go away !

VOITSKI. Soon the rain will be over, and all nature will sigh and awake refreshed. Only I am not refreshed by the storm. Day and night the thought haunts me like a fiend, that my life is lost for ever. My past does not count, because I frittered it away on trifles, and the present has so terribly miscarried! What shall I do with my life and my love? What is to become of them? This wonderful feeling of mine will be wasted and lost as a ray of sunlight is lost that falls into a dark chasm, and my life will go with it.

HELENA. I am as it were benumbed when you speak to me of your love, and I don't know how to answer you. Forgive me, I have nothing to say to you. [*She tries to go out*] Good night!

VOITSKI. [*Barring the way*] If you only knew how I am tortured by the thought that beside me in this house is another life that is being lost for ever—it is yours! What are you waiting for? What accursed philosophy stands in your way? Oh, understand, understand——

HELENA. [*Looking at him intently*] Ivan, you are drunk!

VOITSKI. Perhaps. Perhaps.

HELENA. Where is the doctor?

VOITSKI. In there, spending the night with me. Perhaps I am drunk, perhaps I am; nothing is impossible.

HELENA. Have you just been drinking together? Why do you do that?

VOITSKI. Because in that way I get a taste of life. Let me do it, Helena!

HELENA. You never used to drink, and you never used to talk so much. Go to bed, I am tired of you.

VOITSKI. [*Falling on his knees before her*] My sweetheart, my beautiful one——

HELENA. [*Angrily*] Leave me alone! Really, this has become too disagreeable.

HELENA *goes out. A pause.*

VOITSKI. [*Alone*] She is gone! I met her first ten years

ago, at her sister's house, when she was seventeen and I was
thirty-seven. Why did I not fall in love with her then
and propose to her? It would have been so easy! And
now she would have been my wife. Yes, we would both
have been wakened to-night by the thunderstorm, and she
would have been frightened, but I would have held her in
my arms and whispered : " Don't be afraid! I am here."
Oh, enchanting dream, so sweet that I laugh to think of it.
[*He laughs*] But my God! My head reels! Why am I so
old? Why won't she understand me? I hate all that
rhetoric of hers, that morality of indolence, that absurd
talk about the destruction of the world— [*A pause*] Oh,
how I have been deceived! For years I have worshipped
that miserable gout-ridden professor. Sonia and I have
squeezed this estate dry for his sake. We have bartered
our butter and curds and peas like misers, and have never
kept a morsel for ourselves, so that we could scrape enough
pennies together to send to him. I was proud of him and
of his learning; I received all his words and writings as
inspired, and now? Now he has retired, and what is the
total of his life? A blank! He is absolutely unknown,
and his fame has burst like a soap bubble. I have been
deceived ; I see that now, basely deceived.

> ASTROFF *comes in.   He has his coat on, but is without
> his waistcoat or collar, and is slightly drunk.*
> TELEGIN *follows him, carrying a guitar.*

ASTROFF.   Play !

TELEGIN.   But everyone is asleep.

ASTROFF.   Play !

> TELEGIN *begins to play softly.*

ASTROFF.   Are you alone here ?   No women about ?

> [*Sings with his arms akimbo.*

" The hut is cold, the fire is dead ;
Where shall the master lay his head ? "

The thunderstorm woke me. It was a heavy shower. What time is it ?

VOITSKI. The devil only knows.

ASTROFF. I thought I heard Helena's voice.

VOITSKI. She was here a moment ago.

ASTROFF. What a beautiful woman ! [*Looking at the medicine bottles on the table*] Medicine, is it ? What a variety we have ; prescriptions from Moscow, from Kharkoff, from Tula ! Why, he has been pestering all the towns of Russia with his gout ! Is he ill, or simply shamming ?

VOITSKI. He is really ill.

ASTROFF. What is the matter with you to-night ? You seem sad. Is it because you are sorry for the professor ?

VOITSKI. Leave me alone.

ASTROFF. Or in love with the professor's wife ?

VOITSKI. She is my friend.

ASTROFF. Already ?

VOITSKI. What do you mean by " already ? "

ASTROFF. A woman can only become a man's friend after having first been his acquaintance and then his beloved—then she becomes his friend.

VOITSKI. What vulgar philosophy !

ASTROFF. What do you mean ? Yes, I must confess I am getting vulgar, but then, you see, I am drunk. I usually only drink like this once a month. At such times my audacity and temerity know no bounds. I feel capable of anything. I attempt the most difficult operations and do them magnificently. The most brilliant plans for the future take shape in my head. I am no longer a poor fool of a doctor, but mankind's greatest benefactor. I evolve my own system of philosophy and all of you seem to crawl at my feet like so many insects or microbes. [*To* TELEGIN] Play, Waffles !

TELEGIN. My dear boy, I would with all my heart, but do listen to reason ; everybody in the house is asleep.

ASTROFF. Play !

TELEGIN *plays softly.*

ASTROFF. I want a drink. Come, we still have some brandy left. And then, as soon as it is day, you will come home with me. [*He sees* SONIA, *who comes in at that moment.*

ASTROFF. I beg your pardon, I have no collar on.

[*He goes out quickly, followed by* TELEGIN.

SONIA. Uncle Vanya, you and the doctor have been drinking ! The good fellows have been getting together ! It is all very well for him, he has always done it, but why do you follow his example ? It looks dreadful at your age.

VOITSKI. Age has nothing to do with it. When real life is wanting one must create an illusion. It is better than nothing.

SONIA. Our hay is all cut and rotting in these daily rains, and here you are busy creating illusions ! You have given up the farm altogether. I have done all the work alone until I am at the end of my strength— [*Frightened*] Uncle ! Your eyes are full of tears !

VOITSKI. Tears ? Nonsense, there are no tears in my eyes. You looked at me then just as your dead mother used to, my darling— [*He eagerly kisses her face and hands*] My sister, my dearest sister, where are you now ? Ah, if you only knew, if you only knew !

SONIA. If she only knew what, Uncle ?

VOITSKI. My heart is bursting. It is awful. No matter, though. I must go.   [*He goes out.*

SONIA. [*Knocks at the door*] Dr. Astroff ! Are you awake ? Please come here for a minute.

ASTROFF. [*Behind the door*] In a moment.

He appears in a few seconds. He has put on his collar and waistcoat.

ASTROFF. What do you want ?

SONIA. Drink as much as you please yourself, if you don't find it revolting, but I implore you not to let my uncle do it. It is bad for him.

ASTROFF. Very well; we won't drink any more. I am going home at once. That is settled. It will be dawn by the time the horses are harnessed.

SONIA. It is still raining; wait till morning.

ASTROFF. The storm is blowing over. This is only the edge of it. I must go. And please don't ask me to come and see your father any more. I tell him he has gout, and he says it is rheumatism. I tell him to lie down, and he sits up. To-day he refused to see me at all.

SONIA. He has been spoilt. [*She looks in the sideboard*] Won't you have a bite to eat?

ASTROFF. Yes, please. I believe I will.

SONIA. I love to eat at night. I am sure we shall find something in here. They say that he has made a great many conquests in his life, and that the women have spoiled him. Here is some cheese for you.

> [*They stand eating by the sideboard.*

ASTROFF. I haven't eaten anything to-day. Your father has a very difficult nature. [*He takes a bottle out of the sideboard*] May I? [*He pours himself a glass of vodka*] We are alone here, and I can speak frankly. Do you know, I could not stand living in this house for even a month? This atmosphere would stifle me. There is your father, entirely absorbed in his books, and his gout; there is your Uncle Vanya with his hypochondria, your grandmother, and finally, your stepmother——

SONIA. What about her?

ASTROFF. A human being should be entirely beautiful: the face, the clothes, the mind, the thoughts. Your stepmother is, of course, beautiful to look at, but don't you see? She does nothing but sleep and eat and walk and bewitch us, and that is all. She has no responsibilities,

O

everything is done for her—am I not right ? And an idle life can never be a pure one. [*A pause*] However, I may be judging her too severely. Like your Uncle Vanya, I am discontented, and so we are both grumblers.

SONIA. Aren't you satisfied with life ?

ASTROFF. I like life as life, but I hate and despise it in a little Russian country village, and as far as my own personal life goes, by heaven ! there is absolutely no redeeming feature about it. Haven't you noticed if you are riding through a dark wood at night and see a little light shining ahead, how you forget your fatigue and the darkness and the sharp twigs that whip your face ? I work, that you know—as no one else in the country works. Fate beats me on without rest ; at times I suffer unendurably and I see no light ahead. I have no hope ; I do not like people. It is long since I have loved anyone.

SONIA. You love no one ?

ASTROFF. Not a soul. I only feel a sort of tenderness for your old nurse for old-times' sake. The peasants are all alike ; they are stupid and live in dirt, and the educated people are hard to get along with. One gets tired of them. All our good friends are petty and shallow and see no farther than their own noses ; in one word, they are dull. Those that have brains are hysterical, devoured with a mania for self-analysis. They whine, they hate, they pick faults everywhere with unhealthy sharpness. They sneak up to me sideways, look at me out of a corner of the eye, and say : " That man is a lunatic," " That man is a wind-bag." Or, if they don't know what else to label me with, they say I am strange. I like the woods ; that is strange. I don't eat meat ; that is strange, too. Simple, natural relations between man and man or man and nature do not exist.

[*He tries to go out ;* SONIA *prevents him.*

SONIA. I beg you, I implore you, not to drink any more !

ASTROFF. Why not ?

Sonia. It is so unworthy of you. You are well-bred, your voice is sweet, you are even—more than anyone I know—handsome. Why do you want to resemble the common people that drink and play cards ? Oh, don't, I beg you ! You always say that people do not create any-thing, but only destroy what heaven has given them. Why, oh, why do you destroy yourself ? Oh, don't, I implore you not to ! I entreat you !

Astroff. [*Gives her his hand*] I won't drink any more.

Sonia. Promise me.

Astroff. I give you my word of honour.

Sonia. [*Squeezing his hand*] Thank you.

Astroff. I have done with it. You see, I am perfectly sober again, and so I shall stay till the end of my life. [*He looks at his watch*] But, as I was saying, life holds nothing for me ; my race is run. I am old, I am tired, I am trivial ; my sensibilities are dead. I could never attach myself to anyone again. I love no one, and—never shall ! Beauty alone has the power to touch me still. I am deeply moved by it. Helena could turn my head in a day if she wanted to, but that is not love, that is not affection——

[*He shudders and covers his face with his hands.*

Sonia. What is it ?

Astroff. Nothing. During Lent one of my patients died under chloroform.

Sonia. It is time to forget that. [*A pause*] Tell me, doctor, if I had a friend or a younger sister, and if you knew that she, well—loved you, what would you do ?

Astroff. [*Shrugging his shoulders*] I don't know. I don't think I should do anything. I should make her understand that I could not return her love—however, my mind is not bothered about those things now. I must start at once if I am ever to get off. Good-bye, my dear girl. At this rate we shall stand here talking till morning.

[*He shakes hands with her*] I shall go out through the sitting-room, because I am afraid your uncle might detain me.   [*He goes out.*

SONIA. [*Alone*] Not a word! His heart and soul are still locked from me, and yet for some reason I am strangely happy. I wonder why? [*She laughs with pleasure*] I told him that he was well-bred and handsome and that his voice was sweet. Was that a mistake? I can still feel his voice vibrating in the air; it caresses me. [*Wringing her hands*] Oh! how terrible it is to be plain! I am plain, I know it. As I came out of church last Sunday I overheard a woman say, " She is a dear, noble girl, but what a pity she is so ugly ! " So ugly !

HELENA *comes in and throws open the window.*

HELENA. The storm is over. What delicious air! [*A pause*] Where is the doctor?

SONIA. He has gone.   [*A pause.*

HELENA. Sonia !

SONIA. Yes ?

HELENA. How much longer are you going to sulk at me ? We have not hurt each other. Why not be friends ? We have had enough of this.

SONIA. I myself—[*She embraces* HELENA] Let us make peace.

HELENA. With all my heart.   '   [*They are both moved.*

SONIA. Has papa gone to bed ?

HELENA. No, he is sitting up in the drawing-room. Heaven knows what reason you and I had for not speaking to each other for weeks. [*Sees the open sideboard*] Who left the sideboard open ?

SONIA. Dr. Astroff has just had supper.

HELENA. There is some wine. Let us seal our friendship.

SONIA. Yes, let us.

HELENA. Out of one glass. [*She fills a wine glass*] So, we are friends, are we ?

SONIA. Yes. [*They drink and kiss each other*] I have long wanted to make friends, but somehow, I was ashamed to.   [*She weeps.*

HELENA. Why are you crying ?

SONIA. I don't know. It is nothing.

HELENA. There, there, don't cry. [*She weeps*] Silly ! Now I am crying too. [*A pause*] You are angry with me because I seem to have married your father for his money, but don't believe the gossip you hear. I swear to you I married him for love. I was fascinated by his fame and learning. I know now that it was not real love, but it seemed real at the time. I am innocent, and yet your clever, suspicious eyes have been punishing me for an imaginary crime ever since my marriage.

SONIA. Peace, peace ! Let us forget the past.

HELENA. You must not look so at people. It is not becoming to you. You must trust people, or life becomes impossible.

SONIA. Tell me truly, as a friend, are you happy ?

HELENA. Truly, no.

SONIA. I knew it. One more question : do you wish your husband were young ?

HELENA. What a child you are ! Of course I do. Go on, ask something else.

SONIA. Do you like the doctor ?

HELENA. Yes, very much indeed.

SONIA. [*Laughing*] I have a stupid face, haven't I ? He has just gone out, and his voice is still in my ears ; I hear his step ; I see his face in the dark window. Let me say all I have in my heart ! But no, I cannot speak of it so loudly. I am ashamed. Come to my room and let me tell you there. I seem foolish to you, don't I ? Talk to me of him.

HELENA. What can I say?

SONIA. He is clever. He can do everything. He can cure the sick, and plant woods.

HELENA. It is not a question of medicine and woods, my dear, he is a man of genius. Do you know what that means? It means he is brave, profound, and of clear insight. He plants a tree and his mind travels a thousand years into the future, and he sees visions of the happiness of the human race. People like him are rare and should be loved. What if he does drink and act roughly at times? A man of genius cannot be a saint in Russia. There he lives, cut off from the world by cold and storm and endless roads of bottomless mud, surrounded by a rough people who are crushed by poverty and disease, his life one continuous struggle, with never a day's respite; how can a man live like that for forty years and keep himself sober and unspotted? [*Kissing* SONIA] I wish you happiness with all my heart; you deserve it. [*She gets up*] As for me, I am a worthless, futile woman. I have always been futile; in music, in love, in my husband's house—in a word, in everything. When you come to think of it, Sonia, I am really very, very unhappy. [*Walks excitedly up and down*] Happiness can never exist for me in this world. Never. Why do you laugh?

SONIA. [*Laughing and covering her face with her hands*] I am so happy, so happy!

HELENA. I want to hear music. I might play a little.

SONIA. Oh, do, do! [*She embraces her*] I could not possibly go to sleep now. Do play!

HELENA. Yes, I will. Your father is still awake. Music irritates him when he is ill, but if he says I may, then I shall play a little. Go, Sonia, and ask him.

SONIA. Very well.

> [*She goes out. The* WATCHMAN'S *rattle is heard in the garden.*

HELENA. It is long since I have heard music. And now, I shall sit and play, and weep like a fool. [*Speaking out of the window*] Is that you rattling out there, Ephim?

VOICE OF THE WATCHMAN. It is I.

HELENA. Don't make such a noise. Your master is ill.

VOICE OF THE WATCHMAN. I am going away this minute.   [*Whistles a tune.*

SONIA. [*Comes back*] He says, no.

The curtain falls.

ACT THREE

The drawing-room of SEREBRAKOFF'S *house. There are three doors : one to the right, one to the left, and one in the centre of the room.* VOITSKI *and* SONIA *are sitting down.* HELENA *is walking up and down, absorbed in thought.*

VOITSKI. We were asked by the professor to be here at one o'clock. [*Looks at his watch*] It is now a quarter to one. It seems he has some communication to make to the world.

HELENA. Probably a matter of business.

VOITSKI. He never had any business. He writes twaddle, grumbles, and eats his heart out with jealousy ; that's all he does.

SONIA. [*Reproachfully*] Uncle !

VOITSKI. All right. I beg your pardon. [*He points to* HELENA] Look at her. Wandering up and down from sheer idleness. A sweet picture, really.

HELENA. I wonder you are not bored, droning on in the same key from morning till night. [*Despairingly*] I am dying of this tedium. What shall I do ?

SONIA. [*Shrugging her shoulders*] There is plenty to do if you would.

HELENA. For instance ?

SONIA. You could help run this place, teach the children, care for the sick—isn't that enough ? Before you and papa came, Uncle Vanya and I used to go to market ourselves to deal in flour.

HELENA. I don't know anything about such things, and

216

besides, they don't interest me. It is only in novels that
women go out and teach and heal the peasants ; how can
I suddenly begin to do it ?

SONIA. How can you live here and not do it ? Wait
awhile, you will get used to it all. [*Embraces her*] Don't be
sad, dearest. [*Laughing*] You feel miserable and restless,
and can't seem to fit into this life, and your restlessness
is catching. Look at Uncle Vanya, he does nothing now
but haunt you like a shadow, and I have left my work
to-day to come here and talk with you. I am getting lazy,
and don't want to go on with it. Dr. Astroff hardly ever
used to come here ; it was all we could do to persuade him
to visit us once a month, and now he has abandoned his
forestry and his practice, and comes every day. You
must be a witch.

VOITSKI. Why should you languish here ? Come, my
dearest, my beauty, be sensible ! The blood of a Nixey
runs in your veins. Oh, won't you let yourself be one ?
Give your nature the reins for once in your life ; fall head
over ears in love with some other water sprite and plunge
down head first into a deep pool, so that the Herr Professor
and all of us may have our hands free again.

HELENA. [*Angrily*] Leave me alone ! How cruel you
are ! [*She tries to go out.*

VOITSKI. [*Preventing her*] There, there, my beauty,
I apologise. [*He kisses her hand*] Forgive me.

HELENA. Confess that you would try the patience of an
angel.

VOITSKI. As a peace offering I am going to fetch some
flowers which I picked for you this morning : some autumn
roses, beautiful, sorrowful roses. [*He goes out.*

SONIA. Autumn roses, beautiful, sorrowful roses !

[*She and* HELENA *stand looking out of the window.*

HELENA. September already ! How shall we live

through the long winter here ?   [*A pause*] Where is the doctor ?

SONIA. He is writing in Uncle Vanya's room. I am glad Uncle Vanya has gone out, I want to talk to you about something.

HELENA. About what ?

SONIA. About what ?

> [*She lays her head on* HELENA's *breast.*

HELENA. [*Stroking her hair*] There, there, that will do. Don't, Sonia.

SONIA. I am ugly !

HELENA. You have lovely hair.

SONIA. Don't say that ! [*She turns to look at herself in the glass*] No, when a woman is ugly they always say she has beautiful hair or eyes. I have loved him now for six years ; I have loved him more than one loves one's mother. I seem to hear him beside me every moment of the day. I feel the pressure of his hand on mine. If I look up, I seem to see him coming, and as you see, I run to you to talk of him. He is here every day now, but he never looks at me, he does not notice my presence. It is agony. I have absolutely no hope, no, no hope. Oh, my God ! Give me strength to endure. I prayed all last night. I often go up to him and speak to him and look into his eyes. My pride is gone. I am not mistress of myself. Yesterday I told Uncle Vanya. I couldn't control myself, and all the servants know it. Everyone knows that I love him.

HELENA. Does he ?

SONIA. No, he never notices me.

HELENA. [*Thoughtfully*] He is a strange man. Listen, Sonia, will you allow me to speak to him ? I shall be careful, only hint. [*A pause*] Really, to be in uncertainty all these years ! Let me do it !

SONIA *nods an affirmative.*

HELENA. Splendid ! It will be easy to find out whether he loves you or not. Don't be ashamed, sweetheart, don't worry. I shall be careful ; he will not notice a thing. We only want to find out whether it is yes or no, don't we ? [*A pause*] And if it is no, then he must keep away from here, is that so ?

SONIA *nods*.

HELENA. It will be easier not to see him any more. We won't put off the examination an instant. He said he had a sketch to show me. Go and tell him at once that I want to see him.

SONIA. [*In great excitement*] Will you tell me the whole truth ?

HELENA. Of course I will. I am sure that no matter what it is, it will be easier for you to bear than this uncertainty. Trust to me, dearest.

SONIA. Yes, yes. I shall say that you want to see his sketch. [*She starts out, but stops near the door and looks back*] No, it is better not to know—and yet—there may be hope.

HELENA. What do you say ?

SONIA. Nothing.   [*She goes out.*

HELENA. [*Alone*] There is no greater sorrow than to know another's secret when you cannot help them. [*In deep thought*] He is obviously not in love with her, but why shouldn't he marry her ? She is not pretty, but she is so clever and pure and good, she would make a splendid wife for a country doctor of his years. [*A pause*] I can understand how the poor child feels. She lives here in this desperate loneliness with no one around her except these colourless shadows that go mooning about talking nonsense and knowing nothing except that they eat, drink and sleep. Among them appears from time to time this Dr. Astroff, so different, so handsome, so interesting, so charming. It is like seeing the moon rise on a dark night. Oh, to surrender

oneself to his embrace ! To lose oneself in his arms ! I am
a little in love with him myself ! Yes, I am lonely without
him, and when I think of him I smile. That Uncle Vanya
says I have the blood of a Nixey in my veins : " Give rein
to your nature for once in your life ! " Perhaps it is right
that I should. Oh, to be free as a bird, to fly away from
all your sleepy faces and your talk and forget that you have
existed at all ! But I am a coward, I am afraid ; my
conscience torments me. He comes here every day now.
I can guess why, and feel guilty already ; I should like to
fall on my knees at Sonia's feet and beg her forgiveness,
and weep.

    ASTROFF *comes in carrying a portfolio.*

ASTROFF. How do you do ? [*Shakes hands with her*]
Do you want to see my sketch ?

HELENA. Yes, you promised to show me what you had
been doing. Have you time now ?

ASTROFF. Of course I have !

    *He lays the portfolio on the table, takes out the sketch
    and fastens it to the table with thumb-tacks.*

ASTROFF. Where were you born ?

HELENA. [*Helping him*] In St. Petersburg.

ASTROFF. And educated ?

HELENA. At the Conservatoire there.

ASTROFF. You don't find this life very interesting, I dare
say ?

HELENA. Oh, why not ? It is true I don't know the
country very well, but I have read a great deal about it.

ASTROFF. I have my own desk there in Ivan's room.
When I am absolutely too exhausted to go on I drop everything and rush over here to forget myself in this work for
an hour or two. Ivan and Miss Sonia sit rattling at their
counting-boards, the cricket chirps, and I sit beside them
and paint, feeling warm and peaceful. But I don't permit
myself this luxury very often, only once a month. [*Pointing*

to the picture] Look there! That is a map of our country
as it was fifty years ago. The green tints, both dark and
light, represent forests. Half the map, as you see, is covered
with it. Where the green is striped with red the forests
were inhabited by elk and wild goats. Here on this lake,
lived great flocks of swans and geese and ducks; as the old
men say, there was a power of birds of every kind. Now
they have vanished like a cloud. Beside the hamlets and
villages, you see, I have dotted down here and there the
various settlements, farms, hermit's caves, and water-mills.
This country carried a great many cattle and horses, as you
can see by the quantity of blue paint. For instance, see
how thickly it lies in this part; there were great herds of
them here, an average of three horses to every house.
[*A pause*] Now, look lower down. This is the country
as it was twenty-five years ago. Only a third of the map is
green now with forests. There are no goats left and no elk.
The blue paint is lighter, and so on, and so on. Now we
come to the third part; our country as it appears to-day.
We still see spots of green, but not much. The elk, the
swans, the blackcock have disappeared. It is, on the
whole, the picture of a regular and slow decline which it
will evidently only take about ten or fifteen more years to
complete. You may perhaps object that it is the march of
progress, that the old order must give place to the new,
and you might be right if roads had been run through these
ruined woods, or if factories and schools had taken their
place. The people then would have become better educated
and healthier and richer, but as it is, we have nothing of
the sort. We have the same swamps and mosquitoes;
the same disease and want; the typhoid, the diphtheria,
the burning villages. We are confronted by the degradation
of our country, brought on by the fierce struggle for
existence of the human race. It is the consequence of
the ignorance and unconsciousness of starving, shivering,

sick humanity that, to save its children, instinctively
snatches at everything that can warm it and still its
hunger. So it destroys everything it can lay its hands on,
without a thought for the morrow. And almost everything
has gone, and nothing has been created to take its place.
[*Coldly*] But I see by your face that I am not interesting
you.

HELENA. I know so little about such things!

ASTROFF. There is nothing to know. It simply isn't
interesting, that's all.

HELENA. Frankly, my thoughts were elsewhere. Forgive
me! I want to submit you to a little examination, but I
am embarrassed and don't know how to begin.

ASTROFF. An examination?

HELENA. Yes, but quite an innocent one. Sit down.
[*They sit down*] It is about a certain young girl I know. Let
us discuss it like honest people, like friends, and then forget
what has passed between us, shall we?

ASTROFF. Very well.

HELENA. It is about my stepdaughter, Sonia. Do
you like her?

ASTROFF. Yes I respect her.

HELENA. Do you like her—as a woman?

ASTROFF. [*Slowly*] No.

HELENA. One more word, and that will be the last.
You have not noticed anything?

ASTROFF. No, nothing.

HELENA. [*Taking his hand*] You do not love her. I see
that in your eyes. She is suffering. You must realise
that, and not come here any more.

ASTROFF. My sun has set, yes, and then I haven't the
time. [*Shrugging his shoulders*] Where shall I find time for
such things?   [*He is embarrassed.*

HELENA. Bah! What an unpleasant conversation!
I am as out of breath as if I had been running three miles

uphill. Thank heaven that is over! Now let us forget everything as if nothing had been said. You are sensible. You understand. [*A pause*] I am actually blushing.

ASTROFF. If you had spoken a month ago I might perhaps have considered it, but now— [*He shrugs his shoulders*] Of course, if she is suffering—but I cannot understand why you had to put me through this examination. [*He searches her face with his eyes, and shakes his fingers at her*] Oho, you are wily!

HELENA. What does this mean?

ASTROFF. [*Laughing*] You are a wily one! I admit that Sonia is suffering, but what does this examination of yours mean? [*He prevents her from retorting, and goes on quickly*] Please don't put on such a look of surprise; you know perfectly well why I come here every day. Yes, you know perfectly why and for whose sake I come! Oh, my sweet tigress! don't look at me in that way; I am an old bird!

HELENA. [*Perplexed*] A tigress? I don't understand you.

ASTROFF. Beautiful, sleek tigress, you must have your victims! For a whole month I have done nothing but seek you eagerly. I have thrown over everything for you, and you love to see it. Now then, I am sure you knew all this without putting me through your examination. [*Crossing his arms and bowing his head*] I surrender. Here you have me—now, eat me.

HELENA. You have gone mad!

ASTROFF. You are afraid!

HELENA. I am a better and stronger woman than you think me. Good-bye. [*She tries to leave the room.*

ASTROFF. Why good-bye? Don't say good-bye, don't waste words. Oh, how lovely you are—what hands!

[*He kisses her hands.*

HELENA. Enough of this! [*She frees her hands*] Leave the room! You have forgotten yourself.

ASTROFF. Tell me, tell me, where can we meet
to-morrow? [*He puts his arm around her*] Don't you see
that we must meet, that it is inevitable?

> *He kisses her.* VOITSKI *comes in carrying a bunch of
> roses, and stops in the doorway.*

HELENA. [*Without seeing* VOITSKI] Have pity! Leave
me. [*Lays her head on* ASTROFF'S *shoulder*] Don't!
> [*She tries to break away from him.*

ASTROFF. [*Holding her by the waist*] Be in the forest
to-morrow at two o'clock. Will you? Will you?

HELENA. [*Sees* VOITSKI] Let me go! [*Goes to the window
deeply embarrassed*] This is appalling!

VOITSKI. [*Throws the flowers on a chair, and speaks in
great excitement, wiping his face with his handkerchief*]
Nothing—yes, yes, nothing.

ASTROFF. The weather is fine to-day, my dear Ivan;
the morning was overcast and looked like rain, but now the
sun is shining again. Honestly, we have had a very fine
autumn, and the wheat is looking fairly well. [*Puts his
map back into the portfolio*] But the days are growing short.

HELENA. [*Goes quickly up to* VOITSKI] You must do your
best; you must use all your power to get my husband and
myself away from here to-day! Do you hear? I say, this
very day!

VOITSKI. [*Wiping his face*] Oh! Ah! Oh! All right!
I—Helena, I saw everything!

HELENA. [*In great agitation*] Do you hear me? I must
leave here this very day!

> SEREBRAKOFF, SONIA, MARINA, *and* TELEGIN *come
> in.*

TELEGIN. I am not very well myself, your Excellency.
I have been limping for two days, and my head——

SEREBRAKOFF. Where are the others? I hate this
house. It is a regular labyrinth. Everyone is always
scattered through the twenty-six enormous rooms; one

never can find a soul. [*Rings*] Ask my wife and Mædame Voitskaya to come here !

HELENA. I am here already.

SEREBRAKOFF. Please, all of you, sit down.

SONIA. [*Goes up to* HELENA *and asks anxiously*] What did he say ?

HELENA. I'll tell you later.

SONIA. You are moved. [*Looking quickly and inquiringly into her face*] I understand ; he said he would not come here any more. [*A pause*] Tell me, did he ?

HELENA *nods*.

SEREBRAKOFF. [*To* TELEGIN] One can, after all, become reconciled to being an invalid, but not to this country life. The ways of it stick in my throat and I feel exactly as if I had been whirled off the earth and landed on a strange planet. Please be seated, ladies and gentlemen. Sonia ! [SONIA *does not hear. She is standing with her head bowed sadly forward on her breast*] Sonia ! [*A pause*] She does not hear me. [*To* MARINA] Sit down too, nurse. [MARINA *sits down and begins to knit her stocking*] I crave your indulgence, ladies and gentlemen ; hang your ears, if I may say so, on the peg of attention.   [*He laughs.*

VOITSKI. [*Agitated*] Perhaps you do not need me—may I be excused ?

SEREBRAKOFF. No, you are needed now more than any one.

VOITSKI. What is it you want of me ?

SEREBRAKOFF. You—but what are you angry about ? If it is anything I have done, I ask you to forgive me.

VOITSKI. Oh, drop that and come to business ; what do you want ?

MME. VOITSKAYA *comes in*.

SEREBRAKOFF. Here is mother. Ladies and gentlemen, I shall begin. I have asked you to assemble here, my friends, in order to discuss a very important matter. I want to ask you for your assistance and advice, and knowing your unfailing amiability I think I can count on both. I am a book-worm and a scholar, and am unfamiliar with practical affairs. I cannot, I find, dispense with the help of well-informed people such as you, Ivan, and you, Telegin, and you, mother. The truth is, *manet omnes una nox*, that is to say, our lives are in the hands of God, and as I am old and ill, I realise that the time has come for me to dispose of my property in regard to the interests of my family. My life is nearly over, and I am not thinking of myself, but I have a young wife and daughter. [*A pause*] I cannot continue to live in the country; we were not made for country life, and yet we cannot afford to live in town on the income derived from this estate. We might sell the woods, but that would be an expedient we could not resort to every year. We must find some means of guaranteeing to ourselves a certain more or less fixed yearly income. With this object in view, a plan has occurred to me which I now have the honour of presenting to you for your consideration. I shall only give you a rough outline, avoiding all details. Our estate does not pay on an average more than two per cent. on the money invested in it. I propose to sell it. If we then invest our capital in bonds, it will earn us four to five per cent. and we should probably have a surplus over of several thousand roubles, with which we could buy a summer cottage in Finland——

VOITSKI. Hold on! Repeat what you just said; I don't think I heard you quite right.

SEREBRAKOFF. I said we would invest the money in bonds and buy a cottage in Finland with the surplus.

VOITSKI. No, not Finland—you said something else.

SEREBRAKOFF. I propose to sell this place.

VOITSKI. Aha! That was it! So you are going to sell the place? Splendid. The idea is a rich one. And what do you propose to do with my old mother and me and with Sonia here ?

SEREBRAKOFF. That will be decided in due time. We can't do everything at once.

VOITSKI. Wait! It is clear that until this moment I have never had a grain of sense in my head. I have always been stupid enough to think that the estate belonged to Sonia. My father bought it as a wedding present for my sister, and I foolishly imagined that as our laws were made for Russians and not Turks, my sister's estate would come down to her child.

SEREBRAKOFF. Of course it is Sonia's. Has anyone denied it ? I don't want to sell it without Sonia's consent ; on the contrary, what I am doing is for Sonia's good.

VOITSKI. This is absolutely incomprehensible. Either I have gone mad or—or——

MME. VOITSKAYA. Jean, don't contradict Alexander. Trust to him ; he knows better than we do what is right and what is wrong.

VOITSKI. I shan't. Give me some water. [*He drinks*] Go ahead ! Say anything you please—anything !

SEREBRAKOFF. I can't imagine why you are so upset. I don't pretend that my scheme is an ideal one, and if you all object to it I shall not insist. [*A pause.*

TELEGIN. [*With embarrassment*] I not only nourish feelings of respect toward learning, your Excellency, but I am also drawn to it by family ties. My brother Gregory's wife's brother, whom you may know ; his name is Constantine Lakedemonoff, and he used to be a magistrate——

VOITSKI. Stop, Waffles. This is business ; wait a bit, we will talk of that later. [*To* SEREBRAKOFF] There now, ask him what he thinks ; this estate was bought from his uncle.

SEREBRAKOFF. Ah ! Why should I ask questions ? What good would it do ?

VOITSKI. The price was ninety-five thousand roubles. My father paid seventy and left a debt of twenty-five. Now listen! This place could never have been bought had I not renounced my inheritance in favour of my sister, whom I deeply loved—and what is more, I worked for ten years like an ox, and paid off the debt.

SEREBRAKOFF. I regret ever having started this conversation.

VOITSKI. Thanks entirely to my own personal efforts, the place is entirely clear of debts, and now, when I have grown old, you want to throw me out, neck and crop!

SEREBRAKOFF. I can't imagine what you are driving at.

VOITSKI. For twenty-five years I have managed this place, and have sent you the returns from it like the most honest of servants, and you have never given me one single word of thanks for my work, not one—neither in my youth nor now. You allowed me a meagre salary of five hundred roubles a year, a beggar's pittance, and have never even thought of adding a rouble to it.

SEREBRAKOFF. What did I know about such things, Ivan? I am not a practical man and don't understand them. You might have helped yourself to all you wanted.

VOITSKI. Yes, why did I not steal? Don't you all despise me for not stealing, when it would have been only justice? And I should not now have been a beggar!

MME. VOITSKAYA. [Sternly] Jean!

TELEGIN. [Agitated] Vanya, old man, don't talk in that way. Why spoil such pleasant relations? [He embraces him] Do stop!

VOITSKI. For twenty-five years I have been sitting here with my mother like a mole in a burrow. Our every thought and hope was yours and yours only. By day we talked with pride of you and your work, and spoke your name with veneration; our nights we wasted reading the books and papers which my soul now loathes.

TELEGIN. Don't, Vanya, don't. I can't stand it.

SEREBRAKOFF. [*Wrathfully*] What under heaven do you want, anyway ?

VOITSKI. We used to think of you as almost superhuman, but now the scales have fallen from my eyes and I see you as you are ! You write on art without knowing anything about it. Those books of yours which I used to admire are not worth one copper kopeck. You are a hoax !

SEREBRAKOFF. Can't anyone make him stop ? I am going !

HELENA. Ivan, I command you to stop this instant ! Do you hear me ?

VOITSKI. I refuse ! [SEREBRAKOFF *tries to get out of the room, but* VOITSKI *bars the door*] Wait ! I have not done yet ! You have wrecked my life. I have never lived. My best years have gone for nothing, have been ruined, thanks to you. You are my most bitter enemy !

TELEGIN. I can't stand it ; I can't stand it. I am going.   [*He goes out in great excitement.*

SEREBRAKOFF. But what do you want ? What earthly right have you to use such language to me ? Ruination ! If this estate is yours, then take it, and let me be ruined !

HELENA. I am going away out of this hell this minute. [*Shrieks*] This is too much !

VOITSKI. My life has been a failure. I am clever and brave and strong. If I had lived a normal life I might have become another Schopenhauer or Dostoieffski. I am losing my head ! I am going crazy ! Mother, I am in despair ! Oh, mother !

MME. VOITSKAYA. [*Sternly*] Listen, Alexander !

    SONIA *falls on her knees beside the nurse and nestles against her.*

SONIA. Oh, nurse, nurse !

VOITSKI. Mother ! What shall I do ? But no, don't

speak! I know what to do. [*To* SEREBRAKOFF] And you
will understand me!

> *He goes out through the door in the centre of the room
> and* MME. VOITSKAYA *follows him.*

SEREBRAKOFF. Tell me, what on earth is the matter?
Take this lunatic out of my sight! I cannot possibly live
under the same roof with him. His room [*He points to the
centre door*] is almost next door to mine. Let him take
himself off into the village or into the wing of the
house, or I shall leave here at once. I cannot stay in
the same house with him.

HELENA. [*To her husband*] We are leaving to-day; we
must get ready at once for our departure.

SEREBRAKOFF. What a perfectly dreadful man!

SONIA. [*On her knees beside the nurse and turning to her
father. She speaks with emotion*] You must be kind to us,
papa. Uncle Vanya and I are so unhappy! [*Controlling her
despair*] Have pity on us. Remember how Uncle Vanya
and Granny used to copy and translate your books for you
every night—every, every night. Uncle Vanya has toiled
without rest; he would never spend a penny on us, we sent
it all to you. We have not eaten the bread of idleness. I
am not saying this as I should like to, but you must understand us, papa, you must be merciful to us.

HELENA. [*Very excited, to her husband*] For heaven's
sake, Alexander, go and have a talk with him—explain!

SEREBRAKOFF. Very well, I shall have a talk with him,
but I won't apologise for a thing. I am not angry with
him, but you must confess that his behaviour has been
strange, to say the least. Excuse me, I shall go to him.

> [*He goes out through the centre door.*

HELENA. Be gentle with him; try to quiet him.

> [*She follows him out.*

SONIA. [*Nestling nearer to* MARINA] Nurse, oh, nurse!

MARINA. It's all right, my baby. When the geese

have cackled they will be still again.   First they cackle and
then they stop.

SONIA.   Nurse!

MARINA.   You are trembling all over, as if you were
freezing.   There, there, little orphan baby, God is merciful.
A little linden-tea, and it will all pass away.   Don't cry,
my sweetest.   [*Looking angrily at the door in the centre
of the room*] See, the geese have all gone now.   The devil
take them!

> *A shot is heard.* HELENA *screams behind the scenes.*
> SONIA *shudders.*

MARINA.   Bang!   What's that?

SEREBRAKOFF.   [*Comes in reeling with terror*] Hold him!
hold him!   He has gone mad!

> HELENA *and* VOITSKI *are seen struggling in the
> doorway.*

HELENA.   [*Trying to wrest the revolver from him*] Give
it to me;   give it to me, I tell you!

VOITSKI.   Let me go, Helena, let me go!   [*He frees
himself and rushes in, looking everywhere for* SEREBRAKOFF]
Where is he?   Ah, there he is!   [*He shoots at him.   A pause*]
I didn't get him?   I missed again?   [*Furiously*] Damnation!
Damnation!   To hell with him!

> *He flings the revolver on the floor, and drops helpless
> into a chair.* SEREBRAKOFF *stands as if stupefied.*
> HELENA *leans against the wall, almost fainting.*

HELENA.   Take me away!   Take me away!   I can't
stay here—I can't!

VOITSKI.   [*In despair*] Oh, what shall I do?   What shall
I do?

SONIA.   [*Softly*] Oh, nurse, nurse!

The curtain falls.

ACT FOUR

VOITSKI's *bedroom, which is also his office. A table stands near the window; on it are ledgers, letter scales, and papers of every description. Near-by stands a smaller table belonging to* ASTROFF, *with his paints and drawing materials. On the wall hangs a cage containing a starling. There is also a map of Africa on the wall, obviously of no use to anybody. There is a large sofa covered with buckram. A door to the left leads into an inner room; one to the right leads into the front hall, and before this door lies a mat for the peasants with their muddy boots to stand on. It is an autumn evening. The silence is profound.* TELEGIN *and* MARINA *are sitting facing one another, winding wool.*

TELEGIN. Be quick, Marina, or we shall be called away to say good-bye before you have finished. The carriage has already been ordered.

MARINA. [*Trying to wind more quickly*] I am a little tired.

TELEGIN. They are going to Kharkoff to live.

MARINA. They do well to go.

TELEGIN. They have been frightened. The professor's wife won't stay here an hour longer. "If we are going at all, let's be off," says she, "we shall go to Kharkoff and look about us, and then we can send for our things." They are travelling light. It seems, Marina, that fate has decreed for them not to live here.

MARINA. And quite rightly. What a storm they have just raised! It was shameful!

232

TELEGIN. It was indeed. The scene was worthy of the brush of Aibazofski.

MARINA. I wish I'd never laid eyes on them. [*A pause*] Now we shall have things as they were again : tea at eight, dinner at one, and supper in the evening ; everything in order as decent folk, as Christians like to have it. [*Sighs*] It is a long time since I have eaten noodles.

TELEGIN. Yes, we haven't had noodles for ages. [*A pause*] Not for ages. As I was going through the village this morning, Marina, one of the shop-keepers called after me, " Hi ! you hanger-on ! " I felt it bitterly.

MARINA. Don't pay the least attention to them, master ; we are all dependants on God. You and Sonia and all of us. Everyone must work, no one can sit idle. Where is Sonia ?

TELEGIN. In the garden with the doctor, looking for Ivan. They fear he may lay violent hands on himself.

MARINA. Where is his pistol ?

TELEGIN. [*Whispers*] I hid it in the cellar.

VOITSKI *and* ASTROFF *come in.*

VOITSKI. Leave me alone ! [*To* MARINA *and* TELEGIN] Go away ! Go away and leave me to myself, if but for an hour. I won't have you watching me like this !

TELEGIN. Yes, yes, Vanya.   [*He goes out on tiptoe.*

MARINA. The gander cackles ; ho ! ho ! ho !

                        [*She gathers up her wool and goes out.*

VOITSKI. Leave me by myself !

ASTROFF. I would, with the greatest pleasure. I ought to have gone long ago, but I shan't leave you until you have returned what you took from me.

VOITSKI. I took nothing from you.

ASTROFF. I am not jesting, don't detain me, I really nust go.

VOITSKI. I took nothing of yours.

ASTROFF. You didn't ? Very well, I shall have to wait

a little longer, and then you will have to forgive me if I
resort to force. We shall have to bind you and search
you. I mean what I say.

VOITSKI. Do as you please. [*A pause*] Oh, to make such
a fool of myself! To shoot twice and miss him both
times! I shall never forgive myself.

ASTROFF. When the impulse came to shoot, it would
have been as well had you put a bullet through your own
head.

VOITSKI. [*Shrugging his shoulders*] Strange! I attempted
murder, and am not going to be arrested or brought to
trial. That means that they think me mad. [*With a
bitter laugh*] Me! I am mad, and those who hide their
worthlessness, their dullness, their crying heartlessness
behind a professor's mask, are sane! Those who marry old
men and then deceive them under the noses of all, are sane!
I saw you kiss her; I saw you in each other's arms!

ASTROFF. Yes, sir, I did kiss her; so there.

[*He puts his thumb to his nose.*

VOITSKI. [*His eyes on the door*] No, it is the earth that is
mad, because she still bears us on her breast.

ASTROFF. That is nonsense.

VOITSKI. Well? Am I not a madman, and therefore
irresponsible? Haven't I the right to talk nonsense?

ASTROFF. This is a farce! You are not mad; you are
simply a ridiculous fool. I used to think every fool was
out of his senses, but now I see that lack of sense is a man's
normal state, and you are perfectly normal.

VOITSKI. [*Covers his face with his hands*] Oh! If you
knew how ashamed I am! These piercing pangs of shame
are like nothing on earth. [*In an agonised voice*] I can't
endure them! [*He leans against the table*] What can I do?
What can I do?

ASTROFF. Nothing.

VOITSKI. You must tell me something! Oh, my God!

I am forty-seven years old. I may live to sixty; I
still have thirteen years before me; an eternity! How
shall I be able to endure life for thirteen years? What shall
I do? How can I fill them? Oh, don't you see? [*He
presses* ASTROFF'S *hand convulsively*] Don't you see, if
only I could live the rest of my life in some new way!
if I could only wake some still, bright morning and feel
that life had begun again; that the past was forgotten
and had vanished like smoke. [*He weeps*] Oh, to begin
life anew! Tell me, tell me how to begin.

ASTROFF. [*Crossly*] What nonsense! What sort of a new
life can you and I look forward to? We can have no hope.

VOITSKI. None?

ASTROFF. None. Of that I am convinced.

VOITSKI. Tell me what to do. [*He puts his hand to
his heart*] I feel such a burning pain here.

ASTROFF. [*Shouts angrily*] Stop! [*Then, more gently*]
It may be that posterity, which will despise us for our blind
and stupid lives, will find some road to happiness; but we—
you and I—have but one hope, the hope that we may be
visited by visions, perhaps by pleasant ones, as we lie
resting in our graves. [*Sighing*] Yes, brother, there were
only two respectable, intelligent men in this county, you
and I. Ten years or so of this life of ours, this miserable
life, have sucked us under, and we have become as con-
temptible and petty as the rest. But don't try to talk
me out of my purpose! Give me what you took from
me, will you?

VOITSKI. I took nothing from you.

ASTROFF. You took a little bottle of morphine out of
my medicine case. [*A pause*] Listen! If you are positively
determined to make an end to yourself, go into the woods
and shoot yourself there. Give up the morphine, or there
will be a lot of talk and guesswork; people will think I

gave it to you. I don't fancy having to perform a post-mortem on you. Do you think I should find it interesting ?

SONIA *comes in.*

VOITSKI. Leave me alone.

ASTROFF. [*To* SONIA] Sonia, your uncle has stolen a bottle of morphine out of my medicine case and won't give it up. Tell him that his behaviour is—well, unwise. I haven't time, I must be going.

SONIA. Uncle Vanya, did you take the morphine ?

ASTROFF. Yes, he took it. [*A pause*] I am absolutely sure.

SONIA. Give it up ! Why do you want to frighten us ? [*Tenderly*] Give it up, Uncle Vanya ! My misfortune is perhaps even greater than yours, but I am not plunged in despair. I endure my sorrow, and shall endure it until my life comes to a natural end. You must endure yours, too. [*A pause*] Give it up ! Dear, darling Uncle Vanya. Give it up ! [*She weeps*] You are so good, I am sure you will have pity on us and give it up. You must endure your sorrow, Uncle Vanya ; you must endure it.

VOITSKI *takes a bottle from the drawer of the table and hands it to* ASTROFF.

VOITSKI. There it is ! [*To* SONIA] And now, we must get to work at once ; we must do something, or else I shall not be able to endure it.

SONIA. Yes, yes, to work ! As soon as we have seen them off we shall go to work. [*She nervously straightens out the papers on the table*] Everything is in a muddle !

ASTROFF. [*Putting the bottle in his case, which he straps together*] Now I can be off.

HELENA *comes in.*

HELENA. Are you here, Ivan ? We are starting in a moment. Go to Alexander, he wants to speak to you.

SONIA. Go, Uncle Vanya. [*She takes* VOITSKI'S *arm*]

Come, you and papa must make peace ; that is absolutely necessary.

        Sonia *and* Voitski *go out.*

HELENA. I am going away. [*She gives* Astroff *her hand*] Good-bye.

ASTROFF. So soon ?

HELENA. The carriage is waiting.

ASTROFF. Good-bye.

HELENA. You promised me you would go away yourself, to-day.

ASTROFF. I have not forgotten. I am going at once. [*A pause*] Were you frightened ? Was it so terrible ?

HELENA. Yes.

ASTROFF. Couldn't you stay ? Couldn't you ? To-morrow—in the forest——

HELENA. No. It is all settled, and that is why I can look you so bravely in the face. Our departure is fixed. One thing I must ask of you : don't think too badly of me ; I should like you to respect me.

ASTROFF. Ah ! [*With an impatient gesture*] Stay, I implore you ! Confess that there is nothing for you to do in this world. You have no object in life ; there is nothing to occupy your attention, and sooner or later your feelings must master you. It is inevitable. It would be better if it happened not in Kharkoff or in Kursk, but here, in nature's lap. It would then at least be poetical, even beautiful. Here you have the forests, the houses half in ruins that Turgenieff writes of.

HELENA. How comical you are ! I am angry with you and yet I shall always remember you with pleasure. You are interesting and original. You and I will never meet again, and so I shall tell you—why should I conceal it ?— that I am just a little in love with you. Come, one more last pressure of our hands, and then let us part good friends. Let us not bear each other any ill will.

ASTROFF. [*Pressing her hand*] Yes, go. [*Thoughtfully*]
You seem to be sincere and good, and yet there is something
strangely disquieting about all your personality. No
sooner did you arrive here with your husband than everyone whom you found busy and actively creating something
was forced to drop his work and give himself up for the
whole summer to your husband's gout and yourself. You
and he have infected us with your idleness. I have been
swept off my feet ; I have not put my hand to a thing for
weeks, during which sickness has been running its course
unchecked among the people, and the peasants have been
pasturing their cattle in my woods and young plantations.
Go where you will, you and your husband will always
carry destruction in your train. I am joking of course,
and yet I am strangely sure that had you stayed here we
should have been overtaken by the most immense
desolation. I would have gone to my ruin, and you—
you would not have prospered. So go ! *E finita la
comedia !*

HELENA. [*Snatching a pencil off* ASTROFF'S *table, and
hiding it with a quick movement*] I shall take this pencil for
memory !

ASTROFF. How strange it is. We meet, and then
suddenly it seems that we must part for ever. That is the
way in this world. As long as we are alone, before Uncle
Vanya comes in with a bouquet—allow me—to kiss you
good-bye—may I ? [*He kisses her on the cheek*] So !
Splendid !

HELENA. I wish you every happiness. [*She glances
about her*] For once in my life, I shall ! and scorn the conse-
quences ! [*She kisses him impetuously, and they quickly
part*] I must go.

ASTROFF. Yes, go. If the carriage is there, then start
at once.   [*They stand listening.*

ASTROFF. *E finita !*

Voitski, Serebrakoff, Mme. Voitskaya *with her book*, Telegin, *and* Sonia *come in.*

Serebrakoff. [*To* Voitski] Shame on him who bears malice for the past. I have gone through so much in the last few hours that I feel capable of writing a whole treatise on the conduct of life for the instruction of posterity. I gladly accept your apology, and myself ask your forgiveness.

[*He kisses* Voitski *three times.*

Helena *embraces* Sonia.

Serebrakoff. [*Kissing* Mme. Voitskaya's *hand*] Mother!

Mme. Voitskaya. [*Kissing him*] Have your picture taken, Alexander, and send me one. You know how dear you are to me.

Telegin. Good-bye, your Excellency. Don't forget us.

Serebrakoff. [*Kissing his daughter*] Good-bye, good-bye all. [*Shaking hands with* Astroff] Many thanks for your pleasant company. I have a deep regard for your opinions and your enthusiasm, but let me, as an old man, give one word of advice at parting : do something, my friend! Work! Do something! [*They all bow*] Good luck to you all.

[*He goes out followed by* Mme. Voitskaya *and* Sonia.

Voitski. [*Kissing* Helena's *hand fervently*] Good-bye— forgive me. I shall never see you again !

Helena. [*Touched*] Good-bye, dear boy.

She lightly kisses his head as he bends over her hand, and goes out.

Astroff. Tell them to bring my carriage round too, Waffles.

Telegin. All right, old man.

Astroff *and* Voitski *are left behind alone.* Astroff *collects his paints and drawing materials on the table and packs them away in a box.*

Astroff. Why don't you go to see them off ?

VOITSKI. Let them go! I—I can't go out there. I feel too sad. I must go to work on something at once. To work! To work!

> *He rummages through his papers on the table. A pause. The tinkling of bells is heard as the horses trot away.*

ASTROFF. They have gone! The professor, I suppose, is glad to go. He couldn't be tempted back now by a fortune.

> MARINA *comes in.*

MARINA. They have gone.

> [*She sits down in an arm-chair and knits her stocking.* SONIA *comes in wiping her eyes.*

SONIA. They have gone. God be with them. [*To her uncle*] And now, Uncle Vanya, let us do something!

VOITSKI. To work! To work!

SONIA. It is long, long, since you and I have sat together at this table. [*She lights a lamp on the table*] No ink! [*She takes the inkstand to the cupboard and fills it from an ink-bottle*] How sad it is to see them go!

> MME. VOITSKAYA *comes slowly in.*

MME. VOITSKAYA. They have gone.

> *She sits down and at once becomes absorbed in her book.* SONIA *sits down at the table and looks through an account book.*

SONIA. First, Uncle Vanya, let us write up the accounts. They are in a dreadful state. Come, begin. You take one and I will take the other.

VOITSKI. In account with——[*They sit silently writing.*

MARINA. [*Yawning*] The sand-man has come.

ASTROFF. How still it is. Their pens scratch, the cricket sings; it is so warm and comfortable. I hate to go.

> [*The tinkling of bells is heard.*

ASTROFF. My carriage has come. There now remains

but to say good-bye to you, my friends, and to my table here, and then—away ! [*He puts the map into the portfolio.*

MARINA. Don't hurry away ; sit a little longer with us.

ASTROFF. Impossible.

VOITSKI. [*Writing*] And carry forward from the old debt two seventy-five——

WORKMAN *comes in.*

WORKMAN. Your carriage is waiting, sir.

ASTROFF. All right. [*He hands the* WORKMAN *his medicine-case, portfolio, and box*] Look out, don't crush the portfolio !

WORKMAN. Very well, sir.

SONIA. When shall we see you again ?

ASTROFF. Hardly before next summer. Probably not this winter, though, of course, if anything should happen you will let me know. [*He shakes hands with them*] Thank you for your kindness, for your hospitality, for everything ! [*He goes up to* MARINA *and kisses her head*] Good-bye, old nurse !

MARINA. Are you going without your tea ?

ASTROFF. I don't want any, nurse.

MARINA. Won't you have a drop of vodka ?

ASTROFF. [*Hesitatingly*] Yes, I might.

MARINA *goes out.*

ASTROFF. [*After a pause*] My off-wheeler has gone lame for some reason. I noticed it yesterday when Peter was taking him to water.

VOITSKI. You should have him re-shod.

ASTROFF. I shall have to go around by the blacksmith's on my way home. It can't be avoided. [*He stands looking up at the map of Africa hanging on the wall*] I suppose it is roasting hot in Africa now.

VOITSKI. Yes, I suppose it is.

MARINA *comes back carrying a tray on which are a glass of vodka and a piece of bread.*

MARINA. Help yourself.

ASTROFF *drinks.*

MARINA. To your good health! [*She bows deeply*]
Eat your bread with it.

ASTROFF. No, I like it so. And now, good-bye. [*To*
MARINA] You needn't come out to see me off, nurse.

> *He goes out.* SONIA *follows him with a candle to light*
> *him to the carriage.* MARINA *sits down in her*
> *arm-chair.*

VOITSKI. [*Writing*] On the 2nd of February, twenty
pounds of butter ; on the 16th, twenty pounds of butter
again. Buckwheat flour——

> [*A pause. Bells are heard tinkling.*

MARINA. He has gone.   [*A pause.*

> SONIA *comes in and sets the candle-stick on the table.*

SONIA. He has gone.

VOITSKI. [*Adding and writing*] Total, fifteen—twenty-
five——

> SONIA *sits down and begins to write.*

MARINA. [*Yawning*] Oh, ho! The Lord have mercy.

> TELEGIN *comes in on tiptoe, sits down near the door,*
> *and begins to tune his guitar.*

VOITSKI. [*To* SONIA, *stroking her hair*] Oh, my child, I
am so miserable ; if you only knew how miserable I am !

SONIA. What can we do ? We must live our lives. [*A
pause*] Yes, we shall live, Uncle Vanya. We shall live
through the long procession of days before us, and through
the long evenings ; we shall patiently bear the trials that
fate imposes on us ; we shall work for others without rest,
both now and when we are old ; and when our last hour
comes we shall meet it humbly, and there, beyond the grave,
we shall say that we have suffered and wept, that our life
was bitter, and God will have pity on us. Ah, then dear,
dear Uncle, we shall see that bright and beautiful life ;
we shall rejoice and look back upon our sorrow here ; a

tender smile — and — we shall rest. I have faith, Uncle,
fervent, passionate faith. [SONIA *kneels down before her
uncle and lays her head on his hands. She speaks in a weary
voice*] We shall rest. [TELEGIN *plays softly on the guitar*]
We shall rest. We shall hear the angels. We shall
see heaven shining like a jewel. We shall see all evil
and all our pain sink away in the great compassion that
shall enfold the world. Our life will be as peaceful and
tender and sweet as a caress. I have faith; I have faith.
[*She wipes away her tears*] My poor, poor Uncle Vanya,
you are crying! [*Weeping*] You have never known what
happiness was, but wait, Uncle Vanya, wait! We shall
rest. [*She embraces him*] We shall rest. [*The* WATCH-
MAN'S *rattle is heard in the garden ;* TELEGIN *plays softly*
MME. VOITSKAYA *writes something on the margin of her
pamphlet* ; MARINA *knits her stocking*] We shall rest.

The curtain slowly falls.

THE CHERRY ORCHARD

A COMEDY IN FOUR ACTS

CHARACTERS

LUBOV ANDREYEVNA RANEVSKY (Mme. RANEVSKY), *a land-owner*

ANYA, *her daughter, aged seventeen*

VARYA (BARBARA), *her adopted daughter, aged twenty-seven*

LEONID ANDREYEVITCH GAEV, *Mme. Ranevsky's brother*

ERMOLAI ALEXEYEVITCH LOPAKHIN, *a merchant*

PETER SERGEYEVITCH TROFIMOV, *a student*

BORIS BORISOVITCH SIMEONOV-PISCHIN, *a landowner*

CHARLOTTA IVANOVNA, *a governess*

SIMEON PANTELEYEVITCH EPIKHODOV, *a clerk*

DUNYASHA (AVDOTYA FEDOROVNA), *a maidservant*

FIERS, *an old footman, aged eighty-seven*

YASHA, *a young footman*

A TRAMP

A STATION-MASTER

POST-OFFICE CLERK

GUESTS·

A SERVANT

The action takes place on MME. RANEVSKY'S *estate*

ACT ONE

A room which is still called the nursery. One of the doors leads into ANYA'S *room. It is close on sunrise. It is May. The cherry-trees are in flower but it is chilly in the garden. There is an early frost. The windows of the room are shut.* DUNYASHA *comes in with a candle, and* LOPAKHIN *with a book in his hand.*

LOPAKHIN. The train's arrived, thank God. What's the time?

DUNYASHA. It will soon be two. [*Blows out candle*] It is light already.

LOPAKHIN. How much was the train late? Two hours at least. [*Yawns and stretches himself*] I have made a rotten mess of it! I came here on purpose to meet them at the station, and then overslept myself . . . in my chair. It's a pity. I wish you'd wakened me.

DUNYASHA. I thought you'd gone away. [*Listening*] I think I hear them coming.

LOPAKHIN. [*Listens*] No. . . . They've got to collect their luggage and so on. . . . [*Pause*] Lubov Andreyevna has been living abroad for five years; I don't know what she'll be like now. . . . She's a good sort—an easy, simple person. I remember when I was a boy of fifteen, my father, who is dead—he used to keep a shop in the village

here—hit me on the face with his fist, and my nose bled. . . .
We had gone into the yard together for something or other,
and he was a little drunk. Lubov Andreyevna, as I remember
her now, was still young, and very thin, and she took me
to the washstand here in this very room, the nursery. She
said, " Don't cry, little man, it'll be all right in time for
your wedding." [*Pause*] "Little man". . . . My father was
a peasant, it's true, but here I am in a white waistcoat and
yellow shoes . . . a pearl out of an oyster. I'm rich now,
with lots of money, but just think about it and examine me,
and you'll find I'm still a peasant down to the marrow of
my bones. [*Turns over the pages of his book*] Here I've
been reading this book, but I understood nothing. I read
and fell asleep.   [*Pause.*

DUNYASHA. The dogs didn't sleep all night ; they know
that they're coming.

LOPAKHIN. What's up with you, Dunyasha . . . ?

DUNYASHA. My hands are shaking. I shall faint.

LOPAKHIN. You're too sensitive, Dunyasha. You dress
just like a lady, and you do your hair like one too. You
oughtn't. You should know your place.

EPIKHODOV. [*Enters with a bouquet. He wears a short
jacket and brilliantly polished boots which squeak audibly.
He drops the bouquet as he enters, then picks it up*] The
gardener sent these ; says they're to go into the dining-
room.   [*Gives the bouquet to* DUNYASHA.

LOPAKHIN. And you'll bring me some kvass.

DUNYASHA. Very well.   [*Exit.*

EPIKHODOV. There's a frost this morning—three degrees,
and the cherry-trees are all in flower. I can't approve of
our climate. [*Sighs*] I can't. Our climate is indisposed to
favour us even this once. And, Ermolai Alexeyevitch, allow
me to say to you, in addition, that I bought myself some

boots two days ago, and I beg to assure you that they squeak in a perfectly unbearable manner. What shall I put on them ?

LOPAKHIN. Go away. You bore me.

EPIKHODOV. Some misfortune happens to me every day. But I don't complain ; I'm used to it, and I can smile. [DUNYASHA *comes in and brings* LOPAKHIN *some kvass*] I shall go. [*Knocks over a chair*] There. . . . [*Triumphantly*] There, you see, if I may use the word, what circumstances I am in, so to speak.   It is even simply marvellous.

[*Exit.*

DUNYASHA. I may confess to you, Ermolai Alexeyevitch, that Epikhodov has proposed to me.

LOPAKHIN. Ah !

DUNYASHA. I don't know what to do about it. He's a nice young man, but every now and again, when he begins talking, you can't understand a word he's saying. I think I like him. He's madly in love with me. He's an unlucky man ; every day something happens. We tease him about it. They call him " Two-and-twenty troubles."

LOPAKHIN. [*Listens*] There they come, I think.

DUNYASHA. They're coming ! What's the matter with me ? I'm cold all over.

LOPAKHIN. There they are, right enough. Let's go and meet them. Will she know me ? We haven't seen each other for five years.

DUNYASHA. [*Excited*] I shall faint in a minute. . . . Oh, I'm fainting !

> *Two carriages are heard driving up to the house.*
> LOPAKHIN *and* DUNYASHA *quickly go out. The*
> *stage is empty. A noise begins in the next room.*
> FIERS, *leaning on a stick, walks quickly across the*
> *stage ; he has just been to meet* LUBOV ANDREYEVNA.

He wears an old-fashioned livery and a tall hat. He is saying something to himself, but not a word of it can be made out. The noise behind the stage gets louder and louder. A voice is heard: " Let's go in there." Enter LUBOV ANDREYEVNA, ANYA, *and* CHARLOTTA IVANOVNA *with a little dog on a chain, and all dressed in travelling clothes,* VARYA *in a long coat and with a kerchief on her head.* GAEV, SIMEONOV-PISCHIN, LOPAKHIN, DUNYASHA *with a parcel and an umbrella, and a servant with luggage —all cross the room.*

ANYA. Let's come through here. Do you remember what this room is, mother ?

LUBOV. [*Joyfully, through her tears*] The nursery !

VARYA. How cold it is ! My hands are quite numb. [*To* LUBOV ANDREYEVNA] Your rooms, the white one and the violet one, are just as they used to be, mother.

LUBOV. My dear nursery, oh, you beautiful room. . . . I used to sleep here when I was a baby. [*Kisses her brother,* VARYA, *then her brother again*] And Varya is just as she used to be, just like a nun.   And I knew Dunyasha.

[*Kisses her.*

GAEV. The train was two hours late. There now ; how's that for punctuality ?

CHARLOTTA. [*To* PISCHIN] My dog eats nuts too.

PISCHIN. [*Astonished*] To think of that, now !

[*All go out except* ANYA *and* DUNYASHA.

DUNYASHA. We did have to wait for you !

[*Takes off* ANYA'S *cloak and hat.*

ANYA. . . . I didn't get any sleep for four nights on the journey. . . . I'm awfully cold.

DUNYASHA. You went away during Lent, when it was snowing and frosty, but now ? Darling ! [*Laughs and kisses her*] We did have to wait for you, my joy, my pet. . . . I must tell you at once, I can't bear to wait a minute.

ANYA. [*Tired*] Something else now . . . ?

DUNYASHA. The clerk, Epikhodov, proposed to me after Easter.

ANYA. Always the same. . . . [*Puts her hair straight*] I've lost all my hairpins. . . .

      [*She is very tired, and even staggers as she walks.*

DUNYASHA. I don't know what to think about it. He loves me, he loves me so much !

ANYA. [*Looks into her room ; in a gentle voice*] My room, my windows, as if I'd never gone away. I'm at home ! To-morrow morning I'll get up and have a run in the garden. . . . Oh, if I could only get to sleep ! I didn't sleep the whole journey, I was so bothered.

DUNYASHA. Peter Sergeyevitch came two days ago.

ANYA. [*Joyfully*] Peter !

DUNYASHA. He sleeps in the bath-house, he lives there. He said he was afraid he'd be in the way. [*Looks at her pocket-watch*] I ought to wake him, but Barbara Mihailovna told me not to. " Don't wake him," she said.

      Enter VARYA, *a bunch of keys on her belt.*

VARYA. Dunyasha, some coffee, quick. Mother wants some.

DUNYASHA. This minute.   [*Exit.*

VARYA. Well, you've come, glory be to God. Home again. [*Caressing her*] My darling is back again ! My pretty one is back again !

ANYA. I did have an awful time, I tell you.

VARYA. I can just imagine it !

ANYA. I went away in Holy Week ; it was very cold then. Charlotta talked the whole way and would go on performing her tricks. Why did you tie Charlotta on to me ?

Varya. You couldn't go alone, darling, at seventeen !

Anya. We went to Paris ; it's cold there and snowing. I talk French perfectly horribly. My mother lives on the fifth floor. I go to her, and find her there with various Frenchmen, women, an old abbé with a book, and everything in tobacco smoke and with no comfort at all. I suddenly became very sorry for mother—so sorry that I took her head in my arms and hugged her and wouldn't let her go. Then mother started hugging me and crying. . . .

Varya. [*Weeping*] Don't say any more, don't say any more. . . .

Anya. She's already sold her villa near Mentone ; she's nothing left, nothing. And I haven't a copeck left either ; we only just managed to get here. And mother won't understand ! We had dinner at a station ; she asked for all the expensive things, and tipped the waiters one rouble each. And Charlotta too. Yasha wants his share too— it's too bad. Mother's got a footman now, Yasha ; we've brought him here.

Varya. I saw the wretch.

Anya. How's business ? Has the interest been paid ?

Varya. Not much chance of that.

Anya. Oh God, oh God . . .

Varya. The place will be sold in August.

Anya. O God. . . .

Lopakhin. [*Looks in at the door and moos*] Moo ! . . .

　　　　　　　　　　　　　　　　　　　　　　[*Exit.*

Varya. [*Through her tears*] I'd like to. . . .

　　　　　　　　　　　　　　　　　　　　[*Shakes her fist.*

Anya. [*Embraces* Varya, *softly*] Varya, has he proposed to you ? [Varya *shakes her head*] But he loves you. . . . Why don't you make up your minds ? Why do you keep on waiting ?

VARYA. I think that it will all come to nothing. He's a busy man. I'm not his affair . . . he pays no attention to me. Bless the man, I don't want to see him. . . . But everybody talks about our marriage, everybody congratulates me, and there's nothing in it at all, it's all like a dream. [*In another tone*] You've got a brooch like a bee.

ANYA. [*Sadly*] Mother bought it. [*Goes into her room, and talks lightly, like a child*] In Paris I went up in a balloon !

VARYA. My darling's come back, my pretty one's come back ! [DUNYASHA *has already returned with the coffee-pot and is making the coffee*] I go about all day, looking after the house, and I think all the time, if only you could marry a rich man, then I'd be happy and would go away somewhere by myself, then to Kiev . . . to Moscow, and so on, from one holy place to another. I'd tramp and tramp. That would be splendid !

ANYA. The birds are singing in the garden. What time is it now ?

VARYA. It must be getting on for three. Time you went to sleep, darling. [*Goes into* ANYA'S *room*] Splendid !

[*Enter* YASHA *with a plaid shawl and a travelling bag.*

YASHA. [*Crossing the stage : Politely*] May I go this way ?

DUNYASHA. I hardly knew you, Yasha. You have changed abroad.

YASHA. Hm . . . and who are you ?

DUNYASHA. When you went away I was only so high. [*Showing with her hand*] I'm Dunyasha, the daughter of Theodore Kozoyedov. You don't remember !

YASHA. Oh, you little cucumber !

Looks round and embraces her. She screams and drops a saucer. YASHA *goes out quickly.*

VARYA. [*In the doorway : In an angry voice*] What's that ?

DUNYASHA. [*Through her tears*] I've broken a saucer.

VARYA. It may bring luck.

ANYA. [*Coming out of her room*] We must tell mother that Peter's here.

VARYA. I told them not to wake him.

ANYA. [*Thoughtfully*] Father died six years ago, and a month later my brother Grisha was drowned in the river— such a dear little boy of seven! Mother couldn't bear it; she went away, away, without looking round. . . . [*Shudders*] How I understand her; if only she knew! And Peter Trofimov was Grisha's tutor, he might tell her. . . .

   Enter FIERS *in a short jacket and white waistcoat.*

FIERS. [*Goes to the coffee-pot, nervously*] The mistress is going to have some food here. . . . [*Puts on white gloves*] Is the coffee ready? [*To* DUNYASHA, *severely*] You! Where's the cream?

DUNYASHA. Oh, dear me . . . !   [*Rapid exit.*

FIERS. [*Fussing round the coffee-pot*] Oh, you bungler. . . . [*Murmurs to himself*] Back from Paris . . . the master went to Paris once . . . in a carriage. . . .   [*Laughs.*

VARYA. What are you talking about, Fiers?

FIERS. I beg your pardon? [*Joyfully*] The mistress is home again. I've lived to see her! Don't care if I die now. . . .   [*Weeps with joy.*

   Enter LUBOV ANDREYEVNA, GAEV, LOPAKHIN, *and*
    SIMEONOV-PISCHIN, *the latter in a long jacket*
    of thin cloth and loose trousers. GAEV, *coming in,*
    moves his arms and body about as if he is playing
    billiards.

LUBOV. Let me remember now. Red into the corner! Twice into the centre!

GAEV. Right into the pocket! Once upon a time you

and I used both to sleep in this room, and now I'm fifty-one; it does seem strange.

LOPAKHIN. Yes, time does go.

GAEV. Who does?

LOPAKHIN. I said that time does go.

GAEV. It smells of patchouli here.

ANYA. I'm going to bed. Good-night, mother.

[*Kisses her.*

LUBOV. My lovely little one. [*Kisses her hand*] Glad to be at home? I can't get over it.

ANYA. Good-night, uncle.

GAEV. [*Kisses her face and hands*] God be with you. How you do resemble your mother! [*To his sister*] You were just like her at her age, Luba.

> ANYA *gives her hand to* LOPAKHIN *and* PISCHIN *and goes out, shutting the door behind her.*

LUBOV. She's awfully tired.

PISCHIN. It's a very long journey.

VARYA. [*To* LOPAKHIN *and* PISCHIN] Well, sirs, it's getting on for three, quite time you went.

LUBOV. [*Laughs*] You're just the same as ever, Varya. [*Draws her close and kisses her*] I'll have some coffee now, then we'll all go. [FIERS *lays a cushion under her feet*] Thank you, dear. I'm used to coffee. I drink it day and night. Thank you, dear old man.   [*Kisses* FIERS.

VARYA. I'll go and see if they've brought in all the luggage.   [*Exit.*

LUBOV. Is it really I who am sitting here? [*Laughs*] I want to jump about and wave my arms. [*Covers her face with her hands*] But suppose I'm dreaming! God knows I love my own country, I love it deeply; I couldn't look out of the railway carriage, I cried so much. [*Through her tears*] Still, I must have my coffee. Thank you, Fiers.

Thank you, dear old man. I'm so glad you're still with us.

FIERS. The day before yesterday.

GAEV. He doesn't hear well.

LOPAKHIN. I've got to go off to Kharkov by the five o'clock train. I'm awfully sorry! I should like to have a look at you, to gossip a little. You're as fine-looking as ever.

PISCHIN. [*Breathes heavily*] Even finer-looking . . . dressed in Paris fashions . . . confound it all.

LOPAKHIN. Your brother, Leonid Andreyevitch, says I'm a snob, a usurer, but that is absolutely nothing to me. Let him talk. Only I do wish you would believe in me as you once did, that your wonderful, touching eyes would look at me as they did before. Merciful God! My father was the serf of your grandfather and your own father, but you—you more than anybody else—did so much for me once upon a time that I've forgotten everything and love you as if you belonged to my family . . . and even more.

LUBOV. I can't sit still, I'm not in a state to do it. [*Jumps up and walks about in great excitement*] I'll never survive this happiness. . . . You can laugh at me; I'm a silly woman. . . . My dear little cupboard. [*Kisses cupboard*] My little table.

GAEV. Nurse has died in your absence.

LUBOV. [*Sits and drinks coffee*] Yes, bless her soul. I heard by letter.

GAEV. And Anastasius has died too. Peter Kosoy has left me and now lives in town with the Commissioner of Police.

> *Takes a box of sugar-candy out of his pocket and sucks a piece.*

PISCHIN. My daughter, Dashenka, sends her love.

LOPAKHIN. I want to say something very pleasant, very delightful, to you. [*Looks at his watch*] I'm going away at once, I haven't much time . . . but I'll tell you all about it in two or three words. As you already know, your cherry orchard is to be sold to pay your debts, and the sale is fixed for August 22 ; but you needn't be alarmed, dear madam, you may sleep in peace ; there's a way out. Here's my plan. Please attend carefully ! Your estate is only thirteen miles from the town, the railway runs by, and if the cherry orchard and the land by the river are broken up into building lots and are then leased off for villas you'll get at least twenty-five thousand roubles a year profit out of it.

GAEV. How utterly absurd !

LUBOV. I don't understand you at all, Ermolai Alexeye-vitch.

LOPAKHIN. You will get twenty-five roubles a year for each dessiatin from the leaseholders at the very least, and if you advertise now I'm willing to bet that you won't have a vacant plot left by the autumn ; they'll all go. In a word, you're saved. I congratulate you. Only, of course, you'll have to put things straight, and clean up. . . . For instance, you'll have to pull down all the old buildings, this house, which isn't any use to anybody now, and cut down the old cherry orchard. . .

LUBOV. Cut it down ? My dear man, you must excuse me, but you don't understand anything at all. If there's anything interesting or remarkable in the whole province, it's this cherry orchard of ours.

LOPAKHIN. The only remarkable thing about the orchard is that it's very large. It only bears fruit every other year, and even then you don't know what to do with them ; nobody buys any.

R

GAEV. This orchard is mentioned in the " Encyclopædic Dictionary."

LOPAKHIN. [*Looks at his watch*] If we can't think of anything and don't make up our minds to anything, then on August 22 both the cherry orchard and the whole estate will be up for auction. Make up your mind ! I swear there's no other way out, I'll swear it again.

FIERS. In the old days, forty or fifty years back, they dried the cherries, soaked them and pickled them, and made jam of them, and it used to happen that . . .

GAEV. Be quiet, Fiers.

FIERS. And then we'd send the dried cherries off in carts to Moscow and Kharkov. And money ! And the dried cherries were soft, juicy, sweet, and nicely scented. . . They knew the way. . . .

LUBOV. What was the way ?

FIERS. They've forgotten. Nobody remembers.

PISCHIN. [*To* LUBOV ANDREYEVNA] What about Paris ? Eh ? Did you eat frogs ?

LUBOV. I ate crocodiles.

PISCHIN. To think of that, now.

LOPAKHIN. Up to now in the villages there were only the gentry and the labourers, and now the people who live in villas have arrived. All towns now, even small ones, are surrounded by villas. And it's safe to say that in twenty years' time the villa resident will be all over the place. At present he sits on his balcony and drinks tea, but it may well come to pass that he'll begin to cultivate his patch of land, and then your cherry orchard will be happy, rich, splendid. . . .

GAEV. [*Angry*] What rot !

Enter VARYA *and* YASHA.

VARYA. There are two telegrams for you, little mother.

[*Picks out a key and noisily unlocks an antique cupboard*] Here they are.

LUBOV. They're from Paris. . . . [*Tears them up without reading them*] I've done with Paris.

GAEV. And do you know, Luba, how old this case is? A week ago I took out the bottom drawer; I looked and saw figures burnt out in it. That case was made exactly a hundred years ago. What do you think of that? What? We could celebrate its jubilee. It hasn't a soul of its own, but still, say what you will, it's a fine bookcase.

PISCHIN. [*Astonished*] A hundred years. . . . Think of that!

GAEV. Yes . . . it's a real thing. [*Handling it*] My dear and honoured case! I congratulate you on your existence, which has already for more than a hundred years been directed towards the bright ideals of good and justice; your silent call to productive labour has not grown less in the hundred years [*Weeping*] during which you have upheld virtue and faith in a better future to the generations of our race, educating us up to ideals of goodness and to the knowledge of a common consciousness. [*Pause.*

LOPAKHIN. Yes.

LUBOV. You're just the same as ever, Leon.

GAEV. [*A little confused*] Off the white on the right, into the corner pocket. Red ball goes into the middle pocket!

LOPAKHIN. [*Looks at his watch*] It's time I went.

YASHA. [*Giving* LUBOV ANDREYEVNA *her medicine*] Will you take your pills now?

PISCHIN. You oughtn't to take medicines, dear madam; they do you neither harm nor good. . . . Give them here, dear madam. [*Takes the pills, turns them out into the palm of his hand, blows on them, puts them into his mouth, and drinks some kvass*] There!

LUBOV. [*Frightened*] You're off your head!

PISCHIN. I've taken all the pills.

LOPAKHIN. Gormandizer!   [*All laugh.*

FIERS. They were here in Easter week and ate half a pailful of cucumbers. . . .   [*Mumbles.*

LUBOV. What's he driving at?

VARYA. He's been mumbling away for three years. We're used to that.

YASHA. Senile decay.

> CHARLOTTA IVANOVNA *crosses the stage, dressed in white: she is very thin and tightly laced; has a lorgnette at her waist.*

LOPAKHIN. Excuse me, Charlotta Ivanovna, I haven't said "How do you do" to you yet. [*Tries to kiss her hand.*

CHARLOTTA. [*Takes her hand away*] If you let people kiss your hand, then they'll want your elbow, then your shoulder, and then . . .

LOPAKHIN. My luck's out to-day! [*All laugh*] Show us a trick, Charlotta Ivanovna!

LUBOV ANDREYEVNA. Charlotta, do us a trick.

CHARLOTTA. It's not necessary. I want to go to bed.
                                                    [*Exit.*

LOPAKHIN. We shall see each other in three weeks. [*Kisses* LUBOV ANDREYEVNA'S *hand*] Now, good-bye. It's time to go. [*To* GAEV] See you again. [*Kisses* PISCHIN] Au revoir. [*Gives his hand to* VARYA, *then to* FIERS *and to* YASHA] I don't want to go away. [*To* LUBOV ANDREYEVNA]. If you think about the villas and make up your mind, then just let me know, and I'll raise a loan of 50,000 roubles at once. Think about it seriously.

VARYA. [*Angrily*] Do go, now!

LOPAKHIN. I'm going, I'm going. . . .   [*Exit.*

GAEV. Snob. Still, I beg pardon. . . . Varya's going to marry him, he's Varya's young man.

VARYA. Don't talk too much, uncle.

LUBOV. Why not, Varya? I should be very glad. He's a good man.

PISCHIN. To speak the honest truth . . . he's a worthy man. . . . And my Dashenka . . . also says that . . . she says lots of things. [*Snores, but wakes up again at once*] But still, dear madam, if you could lend me . . . 240 roubles . . . to pay the interest on my mortgage to-morrow . . .

VARYA. [*Frightened*] We haven't got it, we haven't got it!

LUBOV. It's quite true. I've nothing at all.

PISCHIN. I'll find it all right [*Laughs*] I never lose hope. I used to think, "Everything's lost now. I'm a dead man," when, lo and behold, a railway was built over my land . . . and they paid me for it. And something else will happen to-day or to-morrow. Dashenka may win 20,000 roubles . . . she's got a ticket.

LUBOV. The coffee's all gone, we can go to bed.

FIERS. [*Brushing* GAEV'S *trousers; in an insistent tone*] You've put on the wrong trousers again. What am I to do with you?

VARYA. [*Quietly*] Anya's asleep. [*Opens window quietly*] The sun has risen already; it isn't cold. Look, little mother: what lovely trees! And the air! The starlings are singing!

GAEV. [*Opens the other window*] The whole garden's white. You haven't forgotten, Luba? There's that long avenue going straight, straight, like a stretched strap; it shines on moonlight nights. Do you remember? You haven't forgotten?

LUBOV. [*Looks out into the garden*] Oh, my childhood, days of my innocence! In this nursery I used to sleep; I used to look out from here into the orchard. Happiness used to wake with me every morning, and then it was just as it is now; nothing has changed. [*Laughs from joy*] It's all, all white! Oh, my orchard! After the dark autumns and the cold winters, you're young again, full of happiness, the angels of heaven haven't left you. . . . If only I could take my heavy burden off my breast and shoulders, if I could forget my past!

GAEV. Yes, and they'll sell this orchard to pay off debts. How strange it seems!

LUBOV. Look, there's my dead mother going in the orchard . . . dressed in white! [*Laughs from joy*] That's she.

GAEV. Where?

VARYA. God bless you, little mother.

LUBOV. There's nobody there; I thought I saw somebody. On the right, at the turning by the summer-house, a white little tree bent down, looking just like a woman. [*Enter* TROFIMOV *in a worn student uniform and spectacles*] What a marvellous garden! White masses of flowers, the blue sky. . . .

TROFIMOV. Lubov Andreyena! [*She looks round at him*] I only want to show myself, and I'll go away. [*Kisses her hand warmly*] I was told to wait till the morning, but I didn't have the patience.

[LUBOV ANDREYEVNA *looks surprised.*

VARYA. [*Crying*] It's Peter Trofimov.

TROFIMOV. Peter Trofimov, once the tutor of your Grisha. . . . Have I changed so much?

LUBOV ANDREYEVNA *embraces him and cries softly.*

GAEV. [*Confused*] That's enough, that's enough, Luba.

VARYA. [*Weeps*] But I told you, Peter, to wait till to-morrow.

LUBOV. My Grisha . . . my boy . . . Grisha . . . my son.

VARYA. What are we to do, little mother? It's the will of God.

TROFIMOV. [*Softly, through his tears*] It's all right, it's all right.

LUBOV. [*Still weeping*] My boy's dead; he was drowned. Why? Why, my friend? [*Softly*] Anya's asleep in there. I am speaking so loudly, making such a noise. . . . Well, Peter? What's made you look so bad? Why have you grown so old?

TROFIMOV. In the train an old woman called me a decayed gentleman.

LUBOV. You were quite a boy then, a nice little student, and now your hair is not at all thick and you wear spectacles. Are you really still a student? [*Goes to the door.*

TROFIMOV. I suppose I shall always be a student.

LUBOV. [*Kisses her brother, then* VARYA] Well, let's go to bed. . . . And you've grown older, Leonid.

PISCHIN. [*Follows her*] Yes, we've got to go to bed. . . . Oh, my gout! I'll stay the night here. If only, Lubov Andreyevna, my dear, you could get me 240 roubles to-morrow morning——

GAEV. Still the same story.

PISCHIN. Two hundred and forty roubles . . . to pay the interest on the mortgage.

LUBOV. I haven't any money, dear man.

PISCHIN. I'll give it back . . . it's a small sum. . . .

LUBOV. Well, then, Leonid will give it to you. . . . Let him have it, Leonid.

GAEV. By all means; hold out your hand.

LUBOV. Why not ? He wants it; he'll give it back.

LUBOV ANDREYEVNA, TROFIMOV, PISCHIN, *and* FIERS
go out. GAEV, VARYA, *and* YASHA *remain.*

GAEV. My sister hasn't lost the habit of throwing money about. [*To* YASHA] Stand off, do ; you smell of poultry.

YASHA. [*Grins*] You are just the same as ever, Leonid Andreyevitch.

GAEV. Really ? [*To* VARYA] What's he saying ?

VARYA. [*To* YASHA] Your mother's come from the village ; she's been sitting in the servants' room since yesterday, and wants to see you. . . .

YASHA. Bless the woman !

VARYA. Shameless man.

YASHA. A lot of use there is in her coming. She might have come to-morrow just as well.   [*Exit.*

VARYA. Mother hasn't altered a scrap, she's just as she always was. She'd give away everything, if the idea only entered her head.

GAEV. Yes. . . . [*Pause*] If there's any illness for which people offer many remedies, you may be sure that particular illness is incurable, I think. I work my brains to their hardest. I've several remedies, very many, and that really means I've none at all. It would be nice to inherit a fortune from somebody, it would be nice to marry our Anya to a rich man, it would be nice to go to Yaroslav and try my luck with my aunt the Countess. My aunt is very, very rich.

VARYA. [*Weeps*] If only God helped us.

GAEV. Don't cry. My aunt's very rich, but she doesn't like us. My sister, in the first place, married an advocate, not a noble. . . . [ANYA *appears in the doorway*] She not only married a man who was not a noble, but she behaved herself in a way which cannot be· described as proper.

She's nice and kind and charming, and I'm very fond of her, but say what you will in her favour and you still have to admit that she's wicked; you can feel it in her slightest movements.

VARYA. [*Whispers*] Anya's in the doorway.

GAEV. Really ? [*Pause*] It's curious, something's got into my right eye . . . I can't see properly out of it. And on Thursday, when I was at the District Court . . .

    Enter ANYA.

VARYA. Why aren't you in bed, Anya ?

ANYA. Can't sleep. It's no good.

GAEV. My darling ! [*Kisses* ANYA'S *face and hands*] My child. . . . [*Crying*] You're not my niece, you're my angel, you're my all. . . . Believe in me, believe. . .

ANYA. I do believe in you, uncle. Everybody loves you and respects you . . . but, uncle dear, you ought to say nothing, no more than that. What were you saying just now about my mother, your own sister ? Why did you say those things ?

GAEV. Yes, yes. [*Covers his face with her hand*] Yes, really, it was awful. Save me, my God ! And only just now I made a speech before a bookcase . . . it's so silly ! And only when I'd finished I knew how silly it was.

VARYA. Yes, uncle dear, you really ought to say less. Keep quiet, that's all.

ANYA. You'd be so much happier in yourself if you only kept quiet.

GAEV. All right, I'll be quiet. [*Kisses their hands*] I'll be quiet. But let's talk business. On Thursday I was in the District Court, and a lot of us met there together, and we began to talk of this, that, and the other, and now I think I can arrange a loan to pay the interest into the bank.

VARYA. If only God would help us!

GAEV. I'll go on Tuesday. I'll talk to you about it again. [*To* VARYA] Don't howl. [*To* ANYA] Your mother will have a talk to Lopakhin; he, of course, won't refuse . . . And when you've rested you'll go to Yaroslav to the Countess, your grandmother. So you see, we'll have three irons in the fire, and we'll be safe. We'll pay up the interest. I'm certain. [*Puts some sugar-candy into his mouth*] I swear on my honour, on anything you will, that the estate will not be sold! [*Excitedly*] I swear on my happiness! Here's my hand. You may call me a dishonourable wretch if I let it go to auction! I swear by all I am!

ANYA. [*She is calm again and happy*] How good and clever you are, uncle. [*Embraces him*] I'm happy now! I'm happy! All's well!

    Enter FIERS.

FIERS. [*Reproachfully*] Leonid Andreyevitch, don't you fear God? When are you going to bed?

GAEV. Soon, soon. You go away, Fiers. I'll undress myself. Well, children, bye-bye . . . ! I'll give you the details to-morrow, but let's go to bed now. [*Kisses* ANYA *and* VARYA] I'm a man of the eighties. . . . People don't praise those years much, but I can still say that I've suffered for my beliefs. The peasants don't love me for nothing, I assure you. We've got to learn to know the peasants! We ought to learn how. . . .

ANYA. You're doing it again, uncle!

VARYA. Be quiet, uncle!

FIERS. [*Angrily*] Leonid Andreyevitch!

GAEV. I'm coming, I'm coming. . . . Go to bed now. Off two cushions into the middle! I turn over a new leaf. . . .   [*Exit.* FIERS *goes out after him.*

ANYA. I'm quieter now. I don't want to go to Yaroslav, I don't like grandmother; but I'm calm now, thanks to uncle.   [*Sits down.*

VARYA. It's time to go to sleep. I'll go. There's been an unpleasantness here while you were away. In the old servants' part of the house, as you know, only the old people live—little old Efim and Polya and Evstigney, and Karp as well. They started letting some tramps or other spend the night there—I said nothing. Then I heard that they were saying that I had ordered them to be fed on peas and nothing else; from meanness, you see. . . . And it was all Evstigney's doing. . . . Very well, I thought, if that's what the matter is, just you wait. So I call Evstigney. . . . [*Yawns*] He comes. "What's this," I say, "Evstigney, you old fool. . . . [*Looks at* ANYA] Anya dear! [*Pause*] She's dropped off. . . . [*Takes* ANYA's *arm*] Let's go to bye-bye. . . . Come along! . . . [*Leads her*] My darling's gone to sleep! Come on. . . . [*They go. In the distance, the other side of the orchard, a shepherd plays his pipe.* TROFIMOV *crosses the stage and stops on seeing* VARYA *and* ANYA] Sh! She's asleep, asleep. Come on, dear.

ANYA. [*Quietly, half-asleep*] I'm so tired . . . all the bells . . . uncle, dear! Mother and uncle!

VARYA. Come on, dear, come on!

[*They go into* ANYA's *room.*

TROFIMOV. [*Moved*] My sun! My spring!

Curtain.

ACT TWO

*In a field. An old, crooked shrine, which has been long
abandoned ; near it a well and large stones, which
apparently are old tombstones, and an old garden seat.
The road is seen to GAEV's estate. On one side rise dark
poplars, behind them begins the cherry orchard. In the
distance is a row of telegraph poles, and far, far away
on the horizon are the indistinct signs of a large town,
which can only be seen on the finest and clearest days.
It is close on sunset. CHARLOTTA, YASHA, and DUN-
YASHA are sitting on the seat ; EPIKHODOV stands by and
plays on a guitar ; all seem thoughtful. CHARLOTTA
wears a man's old peaked cap ; she has unslung a rifle
from her shoulders and is putting to rights the buckle on
the strap.*

CHARLOTTA. [*Thoughtfully*] I haven't a real passport.
I don't know how old I am, and I think I'm young. When
I was a little girl my father and mother used to go round
fairs and give very good performances and I used to do
the *salto mortale* and various little things. And when papa
and mamma died a German lady took me to her and
began to teach me. I liked it. I grew up and became a
governess. And where I came from and who I am, I don't
know. . . . Who my parents were—perhaps they weren't
married—I don't know. [*Takes a cucumber out of her pocket
and eats*] I don't know anything. [*Pause*] I do want to

talk, but I haven't anybody to talk to . . . I haven't anybody at all.

EPIKHODOV. [*Plays on the guitar and sings*]

> " What is this noisy earth to me,
>   What matter friends and foes ? "
> I do like playing on the mandoline !

DUNYASHA. That's a guitar, not a mandoline.

[*Looks at herself in a little mirror and powders herself.*

EPIKHODOV. For the enamoured madman, this is a mandoline. [*Sings*]

> " Oh that the heart was warmed,
>   By all the flames of love returned ! "

YASHA *sings too.*

CHARLOTTA. These people sing terribly. . . . Foo ! Like jackals.

DUNYASHA. [*To* YASHA] Still, it must be nice to live abroad.

YASHA. Yes, certainly. I cannot differ from you there.

[*Yawns and lights a cigar.*

EPIKHODOV. That is perfectly natural. Abroad everything is in full complexity.

YASHA. That goes without saying.

EPIKHODOV. I'm an educated man, I read various remarkable books, but I cannot understand the direction I myself want to go—whether to live or to shoot myself, as it were. So, in case, I always carry a revolver about with me. Here it is.   [*Shows a revolver.*

CHARLOTTA. I've done. Now I'll go. [*Slings the rifle*] You, Epikhodov, are a very clever man and very terrible ; women must be madly in love with you. Brrr ! [*Going*] These wise ones are all so stupid. I've nobody to talk to.

I'm always alone, alone; I've nobody at all . . . and I don't know who I am or why I live. [*Exit slowly.*

EPIKHODOV. As a matter of fact, independently of everything else, I must express my feeling, among other things, that fate has been as pitiless in her dealings with me as a storm is to a small ship. Suppose, let us grant, I am wrong; then why did I wake up this morning, to give an example, and behold an enormous spider on my chest, like that. [*Shows with both hands*] And if I do drink some kvass, why is it that there is bound to be something of the most indelicate nature in it, such as a beetle? [*Pause.* Have you read Buckle? [*Pause*] I should like to trouble you, Avdotya Fedorovna, for two words.

DUNYASHA. Say on.

EPIKHODOV. I should prefer to be alone with you. [*Sighs.*

DUNYASHA. [*Shy*] Very well, only first bring me my little cloak. . . . It's by the cupboard. It's a little damp here.

EPIKHODOV. Very well . . . I'll bring it. . . . Now I know what to do with my revolver.

[*Takes guitar and exit, strumming.*

YASHA. Two-and-twenty troubles! A silly man, between you and me and the gatepost. [*Yawns.*

DUNYASHA. I hope to goodness he won't shoot himself. [*Pause*] I'm so nervous, I'm worried. I went into service when I was quite a little girl, and now I'm not used to common life, and my hands are white, white as a lady's. I'm so tender and so delicate now, respectable and afraid of everything. . . . I'm so frightened. And I don't know what will happen to my nerves if you deceive me, Yasha.

YASHA. [*Kisses her*] Little cucumber! Of course, every girl must respect herself; there's nothing I dislike more than a badly behaved girl.

DUNYASHA. I'm awfully in love with you; you're educated, you can talk about everything. [*Pause.*

YASHA. [*Yawns*] Yes. I think this: if a girl loves anybody, then that means she's immoral. [*Pause*] It's nice to smoke a cigar out in the open air. . . . [*Listens*] Somebody's coming. It's the mistress, and people with her. [DUNYASHA *embraces him suddenly*] Go to the house, as if you'd been bathing in the river; go by this path, or they'll meet you and will think I've been meeting you. I can't stand that sort of thing.

DUNYASHA. [*Coughs quietly*] My head's aching because of your cigar.

Exit. YASHA *remains, sitting by the shrine. Enter* LUBOV ANDREYEVNA, GAEV, *and* LOPAKHIN.

LOPAKHIN. You must make up your mind definitely—there's no time to waste. The question is perfectly plain. Are you willing to let the land for villas or no? Just one word, yes or no? Just one word!

LUBOV. Who's smoking horrible cigars here? [*Sits.*

GAEV. They built that railway; that's made this place very handy. [*Sits*] Went to town and had lunch . . . red in the middle! I'd like to go in now and have just one game.

LUBOV. You'll have time.

LOPAKHIN. Just one word! [*Imploringly*] Give me an answer!

GAEV. [*Yawns*] Really!

LUBOV. [*Looks in her purse*] I had a lot of money yesterday, but there's very little to-day. My poor Varya feeds everybody on milk soup to save money, in the kitchen the old people only get peas, and I spend recklessly. [*Drops the purse, scattering gold coins*] There, they are all over the place.

YASHA. Permit me to pick them up.

[*Collects the coins.*

LUBOV. Please do, Yasha. And why did I go and have lunch there ? . . . A horrid restaurant with band and tablecloths smelling of soap. . . . Why do you drink so much, Leon ? Why do you eat so much ? Why do you talk so much ? You talked again too much to-day in the restaurant, and it wasn't at all to the point—about the seventies and about decadents. And to whom ? Talking to the waiters about decadents !

LOPAKHIN. Yes.

GAEV. [*Waves his hand*] I can't be cured, that's obvious. . . . [*Irritably to* YASHA] What's the matter ? Why do you keep twisting about in front of me ?

YASHA. [*Laughs*] I can't listen to your voice without laughing.

GAEV. [*To his sister*] Either he or I . . .

LUBOV. Go away, Yasha ; get out of this. . . .

YASHA. [*Gives purse to* LUBOV ANDREYEVNA] I'll go at once. [*Hardly able to keep from laughing*] This minute. . . .

[*Exit.*

LOPAKHIN. That rich man Deriganov is preparing to buy your estate. They say he'll come to the sale himself.

LUBOV. Where did you hear that ?

LOPAKHIN. They say so in town.

GAEV. Our Yaroslav aunt has promised to send something, but I don't know when or how much.

LOPAKHIN. How much will she send ? A hundred thousand roubles ? Or two, perhaps ?

LUBOV. I'd be glad of ten or fifteen thousand.

LOPAKHIN. You must excuse my saying so, but I've never met such frivolous people as you before, or anybody so unbusinesslike and peculiar. Here I am telling you in plain language that your estate will be sold, and you don't seem to understand.

LUBOV. What are we to do ? Tell us, what ?

LOPAKHIN. I tell you every day. I say the same thing every day. Both the cherry orchard and the land must be leased off for villas and at once, immediately—the auction is staring you in the face : Understand ! Once you do definitely make up your minds to the villas, then you'll have as much money as you want and you'll be saved.

LUBOV. Villas and villa residents—it's so vulgar, excuse me.

GAEV. I entirely agree with you.

LOPAKHIN. I must cry or yell or faint. I can't ! You're too much for me ! [*To* GAEV] You old woman !

GAEV. Really !

LOPAKHIN. Old woman !   [*Going out.*

LUBOV. [*Frightened*] No, don't go away, do stop; be a dear. Please. Perhaps we'll find some way out !

LOPAKHIN. What's the good of trying to think !

LUBOV. Please don't go away. It's nicer when you're here. . . . [*Pause*] I keep on waiting for something to happen, as if the house is going to collapse over our heads.

GAEV. [*Thinking deeply*] Double in the corner . . . across the middle. . . .

LUBOV. We have been too sinful. . . .

LOPAKHIN. What sins have you committed ?

GAEV. [*Puts candy into his mouth*] They say that I've eaten all my substance in sugar-candies.   [*Laughs.*

LUBOV. Oh, my sins. . . . I've always scattered money about without holding myself in, like a madwoman, and I married a man who made nothing but debts. My husband died of champagne—he drank terribly—and to my misfortune, I fell in love with another man and went off

                                                            S

with him, and just at that time—it was my first punishment,
a blow that hit me right on the head—here, in the river
. . . my boy was drowned, and I went away, quite away,
never to return, never to see this river again. . . . I shut
my eyes and ran without thinking, but *he* ran after me . . .
without pity, without respect. I bought a villa near
Mentone because *he* fell ill there, and for three days I
knew no rest either by day or night ; the sick man wore
me out, and my soul dried up. And last year, when they
had sold the villa to pay my debts, I went away to Paris,
and there he robbed me of all I had and threw me over and
went off with another woman. I tried to poison myself.
. . . It was so silly, so shameful. . . . And suddenly I
longed to be back in Russia, my own land, with my little
girl. . . . [*Wipes her tears*] Lord, Lord be merciful to me,
forgive me my sins ! Punish me no more ! [*Takes a telegram
out of her pocket*] I had this to-day from Paris. . . . He begs
my forgiveness, he implores me to return. . . . [*Tears it
up*] Don't I hear music ?   [*Listens.*

GAEV. That is our celebrated Jewish band. You
remember—four violins, a flute, and a double-bass.

LUBOV. So it still exists ? It would be nice if they came
along some evening.

LOPAKHIN. [*Listens*] I can't hear. . . . [*Sings quietly*]
" For money will the Germans make a Frenchman of a
Russian." [*Laughs*] I saw such an awfully funny thing at
the theatre last night.

LUBOV. I'm quite sure there wasn't anything at all funny.
You oughtn't to go and see plays, you ought to go and
look at yourself. What a grey life you lead, what a lot
you talk unnecessarily.

LOPAKHIN. It's true. To speak the straight truth, we
live a silly life. [*Pause*] My father was a peasant, an idiot,

he understood nothing, he didn't teach me, he was always drunk, and always used a stick on me. In point of fact, I'm a fool and an idiot too. I've never learned anything, my handwriting is bad, I write so that I'm quite ashamed before people, like a pig!

LUBOV. You ought to get married, my friend.

LOPAKHIN. Yes . . . that's true.

LUBOV. Why not to our Varya? She's a nice girl.

LOPAKHIN. Yes.

LUBOV. She's quite homely in her ways, works all day, and, what matters most, she's in love with you. And you've liked her for a long time.

LOPAKHIN. Well? I don't mind . . . she's a nice girl.

[*Pause.*

GAEV. I'm offered a place in a bank. Six thousand roubles a year. . . . Did you hear?

LUBOV. What's the matter with you! Stay where you are. . . .

Enter FIERS *with an overcoat.*

FIERS. [*To* GAEV] Please, sir, put this on, it's damp.

GAEV. [*Putting it on*] You're a nuisance, old man.

FIERS. It's all very well. . . . You went away this morning without telling me.   [*Examining* GAEV.

LUBOV. How old you've grown, Fiers!

FIERS. I beg your pardon?

LOPAKHIN. She says you've grown very old!

FIERS. I've been alive a long time. They were already getting ready to marry me before your father was born. . . . [*Laughs*] And when the Emancipation came I was already first valet. Only I didn't agree with the Emancipation and remained with my people. . . . [*Pause*] I remember everybody was happy, but they didn't know why.

LOPAKHIN. It was very good for them in the old days. At any rate, they used to beat them.

FIERS. [*Not hearing*] Rather. The peasants kept their distance from the masters and the masters kept their distance from the peasants, but now everything's all anyhow and you can't understand anything.

GAEV. Be quiet, Fiers. I've got to go to town to-morrow. I've been promised an introduction to a General who may lend me money on a bill.

LOPAKHIN. Nothing will come of it. And you won't pay your interest, don't you worry.

LUBOV. He's talking rubbish. There's no General at all.

Enter TROFIMOV, ANYA, *and* VARYA.

GAEV. Here they are.

ANYA. Mother's sitting down here.

LUBOV. [*Tenderly*] Come, come, my dears. . . . [*Embracing* ANYA *and* VARYA] If you two only knew how much I love you. Sit down next to me, like that. [*All sit down.*

LOPAKHIN. Our eternal student is always with the ladies.

TROFIMOV. That's not your business.

LOPAKHIN. He'll soon be fifty, and he's still a student.

TROFIMOV. Leave off your silly jokes !

LOPAKHIN. Getting angry, eh, silly ?

TROFIMOV. Shut up, can't you.

LOPAKHIN. [*Laughs*] I wonder what you think of me ?

TROFIMOV. I think, Ermolai Alexeyevitch, that you're a rich man, and you'll soon be a millionaire. Just as the wild beast which eats everything it finds is needed for changes to take place in matter, so you are needed too.

[*All laugh.*

VARYA. Better tell us something about the planets, Peter.

LUBOV ANDREYEVNA. No, let's go on with yesterday's talk!

TROFIMOV. About what ?

GAEV. About the proud man.

TROFIMOV. Yesterday we talked for a long time but we didn't come to anything in the end. There's something mystical about the proud man, in your sense. Perhaps you are right from your point of view, but if you take the matter simply, without complicating it, then what pride can there be, what sense can there be in it, if a man is imperfectly made, physiologically speaking, if in the vast majority of cases he is coarse and stupid and deeply unhappy? We must stop admiring one another. We must work, nothing more.

GAEV. You'll die, all the same.

TROFIMOV. Who knows? And what does it mean— you'll die? Perhaps a man has a hundred senses, and when he dies only the five known to us are destroyed and the remaining ninety-five are left alive.

LUBOV. How clever of you, Peter!

LOPAKHIN. [*Ironically*] Oh, awfully!

TROFIMOV. The human race progresses, perfecting its powers. Everything that is unattainable now will some day be near at hand and comprehensible, but we must work, we must help with all our strength those who seek to know what fate will bring. Meanwhile in Russia only a very few of us work. The vast majority of those intellectuals whom I know seek for nothing, do nothing, and are at present incapable of hard work. They call themselves intellectuals, but they use " thou " and " thee " to their servants, they treat the peasants like animals, they learn badly, they read nothing seriously, they do absolutely nothing, about science they only talk, about art they understand little. They are all serious, they all have severe faces, they all talk about important things. They philosophize, and at the same time, the vast majority of us, ninety-nine out of a hundred, live like savages, fighting and cursing at the slightest opportunity, eating filthily, sleeping in the dirt, in stuffiness, with fleas, stinks, smells, moral filth, and so on. . . . And it's obvious that all our nice talk is only carried on to distract ourselves and others. Tell me, where are those créches we hear so much of ? and where are those reading-rooms ? People only write novels about them ; they don't really exist. Only dirt, vulgarity, and Asiatic plagues really exist. . . . I'm afraid, and I don't at all like serious faces ; I don't like serious conversations. Let's be quiet sooner.

LOPAKHIN. You know, I get up at five every morning, I work from morning till evening, I am always dealing with money—my own and other people's—and I see what people are like. You've only got to begin to do anything to find out how few honest, honourable people there are. Sometimes, when I can't sleep, I think : " Oh Lord, you've given us huge forests, infinite fields, and endless horizons, and we, living here, ought really to be giants."

LUBOV. You want giants, do you ? . . . They're only good in stories, and even there they frighten one.

EPIKHODOV *enters at the back of the stage playing his guitar. Thoughtfully :* Epikhodov's there.

ANYA. [*Thoughtfully*] Epikhodov's there.

GAEV. The sun's set.

TROFIMOV. Yes.

GAEV. [*Not loudly, as if declaiming*] O Nature, thou art wonderful, thou shinest with eternal radiance ! Oh, beautiful and indifferent one, thou whom we call mother, thou containest in thyself existence and death, thou livest and destroyest. . . .

VARYA. [*Entreatingly*] Uncle, dear !

ANYA. Uncle, you're doing it again !

TROFIMOV. You'd better double the red into the middle·

GAEV. I'll be quiet, I'll be quiet.

> *They all sit thoughtfully. It is quiet. Only the mumbling of* FIERS *is heard. Suddenly a distant sound is heard as if from the sky, the sound of a breaking string, which dies away sadly.*

LUBOV. What's that ?

LOPAKHIN. I don't know. It may be a bucket fallen down a well somewhere. But it's some way off.

GAEV. Or perhaps it's some bird . . . like a heron.

TROFIMOV. Or an owl.

LUBOV. [*Shudders*] It's unpleasant, somehow.   [*A pause.*

FIERS. Before the misfortune the same thing happened. An owl screamed and the samovar hummed without stopping.

GAEV. Before what misfortune ?

FIERS. Before the Emancipation.   [*A pause.*

LUBOV. You know, my friends, let's go in ; it's evening now. [*To* ANYA] You've tears in your eyes. . . . What is it, little girl ?   [*Embraces her.*

ANYA. It's nothing, mother.

TROFIMOV. Some one's coming.

> *Enter a* TRAMP *in an old white peaked cap and overcoat. He is a little drunk.*

TRAMP. Excuse me, may I go this way straight through to the station ?

GAEV. You may. Go along this path.

TRAMP. I thank you from the bottom of my heart. [*Hiccups*] Lovely weather. . . . [*Declaims*] My brother, my suffering brother. . . . Come out on the Volga, you whose groans . . . [*To* VARYA] Mademoiselle, please give a hungry Russian thirty copecks. . . .

> VARYA *screams, frightened.*

LOPAKHIN. [*Angrily*] There's manners everybody's got to keep!

LUBOV. [*With a start*] Take this . . . here you are. . . . [*Feels in her purse*] There's no silver. . . . It doesn't matter, here's gold.

TRAMP. I am deeply grateful to you! [*Exit. Laughter.*

VARYA. [*Frightened*] I'm going, I'm going. . . . Oh, little mother, at home there's nothing for the servants to eat, and you gave him gold.

LUBOV. What is to be done with such a fool as I am! At home I'll give you everything I've got. Ermolai Alexeyevitch, lend me some more ! . . .

LOPAKHIN. Very well.

LUBOV. Let's go, it's time. And Varya, we've settled your affair; I congratulate you.

VARYA. [*Crying*] You shouldn't joke about this, mother.

LOPAKHIN. Oh, feel me, get thee to a nunnery.

GAEV. My hands are all trembling; I haven't played billiards for a long time.

LOPAKHIN. Oh, feel me, nymph, remember me in thine orisons.

LUBOV. Come along; it'll soon be supper-time.

VARYA. He did frighten me. My heart is beating hard.

LOPAKHIN. Let me remind you, ladies and gentlemen, on August 22 the cherry orchard will be sold. Think of that! . . . Think of that! . . .

All go out except TROFIMOV *and* ANYA.

ANYA. [*Laughs*] Thanks to the tramp who frightened Barbara, we're alone now.

TROFIMOV. Varya's afraid we may fall in love with each other and won't get away from us for days on end. Her narrow mind won't allow her to understand that we are above love. To escape all the petty and deceptive things which prevent our being happy and free, that is the aim and meaning of our lives. Forward ! We go irresistibly on to that bright star which burns there, in the distance ! Don't lag behind, friends !

ANYA. [*Clapping her hands*] How beautifully you talk ! [*Pause*] It is glorious here to-day !

TROFIMOV. Yes, the weather is wonderful.

ANYA. What have you done to me, Peter ? I don't love the cherry orchard as I used to. I loved it so tenderly, I thought there was no better place in the world than our orchard.

TROFIMOV. All Russia is our orchard. The land is great and beautiful, there are many marvellous places in it. [*Pause*] Think, Anya, your grandfather, your great-grandfather, and all your ancestors were serf-owners, they owned living souls ; and now, doesn't something human look at you from every cherry in the orchard, every leaf and every stalk ? Don't you hear voices . . . ? Oh, it's awful, your orchard is terrible ; and when in the evening or at night you walk through the orchard, then the old bark on the trees sheds a dim light and the old cherry-trees seem to be dreaming of all that was a hundred, two hundred years ago, and are oppressed by their heavy visions. Still, at any rate, we've left those two hundred years behind us. So far we've gained nothing at all—we don't yet know what the past is to be to us—we only philosophize, we complain that we are dull, or we drink vodka. For it's so clear that in order to begin to live in the present we must first redeem the past, and that can only be done by suffering, by strenuous, uninterrupted labour. Understand that, Anya.

ANYA. The house in which we live has long ceased to be our house ; I shall go away. I give you my word.

TROFIMOV. If you have the housekeeping keys, throw them down the well and go away. Be as free as the wind.

ANYA. [*Enthusiastically*] How nicely you said that!

TROFIMOV. Believe me, Anya, believe me! I'm not thirty yet, I'm young, I'm still a student, but I have undergone a great deal! I'm as hungry as the winter, I'm ill, I'm shaken. I'm as poor as a beggar, and where haven't I been—fate has tossed me everywhere! But my soul is always my own; every minute of the day and the night it is filled with unspeakable presentiments. I know that happiness is coming, Anya, I see it already. . .

ANYA. [*Thoughtful*] The moon is rising.

> EPIKHODOV *is heard playing the same sad song on his guitar. The moon rises. Somewhere by the poplars* VARYA *is looking for* ANYA *and calling, "Anya, where are you?"*

TROFIMOV. Yes, the moon has risen. [*Pause*] There is happiness, there it comes; it comes nearer and nearer; I hear its steps already. And if we do not see it we shall not know it, but what does that matter? Others will see it!

THE VOICE OF VARYA. Anya! Where are you?

TROFIMOV. That's Varya again! [*Angry*] Disgraceful!

ANYA. Never mind. Let's go to the river. It's nice there.

TROFIMOV. Let's go.   [*They go out.*

THE VOICE OF VARYA. Anya! Anya!

Curtain.

ACT THREE

*A reception-room cut off from a drawing-room by an arch.
Chandelier lighted.   A Jewish band, the one mentioned in
Act II, is heard playing in another room.   Evening.   In
the drawing-room the grand rond is being danced.   Voice
of* SIMEONOV PISCHIN   *"Promenade à une paire!"
Dancers come into the reception-room ; the first pair are*
PISCHIN *and* CHARLOTTA IVANOVNA ;   *the second,* TRO-
FIMOV *and* LUBOV ANDREYEVNA ;   *the third,* ANYA *and
the* POST OFFICE CLERK ;   *the fourth,* VARYA *and the*
STATION-MASTER, *and so on.*   VARYA *is crying gently
and wipes away her tears as she dances.*   DUNYASHA *is
in the last pair.   They go off into the drawing-room,*
PISCHIN *shouting, " Grand rond, balancez : " and " Les
cavaliers à genou et remerciez vos dames!"*   FIERS, *in
a dress-coat, carries a tray with seltzer-water across.
Enter* PISCHIN *and* TROFIMOV *from the drawing-room.*

PISCHIN. I'm full-blooded and have already had two
strokes ; it's hard for me to dance, but, as they say, if you're
in Rome, you must do as Rome does.   I've got the strength
of a horse.   My dead father, who liked a joke, peace to his
bones, used to say, talking of our ancestors, that the ancient
stock of the Simeonov-Pischins was descended from that
identical horse that Caligula made a senator. . . . [*Sits*]
But the trouble is, I've no money ! A hungry dog only
believes in meat. [*Snores and wakes up again immediately*]
So I . . . only believe in money. . . .

TROFIMOV. Yes. There is something equine about your figure.

PISCHIN. Well . . . a horse is a fine animal . . . you can sell a horse.

Billiard playing can be heard in the next room. VARYA *appears under the arch.*

TROFIMOV. [*Teasing*] Madame Lopakhin ! Madame Lopakhin !

VARYA. [*Angry*] Decayed gentleman !

TROFIMOV. Yes, I am a decayed gentleman, and I'm proud of it !

VARYA. [*Bitterly*] We've hired the musicians, but how are they to be paid ?   [*Exit.*

TROFIMOV. If the energy which you, in the course of your life, have spent in looking for money to pay interest had been used for something else, then, I believe, after all, you'd be able to turn everything upside down.

PISCHIN. Nietzsche . . . a philosopher . . . a very great, a most celebrated man . . . a man of enormous brain, says in his books that you can forge bank-notes.

TROFIMOV. And have you read Nietzsche ?

PISCHIN. Well . . . Dashenka told me. Now I'm in such a position, I wouldn't mind forging them . . . I've got to pay 310 roubles the day after to-morrow . . . I've got 130 already. . . . [*Feels his pockets, nervously*] I've lost the money ! The money's gone ! [*Crying*] Where's the money ? [*Joyfully*] Here it is behind the lining . . . I even began to perspire.

Enter LUBOV ANDREYEVNA *and* CHARLOTTA IVANOVNA.

LUBOV. [*Humming a Caucasian dance*] Why is Leonid away so long ? What's he doing in town ? [*To* DUNYASHA] Dunyasha, give the musicians some tea.

TROFIMOV. Business is off, I suppose.

LUBOV. And the musicians needn't have come, and we needn't have got up this ball. . . . Well, never mind. . . .

[*Sits and sings softly.*

CHARLOTTA. [*Gives a pack of cards to* PISCHIN] Here's a pack of cards, think of any one card you like.

PISCHIN. I've thought of one.

CHARLOTTA. Now shuffle. All right, now. Give them here, oh my dear Mr. Pischin. *Ein, zwei, drei!* Now look and you'll find it in your coat-tail pocket.

PISCHIN. [*Takes a card out of his coat-tail pocket*] Eight of spades, quite right! [*Surprised*] Think of that now!

CHARLOTTA. [*Holds the pack of cards on the palm of her hand. To* TROFIMOV] Now tell me quickly. What's the top card?

TROFIMOV. Well, the queen of spades.

CHARLOTTA. Right! [*To* PISCHIN] Well now? What card's on top?

PISCHIN. Ace of hearts.

CHARLOTTA. Right! [*Claps her hands, the pack of cards vanishes*] How lovely the weather is to-day. [*A mysterious woman's voice answers her, as if from under the floor,* "Oh yes, it's lovely weather, madam."] You are so beautiful, you are my ideal. [*Voice,* " You, madam, please me very much too."]

STATION-MASTER. [*Applauds*] Madame ventriloquist, bravo!

PISCHIN' [*Surprised*] Think of that, now! Delightful, Charlotta Ivanovna . . . I'm simply in love. . . .

CHARLOTTA. In love? [*Shrugging her shoulders*] Can you love? *Guter Mensch aber schlechter Musikant.*

TROFIMOV. [*Slaps* PISCHIN *on the shoulder*] Oh, you horse!

CHARLOTTA. Attention please, here's another trick. *Takes a shawl from a chair*] Here's a very nice plaid shawl,

I'm going to sell it. . . . [*Shakes it*] Won't anybody buy it ?

PISCHIN. [*Astonished*] Think of that now !

CHARLOTTA. *Ein, zwei, drei.*

> *She quickly lifts up the shawl, which is hanging down.* ANYA *is standing behind it ; she bows and runs to her mother, hugs her and runs back to the drawing-room amid general applause.*

LUBOV. [*Applauds*] Bravo, bravo !

CHARLOTTA. Once again ! *Ein, zwei, drei !*

> [*Lifts the shawl.* VARYA *stands behind it and bows.*

PISCHIN. [*Astonished*] Think of that, now.

CHARLOTTA. The end !

> *Throws the shawl at* PISCHIN, *curtseys and runs into the drawing-room.*

PISCHIN. [*Runs after her*] Little wretch. . . . What ? Would you ?   [*Exit.*

LUBOV. Leonid hasn't come yet. I don't understand what he's doing so long in town ! Everything must be over by now. The estate must be sold ; or, if the sale never came off, then why does he stay so long ?

VARYA. [*Tries to soothe her*] Uncle has bought it. I'm certain of it.

TROFIMOV. [*Sarcastically*] Oh, yes !

VARYA. Grandmother sent him her authority for him to buy it in her name and transfer the debt to her. She's doing it for Anya. And I'm certain that God will help us and uncle will buy it.

LUBOV. Grandmother sent fifteen thousand roubles from Yaroslav to buy the property in her name—she won't trust us—and that wasn't even enough to pay the interest. [*Covers her face with her hands*] My fate will be settled to-day, my fate. . . .

TROFIMOV. [*Teasing* VARYA] Madame Lopakhin !

VARYA. [*Angry*] Eternal student! He's already been expelled twice from the university.

LUBOV. Why are you getting angry, Varya? He's teasing you about Lopakhin, well what of it? You can marry Lopakhin if you want to, he's a good, interesting man. . . . You needn't if you don't want to; nobody wants to force you against your will, my darling.

VARYA. I do look at the matter seriously, little mother, to be quite frank. He's a good man, and I like him.

LUBOV. Then marry him. I don't understand what you're waiting for.

VARYA. I can't propose to him myself, little mother. People have been talking about him to me for two years now, but he either says nothing, or jokes about it. I understand. He's getting rich, he's busy, he can't bother about me. If I had some money, even a little, even only a hundred roubles, I'd throw up everything and go away. I'd go into a convent.

TROFIMOV. How nice!

VARYA. [*To* TROFIMOV] A student ought to have sense! [*Gently, in tears*] How ugly you are now, Peter, how old you've grown! [*To* LUBOV ANDREYEVNA, *no longer crying*] But I can't go on without working, little mother. I want to be doing something every minute.   [*Enter* YASHA.

YASHA. [*Nearly laughing*] Epikhodov's broken a billiard cue!   [*Exit.*

VARYA. Why is Epikhodov here? Who said he could play billiards? I don't understand these people. [*Exit.*

LUBOV. Don't tease her, Peter, you see that she's quite unhappy without that.

TROFIMOV. She takes too much on herself, she keeps on interfering in other people's business. The whole summer she's given no peace to me or to Anya, she's afraid we'll have a romance all to ourselves. What has it to do with her? As if I'd ever given her grounds to believe I'd stoop to such vulgarity! We are above love.

LUBOV. Then I suppose I must be beneath love. [*In agitation*] Why isn't Leonid here? If I only knew whether the estate is sold or not! The disaster seems to me so improbable that I don't know what to think, I'm all at sea . . . I may scream . . . or do something silly. Save me, Peter. Say something, say something.

TROFIMOV. Isn't it all the same whether the estate is sold to-day or isn't? It's been all up with it for a long time; there's no turning back, the path's grown over. Be calm, dear, you shouldn't deceive yourself; for once in your life at any rate you must look the truth straight in the face.

LUBOV. What truth? You see where truth is, and where untruth is, but I seem to have lost my sight and see nothing. You boldly settle all important questions, but tell me, dear, isn't it because you're young, because you haven't had time to suffer till you settled a single one of your questions? You boldly look forward, isn't it because you cannot foresee or expect anything terrible, because so far life has been hidden from your young eyes? You are bolder, more honest, deeper than we are, but think only, be just a little magnanimous, and have mercy on me. I was born here, my father and mother lived here, my grandfather too, I love this house. I couldn't understand my life without that cherry orchard, and if it really must be sold, sell me with it! [*Embraces* TROFIMOV, *kisses his forehead*]. My son was drowned here. . . . [*Weeps*] Have pity on me, good, kind man.

TROFIMOV. You know I sympathize with all my soul.

LUBOV. Yes, but it ought to be said differently, differently. . . . [*Takes another handkerchief, a telegram falls on the floor*] I'm so sick at heart to-day, you can't imagine. Here it's so noisy, my soul shakes at every sound. I shake all over, and I can't go away by myself, I'm afraid of the silence. Don't judge me harshly, Peter . . . I loved you, as if you belonged to my family. I'd gladly let Anya marry you, I swear it, only dear, you ought to work, finish your studies. You don't do anything, only fate throws you about from place to place, it's so odd. . . . Isn't it true? Yes? And you ought to do something to your beard to make it grow better. [*Laughs*] You are funny!

TROFIMOV. [*Picking up telegram*] I don't want to be a Beau Brummel.

LUBOV. This telegram's from Paris. I get one every day. Yesterday and to-day. That wild man is ill again, he's bad again. . . . He begs for forgiveness, and implores me to come, and I really ought to go to Paris to be near him. You look severe, Peter, but what can I do, my dear, what can I do; he's ill, he's alone, unhappy, and who's to look after him, who's to keep him away from his errors, to give him his medicine punctually? And why should I conceal it and say nothing about it; I love him, that's plain, I love him, I love him. . . . That love is a stone round my neck; I'm going with it to the bottom, but I love that stone and can't live without it. [*Squeezes* TROFIMOV'S *hand*] Don't think hardly of me, Peter, don't say anything to me, don't say . . .

TROFIMOV. [*Weeping*] For God's sake forgive my speaking candidly, but that man has robbed you!

LUBOV. No, no, no, you oughtn't to say that!

[*Stops her ears.*

TROFIMOV. But he's a wretch, you alone don't know it! He's a petty thief, a nobody. . . .

T

LUBOV. [*Angry, but restrained*] You're twenty-six or twenty-seven, and still a schoolboy of the second class !

TROFIMOV. Why not !

LUBOV. You ought to be a man, at your age you ought to be able to understand those who love. And you ought to be in love yourself, you must fall in love ! [*Angry*] Yes, yes ! You aren't pure, you're just a freak, a queer fellow, a funny growth. . . .

TROFIMOV. [*In horror*] What is she saying !

LUBOV. " I'm above love ! " You're not above love, you're just what our Fiers calls a bungler. Not to have a mistress at your age !

TROFIMOV. [*In horror*] This is awful ! What is she saying ? [*Goes quickly up into the drawing-room, clutching his head*] It's awful . . . I can't stand it, I'll go away. [*Exit, but returns at once*] All is over between us !   [*Exit.*

LUBOV. [*Shouts after him*] Peter, wait ! Silly man, I was joking ! Peter ! [*Somebody is heard going out and falling downstairs noisily.* ANYA *and* VARYA *scream ; laughter is heard immediately*] What's that ?

  ANYA *comes running in, laughing.*

ANYA. Peter's fallen downstairs !   [*Runs out again.*

LUBOV. This Peter's a marvel.

  The STATION-MASTER *stands in the middle of the drawing-room and recites " The Magdalen " by Tolstoy. He is listened to, but he has only delivered a few lines when a waltz is heard from the front room, and the recitation is stopped. Everybody dances.* TROFIMOV, ANYA, VARYA, *and* LUBOV ANDREYEVNA *come in from the front room.*

LUBOV. Well, Peter . . . you pure soul . . . I beg your pardon . . . let's dance.

  She dances with PETER. ANYA *and* VARYA *dance.*

ACT THREE

FIERS *enters and stands his stick by a side door.*
YASHA *has also come in and looks on at the dance.*

YASHA. Well, grandfather?

FIERS. I'm not well. At our balls some time back, generals and barons and admirals used to dance, and now we send for post-office clerks and the Station-master, and even they come as a favour. I'm very weak. The dead master, the grandfather, used to give everybody sealing-wax when anything was wrong. I've taken sealing-wax every day for twenty years, and more; perhaps that's why I still live.

YASHA. I'm tired of you, grandfather. [*Yawns*] If you'd only hurry up and kick the bucket.

FIERS. Oh you . . . bungler!   [*Mutters.*

TROFIMOV *and* LUBOV ANDREYEVNA *dance in the reception-room, then into the sitting-room.*

LUBOV. *Merçi.* I'll sit down. [*Sits*] I'm tired.
Enter ANYA.

ANYA. [*Excited*] Somebody in the kitchen was saying just now that the cherry orchard was sold to-day.

LUBOV. Sold to whom.

ANYA. He didn't say to whom. He's gone mad.

[*Dances out into the reception-room with* TROFIMOV.

YASHA. Some old man was chattering about it a long time ago. A stranger!

FIERS. And Leonid Andreyevitch isn't here yet, he hasn't come. He's wearing a light, *demi-saison* overcoat. He'll catch cold. Oh these young fellows.

LUBOV. I'll die of this. Go and find out, Yasha, to whom it's sold.

YASHA. Oh, but he's been gone a long time, the old man.   [*Laughs.*

LUBOV. [*Slightly vexed*] Why do you laugh ? What are you glad about ?

YASHA. Epikhodov's too funny. He's a silly man. Two-and-twenty troubles.

LUBOV. Fiers, if the estate is sold, where will you go ?

FIERS. I'll go wherever you order me to go.

LUBOV. Why do you look like that ? Are you ill ? I think you ought to go to bed. . . .

FIERS. Yes . . . [*With a smile*] I'll go to bed, and who'll hand things round and give orders without me ? I've the whole house on my shoulders.

YASHA. [*To* LUBOV ANDREYEVNA] Lubov Andreyevna ! I want to ask a favour of you, if you'll be so kind ! If you go to Paris again, then please take me with you. It's absolutely impossible for me to stop here. [*Looking round ; in an undertone*] What's the good of talking about it, you see for yourself that this is an uneducated country, with an immoral population, and it's so dull. The food in the kitchen is beastly, and here's this Fiers walking about mumbling various inappropriate things. Take me with you, be so kind !

Enter PISCHIN.

PISCHIN. I come to ask for the pleasure of a little waltz, dear lady. . . . [LUBOV ANDREYEVNA *goes to him*] But all the same, you wonderful woman, I must have 180 little roubles from you. . . . I must. . . . [*They dance*] 180 little roubles. . . . [*They go through into the drawing-room.*

YASHA. [*Sings softly*]

" Oh, will you understand
        My soul's deep restlessness ? "

In the drawing-room a figure in a grey top-hat and in baggy check trousers is waving its hands and jumping about ; there are cries of "Bravo, Charlotta Ivanovna !"

DUNYASHA. [*Stops to powder her face*] The young mistress tells me to dance—there are a lot of gentlemen, but few ladies—and my head goes round when I dance, and my heart beats, Fiers Nicolaevitch ; the Post-office clerk told me something just now which made me catch my breath.

[*The music grows faint.*

FIERS. What did he say to you ?

DUNYASHA. He says, " You're like a little flower."

YASHA. [*Yawns*] Impolite. . . . [*Exit.*

DUNYASHA. Like a little flower. I'm such a delicate girl ; I simply love words of tenderness.

FIERS. You'll lose your head.

Enter EPIKHODOV.

EPIKHODOV. You, Avdotya Fedorovna, want to see me no more than if I was some insect. [*Sighs*] Oh, life !

DUNYASHA. What do you want ?

EPIKHODOV. Undoubtedly, perhaps, you may be right. [*Sighs*] But, certainly, if you regard the matter from the aspect, then you, if I may say so, and you must excuse my candidness, have absolutely reduced me to a state of mind. I know my fate, every day something unfortunate happens to me, and I've grown used to it a long time ago, I even look at my fate with a smile. You gave me your word, and though I . . .

DUNYASHA. Please, we'll talk later on, but leave me alone now. I'm meditating now. [*Plays with her fan.*

EPIKHODOV. Every day something unfortunate happens to me, and I, if I may so express myself, only smile, and even laugh.

VARYA *enters from the drawing-room.*

VARYA. Haven't you gone yet, Simeon ? You really

have no respect for anybody. [*To* DUNYASHA] You go away, Dunyasha. [*To* EPIKHODOV] You play billiards and break a cue, and walk about the drawing-room as if you were a visitor!

EPIKHODOV. You cannot, if I may say so, call me to order.

VARYA. I'm not calling you to order, I'm only telling you. You just walk about from place to place and never do your work. Goodness only knows why we keep a clerk.

EPIKHODOV. [*Offended*] Whether I work, or walk about, or eat, or play billiards, is only a matter to be settled by people of understanding and my elders.

VARYA. You dare to talk to me like that! [*Furious*] You dare? You mean that I know nothing? Get out of this! This minute!

EPIKHODOV. [*Nervous*] I must ask you to express yourself more delicately.

VARYA. [*Beside herself*] Get out this minute. Get out! [*He goes to the door, she follows*] Two-and-twenty troubles! I don't want any sign of you here! I don't want to see anything of you! [EPIKHODOV *has gone out; his voice can be heard outside:* "*I'll make a complaint against you.*"] What, coming back? [*Snatches up the stick left by* FIERS *by the door*] Go . . . go . . . go, I'll show you. . . . Are you going? Are you going? Well, then take that. [*She hits out as* LOPAKHIN *enters.*

LOPAKHIN. Much obliged.

VARYA. [*Angry but amused*] I'm sorry.

LOPAKHIN. Never mind. I thank you for my pleasant reception.

VARYA. It isn't worth any thanks. [*Walks away, then looks back and asks gently*] I didn't hurt you, did I?

LOPAKHIN. No, not at all. There'll be an enormous bump, that's all.

VOICES FROM THE DRAWING-ROOM. Lopakhin's returned! Ermolai Alexeyevitch!

PISCHIN. Now we'll see what there is to see and hear what there is to hear. . . . [*Kisses* LOPAKHIN] You smell of cognac, my dear, my soul. And we're all having a good time.

Enter LUBOV ANDREYEVNA.

LUBOV. Is that you, Ermolai Alexeyevitch? Why were you so long? Where's Leonid?

LOPAKHIN. Leonid Andreyevitch came back with me, he's coming. . . .

LUBOV. [*Excited*] Well, what? Is it sold? Tell me?

LOPAKHIN. [*Confused, afraid to show his pleasure*] The sale ended up at four o'clock. . . . We missed the train, and had to wait till half-past nine. [*Sighs heavily*] Ooh! My head's going round a little.

Enter GAEV; *in his right hand he carries things he has bought, with his left he wipes away his tears.*

LUBOV. Leon, what's happened? Leon, well? [*Impatiently, in tears*] Quick, for the love of God. . . .

GAEV. [*Says nothing to her, only waves his hand; to* FIERS, *weeping*] Here, take this. . . . Here are anchovies, herrings from Kertch. . . . I've had no food to-day. . . . I have had a time! [*The door from the billiard-room is open; the clicking of the balls is heard, and* YASHA'S *voice, " Seven, eighteen! "* GAEV'S *expression changes, he cries no more*] I'm awfully tired. Let me change my clothes, Fiers.

Goes out through the drawing-room; FIERS *after him.*

PISCHIN. What happened? Come on, tell us!

LUBOV. Is the cherry orchard sold?

LOPAKHIN. It is sold.

LUBOV. Who bought it ?

LOPAKHIN. I bought it.

> LUBOV ANDREYEVNA *is overwhelmed ; she would fall
> if she were not standing by an armchair and a
> table.* VARYA *takes her keys off her belt, throws
> them on the floor, into the middle of the room and
> goes out.*

LOPAKHIN. I bought it ! Wait, ladies and gentlemen,
please, my head's going round, I can't talk. . . . [*Laugh*]
When we got to the sale, Deriganov was there already.
Leonid Andreyevitch had only fifteen thousand roubles, and
Deriganov offered thirty thousand on top of the mortgage
to begin with. I saw how matters were, so I grabbed hold
of him and bid forty. He went up to forty-five, I offered
fifty-five. That means he went up by fives and I went up
by tens. . . . Well, it came to an end. I bid ninety more
than the mortgage ; and it stayed with me. The cherry
orchard is mine now, mine ! [*Roars with laughter*] My God,
my God, the cherry orchard's mine ! Tell me I'm drunk,
or mad, or dreaming. . . . [*Stamps his feet*] Don't laugh
at me ! If my father and grandfather rose from their
graves and looked at the whole affair, and saw how their
Ermolai, their beaten and uneducated Ermolai, who used
to run barefoot in the winter, how that very Ermolai has
bought an estate, which is the most beautiful thing in the
world ! I've bought the estate where my grandfather and
my father were slaves, where they weren't even allowed into
the kitchen. I'm asleep, it's only a dream, an illusion. . . .
It's the fruit of imagination, wrapped in the fog of the unknown. . . . [*Picks up the keys, nicely smiling*] She threw
down the keys, she wanted to show she was no longer

mistress here. . . . [*Jingles keys*] Well, it's all one!
[*Hears the band tuning up*] Eh, musicians, play, I want to
hear you! Come and look at Ermolai Lopakhin laying his
axe to the cherry orchard, come and look at the trees falling!
We'll build villas here, and our grandsons and great-
grandsons will see a new life here. . . . Play on, music!
[*The band plays.* LUBOV ANDREYEVNA *sinks into a chair
and weeps bitterly.* LOPAKHIN *continues reproachfully*]
Why then, why didn't you take my advice? My poor, dear
woman, you can't go back now. [*Weeps*] Oh, if only the
whole thing was done with, if only our uneven, unhappy
life were changed!

PISCHIN. [*Takes his arm ; in an undertone*] She's crying.
Let's go into the drawing-room and leave her by herself . . .
come on. . . .   [*Takes his arm and leads him out.*

LOPAKHIN. What's that? Bandsmen, play nicely! Go
on, do just as I want you to! [*Ironically*] The new owner,
the owner of the cherry orchard is coming! [*He accidentally
knocks up against a little table and nearly upsets the candelabra*]
I can pay for everything now!   [*Exit with* PISCHIN.

> *In the reception-room and the drawing-room nobody re-
> mains except* LUBOV ANDREYEVNA, *who sits huddled
> up and weeping bitterly. The band plays softly.*
> ANYA *and* TROFIMOV *come in quickly.* ANYA *goes
> up to her mother and goes on her knees in front of
> her.* TROFIMOV *stands at the drawing-room en-
> trance.*

ANYA. Mother! mother, are you crying? My dear,
kind, good mother, my beautiful mother, I love you!
Bless you! The cherry orchard is sold, we've got it no
longer, it's true, true, but don't cry mother, you've still got
your life before you, you've still your beautiful pure soul. . . .

Come with me, come, dear, away from here, come ! We'll
plant a new garden, finer than this, and you'll see it, and
you'll understand, and deep joy, gentle joy will sink into
your soul, like the evening sun, and you'll smile, mother !
Come, dear, let's go !

Curtain.

ACT FOUR

The stage is set as for Act I. There are no curtains on the windows, no pictures ; only a few pieces of furniture are left ; they are piled up in a corner as if for sale. The emptiness is felt. By the door that leads out of the house and at the back of the stage, portmanteaux and travelling paraphernalia are piled up. The door on the left is open ; the voices of VARYA *and* ANYA *can be heard through it.* LOPAKHIN *stands and waits.* YASHA *holds a tray with little tumblers of champagne. Outside,* EPIKHODOV *is tying up a box. Voices are heard behind the stage. The peasants have come to say good-bye. The voice of* GAEV *is heard :* " *Thank you, brothers, thank you.*"

YASHA. The common people have come to say good-bye. I am of the opinion, Ermolai Alexeyevitch, that they're good people, but they don't understand very much.

> *The voices die away.* LUBOV ANDREYEVNA *and* GAEV *enter. She is not crying but is pale, and her face trembles ; she can hardly speak.*

GAEV. You gave them your purse, Luba. You can't go on like that, you can't !

LUBOV. I couldn't help myself, I couldn't ! [*They go out.*

LOPAKHIN. [*In the doorway, looking after them*] Please, I ask you most humbly ! Just a little glass to say good-bye. I didn't remember to bring any from town and I only found one bottle at the station. Please, do ! [*Pause*] Won't you really have any ? [*Goes away from the door*] If I only knew—I wouldn't have bought any. Well, I shan't drink any either. [YASHA *carefully puts the tray on a chair*] You have a drink, Yasha, at any rate.

YASHA. To those departing! And good luck to those who stay behind! [*Drinks*] I can assure you that this isn't real champagne.

LOPAKHIN. Eight roubles a bottle. [*Pause*] It's devilish cold here.

YASHA. There are no fires to-day, we're going away.

[*Laughs.*

LOPAKHIN. What's the matter with you?

YASHA. I'm just pleased.

LOPAKHIN. It's October outside, but it's as sunny and as quiet as if it were summer. Good for building. [*Looking at his watch and speaking through the door*] Ladies and gentlemen, please remember that it's only forty-seven minutes till the train goes! You must go off to the station in twenty minutes. Hurry up.

TROFIMOV, *in an overcoat, comes in from the grounds.*

TROFIMOV. I think it's time we went. The carriages are waiting. Where the devil are my goloshes? They're lost. [*Through the door*] Anya, I can't find my goloshes! I can't!

LOPAKHIN. I've got to go to Kharkov. I'm going in the same train as you. I'm going to spend the whole winter in Kharkov. I've been hanging about with you people, going rusty without work. I can't live without working. I must have something to do with my hands; they hang about as if they weren't mine at all.

TROFIMOV. We'll go away now and then you'll start again on your useful labours.

LOPAKHIN. Have a glass.

TROFIMOV. I won't.

LOPAKHIN. So you're off to Moscow now ?

TROFIMOV. Yes. I'll see them into town and to-morrow I'm off to Moscow.

LOPAKHIN. Yes. . . . I expect the professors don't lecture nowadays ; they're waiting till you turn up !

TROFIMOV. That's not your business.

LOPAKHIN. How many years have you been going to the university ?

TROFIMOV. Think of something fresh. This is old and flat. [*Looking for his goloshes*] You know, we may not meet each other again, so just let me give you a word of advice on parting : " Don't wave your hands about ! Get rid of that habit of waving them about. And then, building villas and reckoning on their residents becoming freeholders in time—that's the same thing ; it's all a matter of waving your hands about. . . . Whether I want to or not, you know, I like you. You've thin, delicate fingers, like those of an artist, and you've a thin, delicate soul. . . ."

LOPAKHIN. [*Embraces him*] Good-bye, dear fellow. Thanks for all you've said. If you want any, take some money from me for the journey.

TROFIMOV. Why should I ? I don't want it.

LOPAKHIN. But you've nothing !

TROFIMOV. Yes, I have, thank you ; I've got some for a translation. Here it is in my pocket. [*Nervously*] But I can't find my goloshes !

VARYA. [*From the other room*] Take your rubbish away !
          [*Throws a pair of rubber goloshes on to the stage.*

TROFIMOV. Why are you angry, Varya ? Hm ! These aren't my goloshes !

LOPAKHIN. In the spring I sowed three thousand acres of poppies, and now I've made forty thousand roubles net profit. And when my poppies were in flower, what a picture it was ! So I, as I was saying, made forty thousand roubles, and I mean I'd like to lend you some, because I can afford it. Why turn up your nose at it ? I'm just a simple peasant. . . .

TROFIMOV. Your father was a peasant, mine was a chemist, and that means absolutely nothing. [LOPAKHIN *takes out his pocket-book*] No, no. . . . Even if you gave me twenty thousand I should refuse. I'm a free man. And everything that all you people, rich and poor, value so highly and so dearly hasn't the least influence over me ; it's like a flock of down in the wind. I can do without you, I can pass you by. I'm strong and proud. Mankind goes on to the highest truths and to the highest happiness such as is only possible on earth, and I go in the front ranks !

LOPAKHIN. Will you get there ?

TROFIMOV. I will. [*Pause*] I'll get there and show others the way. [*Axes cutting the trees are heard in the distance.*

LOPAKHIN. Well, good-bye, old man. It's time to go. Here we stand pulling one another's noses, but life goes its own way all the time. When I work for a long time, and I don't get tired, then I think more easily, and I think I get to understand why I exist. And there are so many people in Russia, brother, who live for nothing at all. Still, work goes on without that. Leonid Andreyevitch, they say, has accepted a post in a bank ; he will get sixty thousand roubles a year. . . . But he won't stand it ; he's very lazy.

ANYA. [*At the door*] Mother asks if you will stop them cutting down the orchard until she has gone away.

TROFIMOV. Yes, really, you ought to have enough tact not to do that. [*Exit.*

LOPAKHIN. All right, all right . . . . yes, he's right. [*Exit.*

ANYA. Has Fiers been sent to the hospital ?

YASHA. I gave the order this morning. I suppose they've sent him.

ANYA. [*To* EPIKHODOV, *who crosses the room*] Simeon Panteleyevitch, please make inquiries if Fiers has been sent to the hospital.

YASHA. [*Offended*] I told Egor this morning. What's the use of asking ten times !

EPIKHODOV. The aged Fiers, in my conclusive opinion, isn't worth mending ; his forefathers had better have him. I only envy him. [*Puts a trunk on a hat-box and squashes it*] Well, of course. I thought so !   [*Exit.*

YASHA. [*Grinning*] Two-and-twenty troubles.

VARYA. [*Behind the door*] Has Fiers been taken away to the hospital ?

ANYA. Yes.

VARYA. Why didn't they take the letter to the doctor ?

ANYA. It'll have to be sent after him.   [*Exit.*

VARYA. [*In the next room*] Where's Yasha ? Tell him his mother's come and wants to say good-bye to him.

YASHA. [*Waving his hand*] She'll make me lose all patience !

> DUNYASHA *has meanwhile been bustling round the luggage ; now that* YASHA *is left alone, she goes up to him.*

DUNYASHA. If you only looked at me once, Yasha. You're going away, leaving me behind.

> [*Weeps and hugs him round the neck.*

YASHA. What's the use of crying ? [*Drinks champagne*] In six days I'll be again in Paris. To-morrow we get into the express and off we go. I can hardly believe it. Vive la France ! It doesn't suit me here, I can't live here . . . it's no good. Well, I've seen the uncivilized world ; I have had enough of it. [*Drinks champagne*] What do you want to cry for ? You behave yourself properly, and then you won't cry.

DUNYASHA. Somebody's coming.

> *He bustles around the luggage, singing softly. Enter* LUBOV ANDREYEVNA, GAEV, ANYA, *and* CHARLOTTA IVANOVNA.

GAEV. We'd better be off. There's no time left. [*Looks at* YASHA] Somebody smells of herring !

LUBOV. We needn't get into our carriages for ten minutes. . . . [*Looks round the room*] Good-bye, dear house, old grandfather. The winter will go, the spring will come, and then you'll exist no more, you'll be pulled down. How much these walls have seen ! [*Passionately kisses her daughter*] My treasure, you're radiant, your eyes flash like two jewels ! Are you happy ? Very ?

ANYA. Very ! A new life is beginning, mother !

GAEV. [*Gaily*] Yes, really, everything's all right now. Before the cherry orchard was sold we all were excited and we suffered, and then, when the question was solved once and for all, we all calmed down, and even became cheerful. I'm a bank official now, and a financier . . . red in the middle ; and you, Luba, for some reason or other, look better, there's no doubt about it.

LUBOV. Yes. My nerves are better, it's true. [*She puts on her coat and hat*] I sleep well. Take my luggage out, Yasha. It's time. [*To* ANYA] My little girl, we'll soon see each other again. . . . I'm off to Paris. I'll live there on the money your grandmother from Yaroslav sent along to buy the estate—bless her !—though it won't last long.

ANYA. You'll come back soon, soon, mother, won't you ? I'll get ready, and pass the exam. at the Higher School, and then I'll work and help you. We'll read all sorts of books

to one another, won't we ? [*Kisses her mother's hands*]
We'll read in the autumn evenings ; we'll read many books,
and a beautiful new world will open up before us. . . .
[*Thoughtfully*] You'll come, mother. . . .

LUBOV. I'll come, my darling.   [*Embraces her.*

Enter LOPAKHIN. CHARLOTTA *is singing to herself.*

GAEV. Charlotta is happy ; she sings !

CHARLOTTA. [*Takes a bundle, looking like a wrapped-up
baby*] My little baby, bye-bye. [*The baby seems to answer,
"Oua! Oua!"*] Hush, my nice little boy. [" *Oua ! Oua !* "]
I'm so sorry for you ! [*Throws the bundle back*] So please
find me a new place. I can't go on like this.

LOPAKHIN. We'll find one, Charlotta Ivanovna, don't
you be afraid.

GAEV. Everybody's leaving us. Varya's going away. . .
we've suddenly become unnecessary.

CHARLOTTA. I've nowhere to live in town. I must go
away. [*Hums*] Never mind.

Enter PISCHIN.

LOPAKHIN. Nature's marvel !

PISCHIN. [*Puffing*] Oh, let me get my breath back. . . .
I'm fagged out. . . . My most honoured, give me some
water. . . .

GAEV. Come for money, what ? I'm your humble servant, and I'm going out of the way of temptation.   [*Exit.*

PISCHIN. I haven't been here for ever so long . . . dear
madam. [*To* LOPAKHIN] You here ? Glad to see you . . .
man of immense brain . . . take this . . . take it. . . .
[*Gives* LOPAKHIN *money*] Four hundred roubles. . . .
That leaves 840. . . .

LOPAKHIN. [*Shrugs his shoulders in surprise*] As if I
were dreaming. Where did you get this from ?

PISCHIN. Stop . . . it's hot. . . . A most unexpected

U

thing happened. Some Englishmen came along and found some white clay on my land. . . . [*To* LUBOV ANDREYEVNA] And here's four hundred for you . . . beautiful lady. . . . [*Gives her money*] Give you the rest later. . . . [*Drinks water*] Just now a young man in the train was saying that some great philosopher advises us all to jump off roofs. " Jump ! " he says, and that's all. [*Astonished*] To think of that, now ! More water !

LOPAKHIN. Who were these Englishmen ?

PISCHIN. I've leased off the land with the clay to them for twenty-four years. . . . Now, excuse me, I've no time. . . . I must run off. . . . I must go to Znoikov and to Kardamonov . . . I owe them all money. . . . [*Drinks*] Good-bye. I'll come in on Thursday.

LUBOV. We're just off to town, and to-morrow I go abroad.

PISCHIN. [*Agitated*] What ? Why to town ? I see furniture . . . trunks. . . . Well, never mind. [*Crying*] Never mind. These Englishmen are men of immense intellect. . . . Never mind. . . . Be happy. . . . God will help you. . . . Never mind. . . . Everything in this world comes to an end. . . . [*Kisses* LUBOV ANDREYEVNA'S *hand*] And if you should happen to hear that my end has come, just remember this old . . . horse and say: " There was one such and such a Simeonov-Pischin, God bless his soul. . . ." Wonderful weather . . . yes. . . . [*Exit deeply moved, but returns at once and says in the door*] Dashenka sent her love !   [*Exit.*

LUBOV. Now we can go. I've two anxieties, though. The first is poor Fiers. [*Looks at her watch*] We've still five minutes. . . .

ANYA. Mother, Fiers has already been sent to the hospital. Yasha sent him off this morning.

Lubov. The second is Varya. She's used to getting up early and to work, and now she's no work to do she's like a fish out of water. She's grown thin and pale, and she cries, poor thing. . . . [*Pause*] You know very well, Ermolai Alexeyevitch, that I used to hope to marry her to you, and I suppose you are going to marry somebody ? [*Whispers to* Anya, *who nods to* Charlotta, *and they both go out*] She loves you, she's your sort, and I don't understand, I really don't, why you seem to be keeping away from each other. I don't understand !

Lopakhin. To tell the truth, I don't understand it myself. It's all so strange. . . . If there's still time, I'll be ready at once. . . . Let's get it over, once and for all ; I don't feel as if I could ever propose to her without you.

Lubov. Excellent. It'll only take a minute. I'll call her.

Lopakhin. The champagne's very appropriate. [*Looking at the tumblers*] They're empty, somebody's already drunk them. [Yasha *coughs*] I call that licking it up. . . .

Lubov. [*Animated*] Excellent. We'll go out. Yasha, allez. I'll call her in. . . . [*At the door*] Varya, leave that and come here. Come !   [*Exit with* Yasha.

Lopakhin. [*Looks at his watch*] Yes. . . .   [*Pause.*
    There is a restrained laugh behind the door, a whisper,
        then Varya *comes in.*

Varya. [*Looking at the luggage in silence*] I can't seem to find it. . . .

Lopakhin. What are you looking for ?

Varya. I packed it myself and I don't remember. [*Pause.*

Lopakhin. Where are you going to now, Barbara Mihailovna ?

Varya. I ? To the Ragulins. . . . I've got an agreement to go and look after their house . . . as housekeeper or something.

LOPAKHIN. Is that at Yashnevo ? It's about fifty miles. [*Pause*] So life in this house is finished now. . . .

VARYA. [*Looking at the luggage*] Where is it ? . . . perhaps I've put it away in the trunk. . . . Yes, there'll be no more life in this house. . . .

LOPAKHIN. And I'm off to Kharkov at once . . . by this train. I've a lot of business on hand. I'm leaving Epikhodov here . . . I've taken him on.

VARYA. Well, well !

LOPAKHIN. Last year at this time the snow was already falling, if you remember, and now it's nice and sunny. Only it's rather cold. . . . There's three degrees of frost.

VARYA. I didn't look. [*Pause*] And our thermometer's broken. . . .   [*Pause.*

VOICE AT THE DOOR. Ermolai Alexeyevitch !

LOPAKHIN. [*As if he has long been waiting to be called*] This minute.   [*Exit quickly.*

> VARYA, *sitting on the floor, puts her face on a bundle of clothes and weeps gently. The door opens.* LUBOV ANDREYEVNA *enters carefully.*

LUBOV. Well ? [*Pause*] We must go.

VARYA. [*Not crying now, wipes her eyes*] Yes, it's quite time, little mother. I'll get to the Ragulins to-day, if I don't miss the train. . . .

LUBOV. [*At the door*] Anya, put on your things. [*Enter* ANYA, *then* GAEV, CHARLOTTA IVANOVNA. GAEV *wears a warm overcoat with a cape. A servant and drivers come in.* EPIKHODOV *bustles around the luggage*] Now we can go away.

ANYA. [*Joyfully*] Away !

GAEV. My friends, my dear friends ! Can I be silent, in leaving this house for evermore ?—can I restrain myself, in saying farewell, from expressing those feelings which now fill my whole being . . . ?

ANYA. [*Imploringly*] Uncle !

VARYA. Uncle, you shouldn't !

GAEV. [*Stupidly*] Double the red into the middle. . . . I'll be quiet.

     Enter TROFIMOV, *then* LOPAKHIN.

TROFIMOV. Well, it's time to be off.

LOPAKHIN. Epikhodov, my coat !

LUBOV. I'll sit here one more minute. It's as if I'd never really noticed what the walls and ceilings of this house were like, and now I look at them greedily, with such tender love. . . .

GAEV. I remember, when I was six years old, on Trinity Sunday, I sat at this window and looked and saw my father going to church. . . .

LUBOV. Have all the things been taken away ?

LOPAKHIN. Yes, all, I think. [*To* EPIKHODOV, *putting on his coat*] You see that everything's quite straight, Epikhodov.

EPIKHODOV. [*Hoarsely*] You may depend upon me, Ermolai Alexeyevitch !

LOPAKHIN. What's the matter with your voice ?

EPIKHODOV. I swallowed something just now; I was having a drink of water.

YASHA. [*Suspiciously*] What manners. . . .

LUBOV. We go away, and not a soul remains behind.

LOPAKHIN. Till the spring.

VARYA. [*Drags an umbrella out of a bundle, and seems to be waving it about.* LOPAKHIN *appears to be frightened*] What are you doing ? . . . I never thought . . .

TROFIMOV. Come along, let's take our seats . . . it's time! The train will be in directly.

VARYA. Peter, here they are, your goloshes, by that trunk. [*In tears*] And how old and dirty they are. . . .

TROFIMOV. [*Putting them on*] Come on!

GAEV. [*Deeply moved, nearly crying*] The train . . . the station. . . . Cross in the middle, a white double in the corner. . . .

LUBOV. Let's go!

LOPAKHIN. Are you all here? There's nobody else? [*Locks the side-door on the left*] There's a lot of things in there. I must lock them up. Come!

ANYA. Good-bye, home! Good-bye, old life!

TROFIMOV. Welcome, new life.   [*Exit with* ANYA.

    VARYA *looks round the room and goes out slowly.*

    YASHA *and* CHARLOTTA, *with her little dog, go out.*

LOPAKHIN. Till the spring, then! Come on . . . till we meet again!   [*Exit.*

    LUBOV ANDREYEVNA *and* GAEV *are left alone. They might almost have been waiting for that. They fall into each other's arms and sob restrainedly and quietly, fearing that somebody might hear them.*

GAEV. [*In despair*] My sister, my sister. . . .

LUBOV. My dear, my gentle, beautiful orchard! My life, my youth, my happiness, good-bye! Good-bye!

ANYA'S VOICE. [*Gaily*] Mother!

TROFIMOV'S VOICE. [*Gaily, excited*] Coo-ee!

LUBOV. To look at the walls and the windows for the last time. . . . My dead mother used to like to walk about this room. . . .

GAEV. My sister, my sister!

ANYA'S VOICE. Mother!

TROFIMOV'S VOICE. Coo-ee!

Lubov. We're coming!   [*They go out.*

> *The stage is empty. The sound of keys being turned
> in the locks is heard, and then the noise of the
> carriages going away. It is quiet. Then the sound
> of an axe against the trees is heard in the silence,
> sadly and by itself. Steps are heard.* Fiers *comes
> in from the door on the right. He is dressed as usual,
> in a short jacket and white waistcoat; slippers on
> his feet. He is ill. He goes to the door and tries
> the handle.*

Fiers. It's locked. They've gone away. [*Sits on a sofa*]
They've forgotten about me. . . . Never mind, I'll sit
here. . . . And Leonid Andreyevitch will have gone in a
light overcoat instead of putting on his fur coat. . . .
[*Sighs anxiously*] I didn't see. . . . Oh, these young
people! [*Mumbles something that cannot be understood*]
Life's gone on as if I'd never lived. [*Lying down*] I'll lie
down. . . . You've no strength left in you, nothing left
at all. . . . Oh, you . . . bungler!

> *He lies without moving. The distant sound is heard,
> as if from the sky, of a breaking string, dying away
> sadly. Silence follows it, and only the sound is
> heard, some way away in the orchard, of the axe
> falling on the trees.*

Curtain.